Books in the Security Series

Computer Security Fundamentals
ISBN: 0-13-171129-6

Information Security: Principles and Practices
ISBN: 0-13-154729-1

Firewalls and VPNs: Principles and Practices
ISBN: 0-13-154731-3

Security Policies and Procedures: Principles and Practices
ISBN: 0-13-186691-5

Network Defense and Countermeasures: Principles and Practices
ISBN: 0-13-171126-1

Disaster Recovery: Principles and Practices
ISBN: 0-13-171127-X

Computer Forensics: Principles and Practices
ISBN: 0-13-154727-5

Disaster Recovery

Principles and Practices

APRIL J. WELLS

CHARLYNE WALKER

TIMOTHY WALKER

DAVID ABARCA

PEARSON

Prentice
Hall

Upper Saddle River, New Jersey 07458

HD
49
.W46
2007

Library of Congress Cataloging-in-Publication Data

Wells, April J.
   Disaster recovery : principles and practices / April J. Wells, Charlyne Walker, Timothy Walker.
     p.   cm.
   Includes bibliographical references and index.
   ISBN 0-13-171127-X (alk. paper)
   1. Emergency management—Handbooks, manuals, etc.   2. Crisis management—Handbooks, manuals, etc.
3. Computer security—Handbooks, manuals, etc.   4. Data protection—Handbooks, manuals, etc.   5. Data recovery
(Computer science)—Planning—Handbooks, manuals, etc.   6. Business planning—Handbooks, manuals, etc.
   I. Walker, Charlyne.   II. Walker, Timothy.   III. Title.
   HD49.W46 2006
   363.34'8—dc22

                                                                    2006025316

Vice President and Publisher: Natalie E. Anderson
Associate VP/ Executive Acquisitions Editor, Print:
   Stephanie Wall
Executive Acquisitions Editor, Media: Richard Keaveny
Executive Acquisitions Editor: Chris Katsaropoulos
Product Development Manager: Eileen Bien Calabro
Editorial Assistants: Rebecca Knauer, Lora Cimiluca
Executive Producer: Lisa Strite
Content Development Manager: Cathi Profitko
Senior Media Project Manager: Steve Gagliostro
Project Manager, Media: Alana Meyers
Director of Marketing: Margaret Waples
Senior Marketing Manager: Jason Sakos
Marketing Assistant: Ann Baranov

Senior Sales Associate: Rebecca Scott
Managing Editor: Lynda J. Castillo
Production Project Manager: Lynne Breitfeller
Manufacturing Buyer: Chip Poakeart
Production/Editorial Assistant: Sandra K. Bernales
Design Manager: Maria Lange
Art Director/Interior Design/Cover Design:
   Blair Brown
Cover Illustration/Photo: Gettyimages/Photodisc Blue
Composition: Integra
Project Management: BookMasters, Inc.
Cover Printer: RR Donnelley/Harrisonburg
Printer/Binder: RR Donnelley/Harrisonburg

Credits and acknowledgments borrowed from other sources and reproduced, with permission, in this textbook appear on appropriate page within text.

Microsoft[8] and Windows[8] are registered trademarks of the Microsoft Corporation in the U.S.A. and other countries. Screen shots and icons reprinted with permission from the Microsoft Corporation. This book is not sponsored, endorsed by, or affiliated with the Microsoft Corporation.

Pearson Education LTD.
Pearson Education Singapore, Pte. Ltd
Pearson Education, Canada, Ltd
Pearson Education–Japan

Pearson Education Australia PTY, Limited
Pearson Education North Asia Ltd
Pearson Educación de Mexico, S.A. de C.V.
Pearson Education Malaysia, Pte. Ltd

10 9 8 7 6 5 4 3 2
ISBN 0-13-171127-X

This book is dedicated to my husband, Larry, who stood by me through it all and helped me to stay focused and sane, while giving me moral support along the way. It is dedicated to my daughter, Amandya Lynn, and my son, Adam Lonny, who are learning that, if you work hard enough and dream big enough, anything is possible and dreams can come true.

—April Wells

This book is dedicated to our son, Charles, who has supported and encouraged his parents in this endeavor. It is also dedicated to Charlyne's mother, Doris, for her support and encouragement. Without your patience and love, we would not have been able to complete this work.

—Charlyne and Tim Walker

This book is dedicated to my wife, Susan, who has always encouraged me to explore my potential, and to my children, Anna and Anthony, who continue to learn that one's capabilities are only limited by their pursuit of success. This is also dedicated to my parents, Antonio "Tony" and Apolonia "Polly", who taught me that my head was to be used for something more than just a place to hang my had !

—David A. Abarca

Contents in Brief

Contents

Security Series Walk-Through

The Security Series is designed to help you understand the threats to computers and networks, and how to safeguard them from attacks. All of the books in this series are filled with real-world examples to help you apply what you learn in the workplace. This walk-through highlights the key elements you'll find in this book, created to help you along the way.

Chapter Objectives. These objectives give you short-term, attainable goals. They mirror the titles of the step-by-step exercises.

Chapter Introduction. Introductory material at the beginning of each chapter explains why these topics are important and how the chapter fits into the overall organization of the book.

Chapter Objectives

After reading this chapter and completing the exercises, you will be able to do the following:

- Define disaster recovery.
- Defend the need for an organizational disaster recovery plan.
- Define "disaster" as it applies to a business or organization and outline the types of disasters that might befall it.
- Describe how a disaster can affect an organization or business.
- Identify those threats that may be most relevant to an organization.
- Discuss specific threats to organizations.
- Explain the difference between a disaster recovery plan and a business continuity plan.

Introduction

Although you may not realize it in your day-to-day routine, you—and the business you work for—face disaster nearly every day. You may not consider yourself prepared, but in many ways you already are. If you have a job, you and your company pay into an unemployment fund that you have access to if you lose your job. If you have a mortgage on your home, the mortgage company generally requires insurance to protect you (and the mortgage company) from a catastrophic loss if the home burns down. If you own an automobile, most states require that you have proof of insurance to protect you, your passengers, and other drivers in case you cause an accident.

IN PRACTICE: Disaster Recovery in the Real World

Global Information Services (GIS) is an application service provider (ASP) that provides complete Oracle E-Business Suite hosting services for several small and medium-sized businesses in the area. The company processes accounting records and incoming and outgoing invoices, and writes and mails checks with the client's approval. In effect, it is a full-service accounting software, human resources, and Enterprise Resource Planning/Customer Relationship Management (ERP/CRM) services firm.

In Practice. These show you how to take concepts from the book and apply them on your own and in the workplace.

FYI. These boxes offer additional information on topics that go beyond the scope of the book.

perspective, need to protect sensitive and the HIPAA ramifications if proper security alth Insurance Portability and Accountability individual's medical information. Disaster-nly maintain and protect the sensitive and ect information about the functions of the cal processes that are centrally unique to the d to the disaster itself

ny identifies, it needs to identify all the assets. This needs to include the damage ge that could impact the information or n estimation of what the effect of the loss tion, both short term and long term, needs

Caution

HIPAA

It is critical for an organization with health-related information to protect access to data during a disaster, throughout the recovery, and even while testing its systems. Records

FYI   Recovery Manager and Funding

One thing that needs to be taken into account when looking at the person filling this position is that it's important for this person to have the signature authority required to allocate funds as a part of the disaster recovery process.

Caution. This flags critical, not-to-be forgotten information that is directly relevant to the surrounding text.

Each chapter ends with exercises designed to reinforce what you've just learned. You'll find four types of evaluation here:

Multiple Choice Questions. Tests your understanding of the text.

MULTIPLE CHOICE QUESTIONS

1. A critical component in the operation of most, if not all, businesses and organizations is _____.
   A. data mining
   B. information resources
   C. security resources
   D. information mining

2. Any event or occurrence that can have a detrimental affect to an organization is known as a(n) _____.
   A. unexpected event
   B. disaster
   C. business disruption
   D. unfortunate event

Exercises. Brief, guided projects that help you apply individual concepts found in the chapter.

EXERCISES

Exercise 1.1: Understanding Key Services

1. Select a company, either real or fictitious.
2. Completely describe the company, including the business and where the company is located.
3. Determine the minimum services that must be maintained for that company after a disaster. What services should be restored first? What services do you think can be put off until later?

Projects. Longer, guided projects that combine lessons from the chapter.

PROJECTS

Project 2.1: Small Business DR Team

1. Put yourself in the position of creating a disaster recovery planning team in a small organization with limited resources (capital and human).
2. Describe the organization's business.
3. Determine the most critical roles to fill on the team.
4. Describe how you might best combine or fill roles that you don't have the resources to fill in-house.

Case Study. Each case study introduces a real-world business scenario that you must resolve.

Case Study

Juan was appointed as captain of ABC Company's disaster recovery team. He knows that working as a team is important and therefore is trying to figure out how to build both the team and camaraderie in the new team. Members will be from widely different departments, may have different interests, and come from different backgrounds. Discuss what positions will be most critical to fill first, what traits you would look for in each person for each position, and how you would approach building the team feeling if you were in his position.

This icon appears in the margin wherever more information can be found at the Companion Website, **www.prenhall.com/security.** You'll also find code terms in monospace type, key terms in ***bold italics,*** and URLs in **boldface.**

Preface

Today, security and the ability of an organization—regardless of size—to recover from a disaster situation is becoming uppermost in the minds of management for organizations. With hurricanes, tsunamis, terrorism, and power outages making the news every day, it's become apparent that organizations need to anticipate the unthinkable. This book will help all of those involved in an organization, whether in security, in IT, or in the functional business areas, to have a better idea of all that is involved in recovering the organization in the event of a critical event.

From a security specialist point of view, by the very nature of the act of recovering from a disaster, the entire process will be critical. From a business point of view, the role that the security specialist will play in the event of an emergency situation or a disaster will be every bit as critical. Being prepared for such a situation will make everyone a more effective member of the recovery team. Keeping the data and all associated applications available and accessible to everyone who should legitimately have access and protecting those same data elements and applications from unauthorized access are critical for every security professional.

For the most part, information security specialists will not need any additional training other than what they already have to make use of the information necessary for disaster recovery. There is little different in a disaster situation from a security standpoint that isn't in day-to-day operations. Where there are differences, this book points them out. That existing knowledge will allow them to make better choices as they play their part in the disaster recovery efforts and as they become vital members of their organizational team.

What this book will do is help acquaint them with the information necessary to better perform their duties as they relate to planning and execution of the disaster recovery plan. This knowledge (applying disaster recovery concepts as well as security concepts) will make everyone a better team member.

Audience

This book is intended for readers with a grasp of current trends in security and security risks, particularly for organizations. An in-depth understanding of *all* security practices and methods is not necessary, but an understanding of business practices and common business processes is useful. Knowing what information is "out there" is a critical first step in determining what (and how) to protect it from intrusion. Obviously, the diversity of software and hardware makes it difficult to offer specific solutions, but general knowledge of both is also beneficial. For this same reason, this book is not written from any operating system perspective. Only the smallest organizations usually have the luxury of having only a single operating system.

Disaster Recovery: Principles and Practices is also a valuable resource for business people and information technologists, as being assured that the business will continue is one of their primary responsibilities.

Overview of the Book

Disaster Recovery: Principles and Practices begins with an introduction to what disaster recovery and business continuity are. Chapter 1 discusses what is meant by a disaster and what different levels of disaster might mean to an organization. We look at the difference between a threat and a disaster and what those differences mean to an organization. Further, we look at the differences between a disaster recovery plan and a business continuity plan, and determine why an organization needs each.

Chapter 2, "Preparing to Develop the Disaster Recovery Plan," looks at choosing the recovery team and defines the tasks typically assigned to the disaster recovery team. It looks as the characteristics of the team members and how their roles fit together to benefit the organization. We look at the notification mechanisms that need to be in place for everyone on the recovery team. Finally, we look at engaging resources from the level of upper management to the functional areas to the subject matter experts that need to be engaged along the way. Once we have secured resources, we look at preparing those resources to be called upon in the planning and recovery process.

Chapter 3, "Assessing Risk and Impact," helps us define the risks that may impact an organization. We look at different methods of risk assessment and how those different methods can help us arrive at the business impact for each of the risks we uncover. We can then set priorities on these risks as a means for determining in what order we need to handle them and mitigate their impact. We will look at different assessment methods and tools that can help an organization or an individual come to the necessary conclusions.

Chapter 4, "Prioritizing Systems and Functions for Recovery," covers the identification of assets and functions in an organization. We then look at prioritizing the assets and functions so the task of tackling systems in a recovery situation can be handled in a systematic and logical manner. We determine dependencies that exist between data, between functions, and even between assets so we can re-assess our ideas on the order that recovery needs to occur.

Chapter 5, "Identify Data Storage and Recovery Sites," looks at determining the best way to back up an organization's data so it can be recovered quickly and efficiently. It helps us evaluate our offsite storage options as well as those that are onsite. In this chapter, we acknowledge information as an asset as well as the assets we have already discussed. We look at recovery site options and types and set up some criteria that might be helpful in selection of a recovery site, and we outline our recovery site solution.

Chapter 6, "Developing Plans, Procedures, and Relationships," looks at the need for documents and contact information to support our recovery efforts. We look at tools that can help support the recovery effort and determine the best way to direct the recovery team in a recovery drill or should a recovery become necessary. This chapter covers backup strategies that will affect an organization's ability to recover in a given recovery timeline. Through this chapter, we will understand upstream vendors and how they can affect an organization's ability to do work and to recover quickly, as well as the organization's determination to declare a disaster and how that might affect downstream clients as well. We look at Service Level Agreements and how best to define them to protect all concerned. Finally, we begin to pull together the recovery documents.

Chapter 7, "Developing Procedures for Special Circumstances," helps us identify emergency situations that may impact us during our recovery efforts. We determine what can be done if such a situation occurs in our recovery efforts and assess the risk if this does indeed occur. Finally, we work to identify gaps in our recovery plans that may allow emergency stations to occur and adjust our plans accordingly.

Chapter 8, "Testing the Disaster Recovery Plan," helps us better understand why it is necessary to practice the disaster recovery plan and describes the different kinds of tests that we can perform and why we might need to test our plans before a disaster occurs. We determine what impact testing might have on the organization and the necessity of change control in the disaster recovery plan.

Chapter 9, "Continued Assessment of Needs, Threats, and Solutions," walks us through the lessons learned in the disaster recovery tests and helps us determine the best way to overcome those areas where gaps were uncovered. We look at different ways to analyze our threats as they have been uncovered and plan for the elimination of these and any new threats going forward.

Finally, the appendices offer additional resources that will be helpful to instructors and students alike, including a disaster recovery plan and several tests that might be followed in a testing situation, links to additional resources, and a glossary and references.

Conventions Used in This Book

To help you get the most from the text, we've used a few conventions throughout the book.

Snippets and blocks of code are boxed and numbered, and can be downloaded from the Companion Website (**www.prenhall.com/security**).

New key terms appear in ***bold italics***.

IN PRACTICE: About In Practice

These show readers how to take concepts from the book and apply them in the workplace.

 **FYI** *About FYIs*

These boxes offer additional information on topics that go beyond the scope of the book.

Instructor and Student Resources

Instructor's Resource Center on CD-ROM

The Instructor's Resource Center on CD-ROM (IRC on CD) is distributed only to instructors and is an interactive library of assets and links. It includes:

- **Instructor's Manual.** Provides instructional tips, an introduction to each chapter, teaching objectives, teaching suggestions, and answers to end-of-chapter questions and problems.

- **PowerPoint Slide Presentations.** Provides a chapter-by-chapter review of the book's content for use in the classroom.

- **Test Bank.** This TestGen-compatible test bank file can be used with Prentice Hall's TestGen software (available as a free download at **www.prenhall.com/testgen**). TestGen is a test generator that lets you view and easily edit test bank questions, transfer them to tests, and print in a variety of formats suitable to your teaching situation. The program also offers many options for organizing and displaying test banks and tests. A built-in random number and text generator makes it ideal for creating multiple versions of tests that involve calculations and provides more possible test items than test bank questions. Powerful search and sort functions let you easily locate questions and arrange them in the order you prefer.

Companion Website

The Companion Website (**www.prenhall.com/security**) is a Pearson learning tool that provides students and instructors with online support. Here you will find:

- Interactive Study Guide, a Web-based interactive quiz designed to provide students with a convenient online mechanism for self-testing their comprehension of the book material.

- Additional Web projects and resources to put into practice the concepts taught in each chapter.

About the Authors

April Wells has spent many years in the IT industry, working her way up through programmer, systems analysis, and database administration. She has spent several semesters as a teacher's assistant at a local university campus. As a trusted member of the organizations she has been a part of, she has been a key part of several disaster recovery teams and has seen both successes and failures in the recovery process.

April is an Oracle Certified Professional in 8, 8i and 9i; has her BS in Information Science from the University of Pittsburgh; and her MBA from West Texas A&M in Canyon, Texas. April has been a speaker at Oracle-specific conferences as well as on the topic of Disaster Recovery Planning in independent conferences. She has authored several books on Oracle Databases as well as Grid Database Design and Grid Application Design.

You can reach April by e-mail at awellsdba@gmail.com.

Timothy Walker has worked in the IT industry for nearly 20 years. He has spent that time working as a technical support field technician, system administrator, software developer, and most recently in the network security/information assurance area. He currently holds the position of Network Security Manager at a large college in South Florida. He is part of the disaster recovery team for the central IT department and actively participates in the disaster planning process for the college's information technology resources.

Timothy holds an MS in Education Computing and Technology from Barry University and a BS in Computer Science from Florida International University. He holds several technical certifications related to security and technology products.

You can reach Timothy Walker by e-mail at trw1969@gmail.com.

Charlyne Walker has worked in the IT industry for nearly two decades. She spent nearly a decade providing technical support and training at a large, urban public university. She has also served as the Director of Educational Technology and now holds the position of Director of Educational Research and Evaluation. In her many roles in IT, Charlyne has been called upon to work with planning committees looking at IT implementation and disaster preparedness planning. She has also assisted faculty members and staff in the development of backup strategies for personal and research data.

Charlyne holds a PhD in Leadership and Education, Educational Technology from Barry University, a Master's degree in Adult Education, and a Bachelors degree in Liberal Studies with an emphasis in Computer Science from Florida International University in Miami, Florida. Her area of research interest is human computer interaction, including the influence of technology on student learning. She has been a speaker at conferences focusing on the integration of technology into the educational setting.

You can reach Charlyne by e-mail at charlynew@gmail.com.

David A. Abarca has spent almost 30 years learning about and working with computers. He worked for IBM in several roles including the development of Disaster Recovery and Business Continuity Plans for businesses and organizations in South Texas. After leaving IBM, David became an IT consultant providing many services including Disaster Recovery planning for small and medium-sized businesses.

David is currently completing his Ed.D. in Educational Leadership and holds a MS in Computer Information Systems and a BS in Business Administration all from the University of Phoenix. David is an instructor in the Computer Science and Information Technology department at Del Mar College. He teaches courses in Information Security, Security Management Practices, Intrusion Detection, Network Defense and Countermeasures and other Cyber-Security, Digital Forensic and Computer Networking courses. David has spoken at conferences on various Information Technology and Cyber-Security topics including Disaster Recovery and Business Continuity Planning
.

You can reach David Abarca by email at david@cbrsec.com

Acknowledgments

We would like to thank Emilie Herman for her help in getting this book into print. Her editorial help has been invaluable.

Quality Assurance

We would like to thank our Quality Assurance team for their attention to detail, and their efforts to make sure we got it right.

Technical Editors
Anooshirvan Ghazai
Jaime Sainz

## Chapter 1

Introduction to Disaster Recovery

Chapter Objectives

After reading this chapter and completing the exercises, you will be able to do the following:

- Define disaster recovery.
- Defend the need for an organizational disaster recovery plan.
- Define "disaster" as it applies to a business or organization and outline the types of disasters that might befall it.
- Describe how a disaster can affect an organization or business.
- Identify those threats that may be most relevant to an organization.
- Discuss specific threats to organizations.
- Explain the difference between a disaster recovery plan and a business continuity plan.

Introduction

Although you may not realize it in your day-to-day routine, you—and the business you work for—face disaster nearly every day. You may not consider yourself prepared, but in many ways you already are. If you have a job, you and your company pay into an unemployment fund that you have access to if you lose your job. If you have a mortgage on your home, the mortgage company generally requires insurance to protect you (and the mortgage company) from a catastrophic loss if the home burns down. If you own an automobile, most states require that you have proof of insurance to protect you, your passengers, and other drivers in case you cause an accident.

Organizations and businesses also have to plan ahead to protect the company, its employees, and its customers from those possible "unlucky breaks." For a company, a disaster could range from the breakdown of a piece of equipment (a mailing machine, computer, or phone system) to total destruction of the building through fire, hurricane, or terrorism. As in your personal life, the level of disaster facing a business or organization is all a matter of degree. In all cases, it pays to be prepared and ready to take action to keep the company functioning, clean up the mess or repair the problem, and move forward with a minimum of cost in the shortest amount of time.

Although phone systems and mailing machines are not necessarily what we typically consider to be part of disaster recovery, they are part of the system that allows an organization to function effectively and efficiently. You may not consider replacing a toner cartridge to be critical to an organization's continuation, but an extended period of time during which you cannot print, process payments, or write checks can spell disaster, particularly for an organization surviving on a shoestring.

The chapter begins the central discussion of the book: how you can prepare for the disasters that may occur and either avoid them or mitigate the damages to the organization should they occur. Future chapters will go into greater detail on exactly who should be on the disaster recovery planning team and what should go into the plan. We will look at testing and revising the disaster recovery document and security concerns for the recovery plan along the way.

Why Disaster Recovery?

If business continuity is everything that it takes for the business to continue, regardless of whether there is a disaster or not, then disaster recovery is that portion of business continuity that allows for how the business will continue if a disaster or emergency is declared.

Disaster recovery is the ability of a company to recover from a catastrophe and get back to business as usual. For example, if Lexmark Printing Company is flooded and loses all the printing jobs in progress, its printing and computer systems, and its entire supply of paper, what will it take for the company to recover the documents, equipment, and supplies that were lost? If Lexmark has a backup to the company computer system, and a second location that has paper inventory and can take over the jobs in progress, it may be able to get up and running quickly. If, however, Lexmark has failed to plan ahead in any of these critical categories, the company may or may not survive the flood.

If there is a major disaster, the first goal of the business is to maintain the minimal sustainable level of services for the organization. At the same time, it is critical to restore the company to business as usual as quickly as possible. This indicates that a two-pronged approach is needed for disaster recovery: to act most quickly on the most critical functions and processes, and to concurrently work on restoring all other processes and functions. Planning for the restoration process takes a concerted effort by all the experts in the many functions that the company carries out. Later chapters of this book will provide you with information about the process of planning for the recovery of the business.

Chapter 2 explains the steps required to start the process of developing a disaster recovery plan—what it takes to get the ball rolling. Chapter 3 looks at what exactly a disaster means, and describes assessing the risks to the organization of any given kind of disaster and determining the best plan of action to not only plan for the recovery from such an event, but to mitigate any damages that may occur and to help the company avoid the necessity of recovering at all. Chapter 4 looks at the decisions necessary to prioritize the systems that need to be recovered. Chapter 5 provides insights into data storage locations and disaster recovery site location selections. Chapter 6 covers developing the plans and procedures for disaster recovery, and Chapter 7 covers organizing the relationships needed. Chapter 8 gives some ideas on developing different procedures that may be required for the organization to recover in the light of special circumstances. Finally, Chapters 9 and 10 provide details on implementing the plan and continuing your assessment of the plan and of the organization's needs going into the future.

IN PRACTICE: Disaster Recovery in the Real World

Global Information Services (GIS) is an application service provider (ASP) that provides complete Oracle E-Business Suite hosting services for several small and medium-sized businesses in the area. The company processes accounting records and incoming and outgoing invoices, and writes and mails checks with the client's approval. In effect, it is a full-service accounting software, human resources, and Enterprise Resource Planning/Customer Relationship Management (ERP/CRM) services firm.

GIS found itself the victim of an arson fire that burned the building to the ground. It had what it believed to be a very effective disaster recovery plan. The company backed up all data religiously, and even practiced restoring the data. It practiced, on test servers, restoring the data and connecting to the data one server at a time. The company

▶▶ CONTINUED

even practiced on entire systems so that it could restore any given client system easily from its backups.

When push came to shove, however, it was not a lack of data backups that caused the company so many headaches—it was the lack of business continuity planning that caused GIS to have fines levied against it and to have very dissatisfied customers.

The backup site vendor provided GIS with heating and cooling, all utilities, and a fully functional building in which to work. The vendor provided stocked vending machines and had arrangements with all the local restaurants for delivery, often 24-hour-a-day delivery.

GIS had planned on how it would print reports and checks. It had the hardware lined up with its disaster recovery vendor. Servers, PCs, and printers were all taken into account and provided for. It planned for manning the servers and having bodies to maintain the systems at the PCs, and even planned for having a print room operator to handle the paper and the printing. The flow chart of GIS's plan can be seen in Figure 1.1.

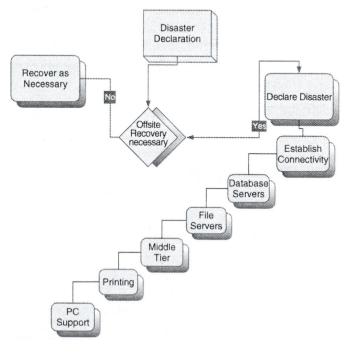

FIGURE 1.1 Original GIS disaster recovery plan.

▶▶ CONTINUED ON NEXT PAGE

What was GIS missing? The company hadn't planned on mail-room people to stuff the envelopes with invoices or checks, nor had it planned on needing supplies (office supplies, custom checks and invoices, or printed envelopes). It hadn't planned on having its own accounting people available to process payments in the system, nor did it provide for bank deposits and withdrawals. It hadn't provided for payroll to provide the input for having employees paid, and it hadn't thought ahead that, in a disaster situation, ready cash for expenses for those having to find their way to the backup site (800 miles away) might be an issue as well.

So GIS's plans went slightly awry.

When GIS recovered from its disaster, more the wiser and somewhat worse off from a balance sheet perspective, it made revisions to its plan. Figure 1.2 shows the alterations to the plan. As you can see, the company learned from its mistakes and bolstered its business continuity plan to better meet the needs of the business—not just to recover the data and access in the event of an actual emergency.

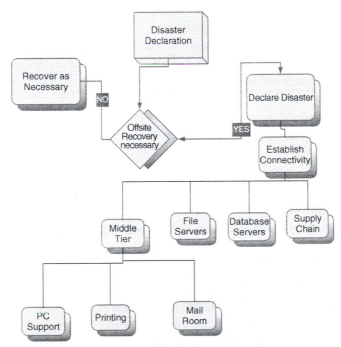

FIGURE 1.2 Revised GIS disaster recovery plan.

> **CONTINUED**
>
> Disaster recovery is often considered as just an information technology (IT) problem. The rationale is that if the IT computer systems can be restored in a reasonable amount of time, the organization will continue on with the company business as before. This is not necessarily true. There are many critical business processes that are either tangential to IT operations or that are critical business functions that are not directly IT related.

Business Functions

Business functions are those functions that provide products and/or services. This is what the business is all about, regardless of what the business is. This is how businesses make their money and, unless they are an Internet service provider (ISP) or an application service provider (ASP) business model, it isn't likely that they make their money strictly through the IT services that they may provide. Many people see Amazon.com as strictly an IT company because it is fundamentally an Internet presence through which you can purchase things, but it also must have the facility to see to it that the product is shipped to the customer.

Critical Support Functions

Critical support functions are not necessarily directly related to the company's core competencies—its main line of business—but are functions without which the business can't operate. This is where IT comes into the picture. It isn't the be all and end all of the critical support functions, but it is an important link in the overall business continuity.

Corporate-Level Support Functions

Corporate-level support functions are the functions that may not be critical to the day-to-day operation of the organization, but are required for the effective and efficient operations of the business functions. Human resources (HR) might fall into this category.

But who is affected by a disaster? What are the consequences and who, besides the company itself, should be concerned?

What Is a Disaster?

On a business level, *disasters* are often thought of as catastrophic occurrences that happen to affect the business or organization, or those occurrences on a grand scale that disrupt the business's ability to function. For example, the British Columbian

Ministry of Human Resources' Emergency Social Services division defines a disaster as "A calamity caused by accident, fire, explosion, or technical failure, or by the forces of nature that has resulted in serious harm to the health, safety or welfare of people, or in widespread damage to property." (**http://www.pep.bc.ca**)

FYI | *British Columbia Ministry of Human Resources*

British Columbia's Ministry of Human Resources has a very complete Web site dedicated to Emergency Social Services and emergency preparedness at **http://www.ess.bc.ca.** It provides in-depth information on the British Columbia Emergency Program Act and numerous resources on disaster preparedness for not only organizations but for personal preparedness as well.

There is an interesting document on the Web site called *It Can Happen to Your Agency! Tools for Change: Emergency Management for Women's Services.* Although directed at women, the information contained in this document applies to everyone and is a worthwhile addition to a disaster recovery library.

Women's Services is little different than any other organization, and the name of the paper speaks to this. However, it really can happen to any agency. The workbook breaks the often-daunting concept of emergency planning into a discrete set of 12 tasks. Any company, regardless of location, complexity, or organization type, can take these steps, and follow or modify them to the company's specific needs. The workbook can help in the overall business continuity planning; it speaks to the whole organization and is a tool that can be used to help it to survive any emergency.

There is a common conception that a disaster is something that affects not only a given organization, but a community as well. Governments often use this concept of disaster (the idea that a disaster is something that affects an entire location as opposed to a single organization) to determine availability or qualification for aid or funding assistance after a disaster. Most employees and managers would probably agree that fires, floods, hurricanes, tornadoes, and terrorist attacks are all disasters that would adversely affect their business and they might define disaster in a similar way. But is this too narrow a scope? This definition does not cover all the potential disasters that can adversely affect businesses or organizations. So how should businesses and organizations really define a potential disaster?

In contrast to the British Ministry of Human Resources disaster definition, the Tasmanian government Web site provides a more comprehensive explanation of a disaster (found in **http://www.ses.tas.gov.au/Library/Tasmanian%20 Emergency%20Management%20Plan%20Issue%205%20-%20 September% 202005.pdf**). The Tasmanian government defines disaster as "a condition in which an information resource is unavailable, as a result of a natural or man-made occurrence that is of sufficient duration to cause significant disruption in the accomplishment of agency program objectives, as determined by agency management."

The Tasmanian government's definition might serve a business or organization better. It indicates that a disaster involves information resources, which is a critical component in the operation of most, if not all, businesses and organizations. It allows the affected organization or business to determine exactly what constitutes a disaster and its impact. Finally, it suggests that any situation that disrupts normal day-to-day business may be considered a disaster. However, this definition may be self-limiting to the detriment of those using it as their sole basis for the definition of disaster. This limitation is due greatly to the fact that it limits the scope to information resources. Although information resources are what IT departments are primarily interested in, they are not necessarily all that the organization is interested in, and even the definition of information resources can vary widely. Rarely, however, does the information resources definition include microfilm, microfiche, or paper documents, although many organizations still rely heavily on these information resources.

Dictionary.com defines disaster as "An occurrence causing widespread destruction and distress; a catastrophe" or "A grave misfortune" (**http://dictionary. reference.com/search?q=disaster&r=67**). Not only is this definition more relevant for not only information technology but also for all sectors of a given organization. A disaster not only disrupts the information technology resources of a given organization, it disrupts the organization in any and often all facets of its business. Thinking of a disaster as any unforeseen or sudden event that causes damage to a company or organization, it's possible to extend the scope of what is classified as a disaster. This expanded definition may also allow for more complete planning for the consequences of any disaster and for exploring the ramifications to all involved parties of the possible event. Only through this exploration, and carefully thinking and planning ahead, will a business become prepared for any eventuality.

For the remainder of this book, we will consider a disaster to be defined as any event or occurrence that can have a detrimental effect on an organization either in whole or in part. This definition is broad enough to allow for nearly any event that can harm any part of the organization, and narrow enough to only encompass the organization itself and not necessarily the surrounding environment, while not limiting the resources that may be involved or affected.

To a great degree, how a business defines a disaster is dependent on the type of business, what is required for that business to continue to function as a business, and where that business is located.

FYI *U.S. Government Assistance with Disaster Planning and Recovery*

The Federal Emergency Management Agency (FEMA, **http://www. fema.org** or **http://www.fema.gov**), in cooperation with the Department of Homeland Security, offers resources, independent study classes, and exams (**http://training.fema.gov/EMIWeb/ IS/crslist.asp**) that you can take to ensure that you are prepared for of an actual disaster. Although most of the information in the self-study courses is designed for either individuals or for government and community action and reaction in emergency situations, the information within the pages is invaluable, applicable, and extensible to business situations. One of the most invaluable resources on the FEMA site is the library of disasters and emergencies. This section includes itemized lists, by state and counties within a state, of the declared disasters on a yearly basis. This information can assist you in determining your risk for a given situation.

What Kinds of Disasters Are There?

Disasters can take on many different forms and severities, from earthquakes and other acts of nature to sabotage by a disgruntled employee or an attack on a network by malevolent external sources. The various dangers a business faces vary by degree. Some may be perceived as a total disaster, and others may simply be a nuisance. However, by looking at the definitions of disaster spelled out previously, all disasters—both large and small—meet the criteria: an event that creates a detrimental effect on the business practices of the organization. In more conversational language, a disaster is anything that happens to or around an organization that has any harmful (either in actuality or perceived) effect on the organization.

The major threats of disaster facing companies are:

- Accidents
- Technological breakdowns
- Acts of nature
- Deliberate acts of sabotage

The sheer number of possible events that can occur is mind-boggling and each event comes with its own range of severities. But the more a company can face the possibilities and prepare for those disruptions that may be most likely, given the company's geographic location and type of business, the less likely that a disaster will destroy the business.

It is often said simply that "accidents can happen to everyone." Although this is true, and it is also true that many are unavoidable, some accidents (even avoidable or preventable ones) can have a major impact on a business.

Lack of Computer Security

The following situations are caused by a lack of computer security. Lack of security in a computer system is often one of the leading causes of system loss seen by organizations.

Hackers Hackers get in without any notice though standard ports that are left open, or through software products that can be leveraged to allow them through. Hackers may "just" attempt to access data or may use the company network as a launching point to get to other networks, or may be interested in disabling or causing harm to the networks into which they are hacking.

Viruses Viruses may not seem like disasters, but ask the companies who struggled with the "I LOVE YOU" virus and its offshoots about the havoc it wrought on their systems. Many organizations had to shut down networks and disable e-mail systems for extended periods of time in order to combat the virus and its effects.

Spam Spam, as a disaster in the making? As unusual as it sounds, it can be. Spam causes major issues for organizations. End users tend to see it as a nuisance or something to poke fun at in jokes, but when an e-mail server is flooded with tens of thousands of spam messages a day, or even an hour, valuable resources are being used in the delivery of spam to those who have no desire to get it.

Some organizations have had to dedicate a dozen or more servers to the filtering of spam from useful e-mail. These servers cost money that could be spent in other areas and take resources from other jobs that would be more productive to the organization keeping e-mail servers from crashing from overwork.

Death of Key Employees

Employee death or long-term incapacitation is also not usually seen as a disaster for a company, but depending on the size of the company and the employee in question, it can be.

Owner In a small company, the death of the owner can mean dissolution of the company. Even if there isn't total dissolution, it can mean disruption or upheaval for an extended period of time. The owner may be the only one who has access to certain reports or key information. Sudden death may mean that the accessibility of that information is limited for an extended period of time, or that people simply don't know that the accessibility is necessary. This kind of disaster may not be the kind that causes you to recover the company in another location; it may mean that the company is unrecoverable.

CEO　　The same thing is true for a company president or the CEO of a larger organization. Although the knowledge of the information's existence is likely to be more widespread in this case, accessibility to that information may not be any easier.

Other Key Personnel　　In most organizations there are people who have specialized knowledge of the organization, its inner workings, different pieces of software or hardware, or of how different pieces work together. These people may not have written anything down pertaining to their specialized knowledge, and their sudden unavailability can mean that processes will break or that broken processes have to be thoroughly researched before fixes can even be considered.

　　Similar to the loss of the owner, the loss of key people can mean extensive resources expended in the pursuit of stability. These losses are usually better mitigated by avoiding the situation where one person has all the information.

Strikes

Strikes are usually only seen as disruptions to business and production, but if strikes turn ugly, people can attempt to disrupt the flow of information into and out of an organization, either by affecting the conduit through which the information flows or by tampering with the information systems from inside the organization.

　　Special security measures need to be put into place when considering strike situations either in process or threatened in the near future.

Accidents

Any location housing a business is at risk from a multitude of potential disasters. Some are directly attributable to individuals, whereas others can't easily be blamed on a person or on a natural occurrence.

　　Accidents that affect buildings that are attributable to individuals are said to be vandalism when intentional. These accidents can be breakage of glass in doors and windows or even a vehicle driving through the wall of a building.

　　Accidents that cannot be attributed to individuals may range from flooding caused by a waterline break or sewer line backups, rodents chewing through wiring, or structural vulnerabilities caused by earthquake or volcanic activity.

Created by People　　Company employees use the company's resources, access and manipulate valuable data, and rely on these things for the work they do. Therefore, it is critical that the data remain intact, available, and accessible to employees in order for the company to continue to function. Because so many people use the company computer files, and often take the use of the data and its continuous availability for granted, that data is always at risk to accidents by the people who access it (either those accessing it legitimately or those accessing it for nefarious purposes). The need for constant access also makes restoration—in case of accident—a difficult task.

The accidents that may occur include deletion of data at the file or record levels, data corruption, or data intrusion. These losses are insidious and harder to pinpoint than some other threats because the loss may be limited to a particular file or record and may go unnoticed for an extended period of time. Further, if the only "loss" of data is that the data was accessed and then copied for less-than-honest purposes (leaking information to other companies, for example) the intrusion and loss may only be discovered when the data shows up in places where it is not supposed to be. Although it would be helpful if a user who accidentally deleted data were to request assistance in retrieving the information as soon as the accident happens, these disasters often go unreported for an extended time, making restoration of the data difficult or impossible.

Spills

If a company uses or stores toxic chemicals, there is a risk of a spill, either within the company or during shipping. Chemical spills could have far-reaching effects depending on the type of chemical and the location of the spill. There may be extensive damage to the building, groundwater, property, and to personnel safety. Although it's possible for some chemical spills to be contained quickly, the company may face serious financial consequences in fines and cleanup costs.

Chemical spills can aversely affect access to critical data if the spill is in an area of a building where either servers or access points are located. Many companies have their PCs sitting on the floor of the offices. A spill, and the resulting cleanup effort, can cause damage to valuable equipment and make the data inaccessible for an extended period of time.

Another kind of spill that can cause significant problems for organizations is a spill of the product being manufactured. Plastics plants, steel manufacturers, and oil refineries are all examples of types of businesses that can see downtime related to a spill.

One steel firm housed its computer systems on the second story of the building where heats of steel were transferred from the furnace to tank cars. When a heat of steel (a batch of steel) was accidentally spilled on the floor, however, poorly placed electrical and computer network cabling was affected, causing an outage to critical computers. In this case, moving the computer systems to another part of the plant while services to the main computer room were being restored was already in the firm's recovery plans and was easy enough to do.

Explosions

Depending on the type of business, explosives may be a part of the day-to-day operations of the business. For example, a taconite plant in northern Minnesota or a gravel quarry in the Midwest requires explosives to operate. Accidents can happen, and it's important that all personnel are trained in the safe use of explosives and that an accident contingency plan be a part of the training employees receive. For other businesses, such as a refinery in Texas or a grain elevator in Nebraska, explosions are a dreaded occurrence, but can happen because of the volatile compounds present.

Although it is true that most organizations will not have explosives on site, there is an increased chance of terrorist threats dealing with the use of explosives. It may not be that you have to worry about your own explosives, but you may need to remain aware of the threat of destruction associated with explosives.

Technological Breakdowns

Technological threats include utility failures, hardware and software failures, and heating, ventilation, and air conditioning or other environmental-control failures.

Electrical   Electricity is such a vital part of every company's business that it is easy to forget that at times it can fail without warning. In a windowless building, working is difficult without electric lights, and even getting out of the building is a challenge. A food manufacturing plant depends on refrigeration and freezing to maintain its products. Every business relies on computers for some part of the business: inventory control, client records, data processing, and myriad other vital functions. Power failure caused by a breaker blowing or a transformer going down in the area can cause major headaches for a company.

But what if it isn't "just" a transformer going down? For example, let's look at the enormous power outage that hit the United States in August 2003. In just about 3 minutes, 21 power plants in the Northeast and Midwest shut down, stopping trains, elevators, and all data processing. Over a million and a half people in New Jersey alone were affected by the blackout. Companies with uninterruptible power supplies (UPS) or independent generators were able to bring down systems without causing crashes, or even were able to function (for those where power was restored within an hour or two or for those who had generators) during the outage. Others were not so lucky. Computer crashes had to be recovered from. Spoilage of food was a major problem for many grocers. The inability to meet deadlines due to the physical inability to do work caused many issues with a large number of companies. But who thinks that a power outage will occur that has this far reaching of an effect?

Loss of electric power may lead to a communications failure as people are unable to communicate via e-mail and perhaps even by phone. Again, in the blackout of August 2003, the inability to communicate in nearly every way was affected, from TV stations, newspapers, and radio stations to faxes and other means of communication that rely in part or in whole on the electrical grid's availability. Communications failures may be critical because important clients, vendors, or suppliers may be unable to contact the organizations' personnel to verify orders, shipments, or crucial information about ongoing operations.

Many companies have the ability to mitigate the damage caused by an electrical outage through the use of generators. This is of particular concern to hospitals and nursing homes, where patients may be on critical life-support functions and where surgeries can't be performed without electricity.

At the other end of the spectrum, a power surge may cause irreparable damage to a computer system, may make a hard drive unreadable, or may destroy other electrical equipment or machinery.

Gas Gas leaks can happen internally or externally to the company's facilities. They can cause additional problems of explosions or fire, or may just make a building uninhabitable for a period of time. Given the amount of electrical equipment in even a modest data center, gas leaks can mean extended downtime while safe operation is restored.

Hardware and Software Failure Electrical failure can lead to hardware failure, which in turn can lead to software failure. Power failure without adequate uninterruptible power supply (UPS) can lead to hardware failure. Hard drives, or disk drives, are more reliable than ever; however, it is also true that power surges and power failures happen, and anything mechanical that relies on a constant source of power is susceptible to breakdown if that power supply isn't maintained. Not only can hard drives crash, causing issues with data and software corruption, but many components could be physically damaged in the sudden loss of power or in the return of the power in an inelegant manner.

Heating, Ventilation, and Air Conditioning (HVAC) Heating, ventilation, and air conditioning all rely in total or in part on the availability of a source of electricity. Heating may rely on the availability of natural gas, fuel oil, or entirely on electricity for its power source. Although many people consider HVAC systems to be more directly associated with the people aspect of an organization, as it can get very uncomfortable if not seriously unhealthy if the HVAC system goes out in a building (think of the fact that HVAC is the only way that many buildings provide an adequate supply of exchanged air into the building), computer systems find it equally as unhealthy to be without adequate heating and cooling.

HVAC is critical to the efficient operation of the data center. Without it there would be no control of the ambient environment, and no control over the temperature, humidity, and airflow in the data center. This can mean that expensive servers and mainframes can overheat. Nearly any physical hardware device comes with its own environmental requirements. These requirements are often limited when dealing with personal computers and laptops, but there are often more extensive requirements for not only temperature but also humidity ranges for any hardware product. HVAC is what provides the data center with the ability to maintain the operating environment within these guidelines. Without it, even for a short time, extensive damage can occur to the hardware.

Sabotage and Terrorism

By far the most insidious threat to an organization and its ability to recover and remain viable as a company is sabotage, or a deliberate attack on the company. Sabotage is often well planned, and consequently may be well hidden. Listen to the news on any given day and you can see examples of threats that have the potential to impact organizations of any size all over the globe. Deliberate threats can be internal, from employees, or they can be external acts of terrorism.

The possibilities for intrusion and the damage that can be caused are nearly endless for someone intent on wreaking havoc on a business. Someone intent on causing damage to the business might leave a faucet on and allow a sink to overflow, or may start a fire. In the technology area, the saboteur might cause hardware or software failure, or destroy utilities such as the phone, alarm, or heating/cooling systems. It is possible that the perpetrator might make the sabotage appear to be an accident, or permit non-employees into the building to cause damage. The intruder may cause denial of service for a company connected to the Internet or may cripple a system internally with a well-placed worm or virus.

Another valid concern for company management is that the saboteur may hide misdeeds by leaving a trail pointing to someone else. As we will discuss in Chapter 3, this is one of the reasons why it is important to keep passwords private, not to write a password down and store it where it can be found, and to have multiple levels of authentication and authorization over a system. It is also a reason for not leaving back doors in systems no matter how attractive this might appear on the surface.

FYI   *The Cuckoo's Egg*

The Cuckoo's Egg by Cliff Stoll (Doubleday, 1989) provides entertaining information on how it would be very easy for someone determined to use a network to keep his presence unknown or to look like a regular user.

With the changes in national and corporate security that have been made in recent years, many of the holes in the system exploited in the book have been patched in most systems, and better methods for intruder detection have been created. However, the book points out that, even in what we consider to be extremely secure systems, there may be weaknesses that can be exploited. These may be there

▶▶ CONTINUED

by accident, or they may be left open because of poor training and misinformation.

Although the information is somewhat dated (I read it in 1994 as a freshman undergrad at the University of Pittsburgh's School of Information Sciences), it is a must read for anyone going into information security. It is still relevant today because there are still systems out there with back doors that can be exploited, more sophisticated methods of scavenging users' information have been developed, and users haven't necessarily become more sophisticated. Despite all the warnings that are given by network administrators, users still use the names of their kids, spouse, or pet as passwords and use those same passwords on every system. System administrators don't always look for network access at unusual hours by people who shouldn't be accessing the system at those times. If they do find it, and the people involved are high enough in the organization, the system administrator may feel that it isn't his or her place to question why the CIO is in the system poking around in the financial information of the organization at 3 A.M. on a Sunday morning. It is true that most organizations are much tighter and more secure than they were 10 or 20 years ago, but why take the chance? This book is an entertaining way to realize that more organizations than we think may still be taking that chance.

What Are the Possible Effects of a Disaster?

It is important to realize that, in any disaster situation, it is likely that many people will be affected in some way. An organization must recognize all the individuals who will be affected and understand the ramifications on the business.

For example, there has been a fire at one location of Business Systems Inc., a chain with several offices in Pennsylvania. One location (in Bird in Hand) of the business has been affected by smoke, water, and fire damage. Who is affected? It is simple to say that the employees at that location find it difficult, if not impossible, to perform their jobs because the building is not safe to enter, and much of the office equipment has been destroyed. It is also not a great leap to determine that other business locations will also be affected, because customers and clients have to shift their business, temporarily, to another location. The employees at those locations have to pick up the overflow work. In addition, there are others who will be affected by the fire. The fire may cause a ripple effect to many other individuals; this is true of nearly every disaster.

Within the Organization

Employees of the affected organization are clearly on the front line and the first to feel the impact of the disaster. Depending on the type, duration, and location of the disaster, the effects may or may not be overcome.

The Organizational Structure   Any disaster, whether large or small, will have a ripple effect through the entire organization in its policies, procedures, and even how and whether the company can continue functioning. The disaster may cause individual members to come together as a working team or may drive the members into competition for scarce resources. In part, the actions of the company at this time will be driven by the advance preparations that have taken place to plan for this eventuality.

The Disaster Recovery Team   The disaster recovery team will be made up of many different people in the organization who have a stake in the outcome of recovering from a disaster and who have the ability to do something about the disaster recovery process. Many of these people will have specialized knowledge and will be able to assist with the planning and testing of plans to meet the ultimate goal of being able to recover from any disaster that might befall the organization.

Disasters will, therefore, naturally affect the disaster recovery team, both those involved in the planning aspects and those called upon to carry out the plan. These people have to be provided with training and instructions as well as a disaster call list indicating those parties responsible for all aspects of the disaster recovery scenario and a call list for those software vendors from whom support and information will be required throughout the recovery process.

Employees   Every employee in an organization, regardless of job description, the direct impact of the disaster on immediate responsibilities, or the direct impact the employee can have on the recovery effort, will feel the effects of the disaster.

Some of the individual effects may be temporary loss of income (if the company closes for a short time to repair losses), difficulty in getting to the place of business (if the surrounding area is affected, such as by a flood), having to work in less-than-ideal conditions (if work continues even though the building has been damaged by the disaster), and even loss of employment (if the company permanently closes because of the disaster). In all cases, the uncertainty following the disaster will cause stress and worry for the employees, and most likely some work disruption.

It is important that employees be kept aware of what is going on in the organization and the effects that the changes will have on their future.

Employees' Families   If employees are concerned and stressed, their family members will be also. Family members worry about the safety and wellbeing of the family member who is affected by the disaster and any family member who is cleaning up after the disaster occurs. In addition, loss of income, changed work hours and schedules, or other short- or long-term effects of the disaster on the business and the business's employees also affect family members.

External to the Organization

A disaster doesn't just affect those who work for the company and their families. Many others are directly or indirectly pulled into the chaos that can surround a minor or major catastrophe.

Customers/Clients Customers and clients will have a direct interest in the outcome of the disaster recovery. They will want to be assured that the organization will continue in business or they may switch their business to competitors.

If the disaster affects the geographic region (flood, hurricane, or other similar disaster), many of the customers are also likely to be affected by the disaster. These customers may be more lenient and understanding than those who are not affected by the disaster.

Because many companies are multi-location and either international or interstate, many of the customers interested in the products or services provided by the company will not be affected by the disaster. They will be less tolerant of extended interruptions in service. An exception is a national or international disaster, such as the 9/11 attacks, which may draw people together in a common bond. Customers and clients are likely to be more understanding and go out of their way to support the stricken businesses as they regroup.

Competitors Depending on the duration and severity of the disaster facing a company, the company's competitors may be affected. The competitors may gain a competitive advantage as customers seek products and services the affected company can no longer provide. It is also possible that the competitors may gain so much business that the competitors' employees and ability to provide product may be temporarily stretched to the limit. The companies may not be able to handle the increased business because staff was not prepared.

Suppliers and Receivers Suppliers depend upon their downstream organizations to purchase a given amount of supplies. If the company purchasing a regular amount of supplies unexpectedly can no longer purchase the supplies, the supplier may run into financial difficulties and have an oversupply of product. On the other side, if the company suffering the disaster is no longer able to produce a product desperately needed by another company, another product and revenue stream is affected and may be unable to function.

Utility companies may be affected by the disaster directly or indirectly. They may be affected by an organization's ability to pay for utility service or by the organization's short-term or long-term increased or decreased need for the utilities supplied.

Disaster Aid   Depending on the type of disaster, outside assistance may be enlisted to overcome it. Fire departments, police departments, the National Guard, the Red Cross, and emergency medical technicians (EMTs) may need to be called upon to assist one or more organizations in a disaster. These people may be asked to go "above and beyond the call of duty" and sacrifice their time, energy, and even their lives in the fight to save others during a major disaster.

Banks   Banks will likely to be called upon, in disasters of significant size, to provide interim funding to those affected by disasters. However, if the disaster is extremely localized, or is organization specific, funding may disappear based on a perceived inability for the organization to remain a viable business in the face of adversity.

What Is Business Continuity Planning?

Another term often applied to disaster recovery is often business continuity planning (BCP), a more accurate description of the overall process, but not necessarily synonymous. Business continuity implies that the continuation of the business is the goal, and this is the goal of BCP. Disaster recovery is that part of the business continuity plan that deals with what the company will do in the event of an emergency or a declared disaster.

Although disaster recovery is often aimed at simply picking up the pieces of the business after a disaster strikes and attempting to function until the business can be fully repaired (a reactive response even when planned for), BCP is typically proactive and involves advance planning. The focus of BCP is attempting to avoid a risk or mitigating the consequences of the risk.

Disaster recovery is an integral part of BCP, but business continuity planning is much broader. Disaster recovery implies simply being able to become marginally functional for the duration—likely a short time—of an adverse event. In BCP, you may go beyond the recovery of a company's computer systems and ability to do work; you may need to relocate the entire company.

BCP is interested in avoiding disasters if possible. It looks not only at making sure that the given organization can recover sufficiently to survive, but looks at managing the supply chain if unforeseen circumstances affect either the given organization or the environment in which it operates. It addresses alternate sources of supplies and personnel should that become necessary and training for additional people should they be needed.

Disaster recovery typically looks at the short term and maintaining functionality, for example, the first 72 hours or the first week. BCP typically looks at the longer term.

Disaster recovery plans are often broken down by when each function to be recovered will be required by the organization. This allows the business units to know when they can anticipate their information becoming available, and those performing the recovery to plan and prepare for what needs to be in place and when it needs to be there.

One common method of delineating the plan is to separate the functions into tiers, with each tier having a recovery timeline a little further out than the previous tier.

This can mean that a Tier 1 timeline may include those functions that have to be available within the first 72 hours. This allows those performing the recovery to concentrate on just those functions that the organization has determined to be mission critical to sustaining its business functions during the time that it will take to recover the rest of the systems. This will likely include many of the accounting functions, including accounts receivable and accounts payable, payroll, and any functions that allow clients to interact with the system.

Tier 2 functions may be able to be pushed out to the end of a week or 10 days. This may include those auxiliary functions, like HR and marketing or sales, that need to occur in order to continue or grow the business but that do not have to be operational immediately.

Tier 3 functions may be able to wait until the end of the first month. This will likely include report printing and batch reporting, possibly month-end processing, and time tracking.

There may even be functions that are deemed by the organization as not being required in a disaster recovery situation until business as usual has been restored.

By allowing everyone to know what is likely to be available and what is required to be available, expectations and planning can be managed and stress will be kept to a minimum.

Who and what needs to be taken into account? What functions need to be considered and what functions are often missed?

Summary

Disaster recovery and BCP are activities that all organizations, regardless of their size and complexity, should undertake. The ability of a company to remain profitable and viable through emergency situations is critical. To this end, we are looking at disaster recovery.

What is a disaster? A disaster is any condition in which a resource is unavailable for a period of sufficient duration to cause significant disruption to a business, as determined by that organization's management.

What kinds of disasters are relevant? Although we might think that only great disasters are those from which we would have to recover, it is often the small insidious disasters that cause the most havoc and damage to an organization.

The importance of any given threat to an organization has to be determined by those connected to the organization, and the long-reaching effects also have to be determined.

There are many stakeholders in a disaster situation, and each is impacted in a different way and to a different extent. Many of these stakeholders are not people you would immediately consider to be directly connected to the company or directly affected by the disaster.

Disaster recovery plans are important in order to determine how an organization will react in the face of a disaster and how that organization will recover its ability to do work and perform its functions following the disaster situation.

Test Your Skills

MULTIPLE CHOICE QUESTIONS

1. A critical component in the operation of most, if not all, businesses and organizations is _____.
   A. data mining
   B. information resources
   C. security resources
   D. information mining

2. Any event or occurrence that can have a detrimental affect to an organization is known as a(n) _____.
   A. unexpected event
   B. disaster
   C. business disruption
   D. unfortunate event

3. A leading cause of system loss seen by organizations is _____.
   A. employee death
   B. natural disasters
   C. lack of computer security
   D. strikes

4. In a small company, the _____ can be a disaster for the company.
   A. key personnel
   B. inner workings
   C. death of an employee
   D. extensive resources

5. Individuals who try to gain unauthorized access to data or a company network are known as _____.

   A. intruders

   B. data miners

   C. hackers

   D. worms

6. Don't keep the _____ password that comes with a system.

   A. manager

   B. system

   C. assigned

   D. default

7. Accidents affecting buildings that are attributable to individuals are often said to be _____ of some type.

   A. natural disasters

   B. vandalism

   C. planned events

   D. disruptions

8. Accidents created by people may include the deletion of data at the file or _____ level.

   A. information

   B. security

   C. access

   D. record

9. Threats that include utility failures, hardware and software failures, and heating, ventilation, and air conditioning or other environmental-control failures are known as _____ threats.

   A. human

   B. natural

   C. technological

   D. structural

10. Loss of electrical power may lead to disruption in _____ systems.

    A. standardization

    B. communication

    C. offsite

    D. customer

11. _____ threats may include flooding, fire, seismic activity, wind, snow, ice storms, volcanic eruption, tornado, hurricane, epidemic, famine, and drought.

    A. Adverse

    B. Natural

    C. Technical

    D. Weather

12. The part of the business continuity plan that deals with what the company will do in the event of an emergency or a declared disaster is known as the _____ plan.

    A. update recovery

    B. disaster recovery

    C. short-term recovery

    D. long-term recovery

13. Disaster recovery plans are designed for _____ recovery of business operations.

    A. short-term

    B. long-term

    C. continuing-term

    D. indefinite-term

14. Business continuity planning is interested in _____ disasters if possible.

    A. resisting

    B. organizing

    C. weathering

    D. avoiding

15. In the event of a major disaster, the _____ goal of the business is to maintain the minimal sustainable level of services for the organization.

    A. first

    B. second

    C. third

    D. final

16. The _____ team will be made up of many different people in the organization who have a stake in the outcome of recovering from a disaster and who have the ability to do something about the disaster recovery process.

    A. disaster restructuring

    B. disaster review

    C. disaster recovery

    D. disaster reorganizing

EXERCISES

Exercise 1.1: Understanding Key Services

1. Select a company, either real or fictitious.

2. Completely describe the company, including the business and where the company is located.

3. Determine the minimum services that must be maintained for that company after a disaster. What services should be restored first? What services do you think can be put off until later?

Exercise 1.2: Key Services Based on Disaster Type

1. Select a company, either real or fictitious.

2. Describe the company. Be sure to include the nature of the business, where the company is located, and the size of the company.

3. Determine the minimum services that must be maintained for that company after a disaster. Which service should be restored first? What services do you think can be put off until later? How would the list of services be affected based on the type of disaster (natural, technical, or human)?

Exercise 1.3: Disasters in a Competitive Environment

1. Place a company in a competitive environment. Determine the services that allow it to maintain a competitive advantage in its environment.

2. Determine what services are required to maintain business continuity.

3. How does the presence of competition affect your decisions on what services are maintained or sacrificed?

Exercise 1.4: Technological Breakdowns

1. Make a list of five different technological disasters.

2. List five similarities and differences between these disasters.

Exercise 1.5: Home Offices

1. Most discussions of disaster recovery target businesses with their own separate locations. Consider situations surrounding home computers, either used simply for running the home or for running a home-based business. Is there a need for a disaster recovery plan for home-based businesses and/or home offices?

2. Discuss how disaster recovery planning may be different for home offices than for corporate offices.

3. Explain the differences encountered with computers that are shared between personal and home-office use.

Exercise 1.6: Risk Assessments

1. Choose a business, either real or fictitious.

2. Describe the business, its line of business, its geographic location, and its physical location.

3. Create a risk assessment, for each of the following disasters:
   a. Tornado
   b. Hurricane
   c. Power grid failure
   d. Bacterial/viral outbreak
   e. Mainframe/server failure
   f. CEO and key department figures killed in plane crash
   g. Internal hacker that has deleted all network configurations
   h. Web page html file deleted
   i. HR Equal Employment Opportunity (EEO) database corrupted
   j. Mail server failure

Exercise 1.7: Natural Disaster Determinations

1. Divide the country into four quadrants.

2. Describe, topographically and in terms of population centers, your quadrants.

3. Discuss the types of natural disasters that may affect each quadrant. Use the National Weather Service (**www.nws.noaa.gov**) and U.S. Geological Survey (**www.usgs.gov**) as references to find information on where natural disasters occur.

PROJECTS

Project 1.1: Discovering Disaster Recovery Information

1. Using an Internet search engine of your choice, search on the words "disaster recovery" or "business continuity."

2. List five sites that contain articles relating to disaster recovery.

3. Write a summary for each article.

4. Describe how each article applies to our definition of disaster recovery.

Project 1.2: Disaster Recognition

1. Choose one type of disaster: human, technical, or natural.

2. Describe the disaster as completely as possible, for example, a tornado with a rating of F4 on the Fujita scale touching down and creating a path of destruction over 10 miles long and almost 1 mile wide.

3. Research the type of disaster on the Internet and write a short report on the disaster, how it occurs, and if there are businesses or locations that are more apt to be affected by it. Cite any sources.

4. Choose a company, either real or fictitious, and describe how that business might be affected by the chosen disaster.

Project 1.3: Disasters Affecting the United States

1. Name seven disasters that have occurred in the United States over the last 5 years.

2. Describe the type of disaster that each was.

3. Businesses were affected by these disasters; describe how each disaster affected at least one business in the area. For example, how would a hurricane impacting Miami, FL affect a local Starbucks?

Case **Study**

Choose one of the following department head positions in an organization or another position of equal relevance to a real organization:

Computer Operations

Accounting

Marketing

Payroll

Sales

Distribution

Human Resources

Purchasing

Service (i.e., vehicle maintenance)

Describe the services that your department provides to the organization, the types of disasters will most affect your department, and what you and your department can do to prepare for a disaster situation. Perform a limited risk analysis for the department that you choose (because any given department in an organization can be considered an organization on its own) for one type of disaster mentioned in the chapter and prepare to justify your answers.

Chapter | 2

Preparing to Develop the Disaster Recovery Plan

Chapter Objectives

After reading this chapter and completing the exercises, you will be able to do the following:

- Choose the disaster recovery team.
- Define tasks that typically are assigned to the disaster recovery team.
- Describe the characteristics of disaster recovery team members.
- Create a notification directory.
- Understand what is involved in getting management support.
- Describe and understand the process involved in securing resources.
- Explain how to prepare your resources.

Introduction

The first step in any endeavor is to plan. It has been said that the journey of 1000 miles begins with a single step. In the case of a *disaster recovery plan,* the preparation for the plan is one of the most important steps, and a step that can't be skipped. Knowing the direction that you are going in and who you will be traveling with makes a solid foundation for the trip ahead.

What is a disaster recovery plan? It is, simply, a document that defines all the known resources, actions, tasks, systems, and data that are required to manage a business recovery process in the event of a significant business interruption. It is designed to assist in restoring the business process within the business recovery goals of the organization.

There are many strategies for developing the disaster recovery plan; which one you choose depends on what you want to get out of the recovery.

Each choice has different implications. You can do nothing, recognizing that if there is a disaster you may not be able to continue as a going business. In this scenario, the business will revert to manual processing until such time as you may, or may not, be able to recover the business as usual.

A company can become self-reliant and maintain the ability to recover its systems internally by utilizing multiple sites (either real time or at what is considered to be a standby *disaster recovery site*). If a company chooses a standby recovery site (often referred to as a *hotsite*) it would either contract with a hotsite vendor or maintain a duplicate site on its own. This duplicate site is the location from where the company would run the business if anything were to happen at the primary site. The data at this site is as current as possible, and the failover recovery time would be minimal. Recovery in this kind of situation simply means that the organization fails over to the alternative location, with no loss of business and no loss of time, but this still comes at a cost. We will go further into this scenario in the coming chapters. There are also mobile recovery facilities that can be brought into play, quick ship agreements that can be developed, or reciprocal agreements with other similar or competitive companies in a somewhat partnership relationship to assist both companies for the duration of the disaster.

Why plan to plan? Although it may sound trite, the adage is true, "If you fail to plan, you plan to fail."

Each business has different requirements for its *business continuity plan (BCP).* Equally important is choosing a team to create your disaster recovery plans that recognizes how each business unit interacts within the framework of the organization and with the other business units both upstream and downstream. The process of identifying these individuals and allowing them to form working relationships among themselves fosters the spirit that is needed to provide quick and effective cooperation among the team members. These people make up what will be known as the *disaster recovery team* or the *disaster recovery planning team.*

Why Plan?

Different organizations undertake a disaster recovery plan initiative for different reasons. There are often as many different reasons as there are organizations that make the undertaking. How the plan proceeds often ends up being dictated by the reasons for planning in the first place.

The impetus to undertake a DR plan initiative may be that insurance companies are applying either direct or indirect pressure to organizations to inspire them to develop the disaster recovery plan.

Direct Pressure

Direct pressure implies that the organization can either not get adequate insurance or that it will not be able to afford the insurance that it can get until and unless it can prove to an auditor's satisfaction that it can recover the business to such a point as to be able to continue with the business. Although the pressure is often just what is needed by the organization to spur it on to develop its ability to recover its business, this is not what the insurance companies are after.

Indirect Pressure

Indirect pressure means making the business make the decision based on seeing the end plan as being in its best interest not only for the business but for the purse strings as well, by providing discounts or incentives to the organization for going the extra mile. Direct and indirect pressure are often simply different shades of the same color, and they work to achieve the same end goal: assisting the organization with the decision to begin the disaster recovery planning process.

Not only do insurance companies have regulations concerning the ability for an insured company to recover, there may also be governmental regulatory requirements in place for certain types of organizations, requiring them to be able to recover. This could mean that a company working with chemicals put into place a plan that would enable it to quickly and efficiently clean up after accidents in which it is involved or to be able to protect its employees and neighbors in the event of a localized disaster (a disaster that affects a city or a section of a city). Compliance with regulatory organizations is often one of the primary reasons that an organization undertakes to develop a disaster recovery plan.

Another reason an organization may decide to undertake a disaster recovery plan is that the stakeholders, shareholders, clients, or venture capital firms have made a formalized request that the organization make the effort to be fully recoverable. These people have a vested interest in the organization and their voice often carries a lot of weight. An organization is liable to listen much more closely and deliberately to those holding the purse strings than they might to anyone else.

Now that we've looked at why we need to start disaster recovery planning, let's look at establishing the team. These will be the people on whom the onus of creating and often implementing the plan will fall.

Establishing the Team

Before planning can begin in earnest, you have to get the right people in the right places. You have to find those people and get them into the roles into which they fit.

The people who make up the planning team may not be the same people who will end up going to disaster recovery drills, and they may not be the same people who end up being involved in the actual recovery effort should a disaster be declared. The fact is, they probably won't be. However, they are, and should be, the people who know the business, who know the technology, who know security, and who have a fundamental understanding of what it takes to get back to business as usual. Because each business unit within the organization knows its functions and idiosyncrasies, all business units are critical members of the disaster recovery team.

A well-written disaster recovery (DR) plan, including well-written desk instructions, will come as a result of the planning and testing process. This will enable whoever is on the team performing the recovery either in a disaster situation or in a testing situation to sit down and, without fail, perform the tasks at hand as if they were the people who actually did the writing.

Many companies bring with them brand recognition, goodwill, or corporate reputation. Preserving the reputation and brand recognition are critical to continuing to be a thriving business.

This is true not only for multinational organizations but also for small businesses and individual proprietorships. The fact is, it is often overlooked by companies and their employees that they are considered a brand, and are looked upon as that brand when people do business with them. This understanding of the individual or business as a brand has implications not only in disaster recovery, but also in the field of marketing, corporate structure, and business attitude.

Consider the following example. Mary and John Smith have a specialty grocery store, Ethnically Yours, in a suburb of Pittsburgh, PA. They sell hard-to-find staples and fresh food that target the diverse local population. They have become well known for their ability to either maintain in stock, or acquire on short notice, nearly any requested special ingredient for their customers. The local customers have spread the word on the reliability of this store and their reputation has grown, and as a result so has their customer base. People start to travel from neighboring towns to shop at their store. If you simply mention the name, Ethnically Yours, most people understand to what you are referring. They have, essentially, become a brand name.

Consider that all their internal systems, food temperature control as well as computer systems, are controlled by their central computer system. They fall prey to a computer virus that wreaks havoc not only with their ability to process orders and do business, but with their inventory of fresh foods as well. People have been relying on them for supplies, and there are several significantly large special orders of fresh food.

People who have been relying on Ethnically Yours to fill orders and to supply them with the food that they want initially understand. Everyone finds themselves the victims of accidents or malicious acts. But John and Mary haven't thought very far ahead when it comes to disaster planning, and they realize that this is likely considered to be a disaster. They find that they are not able to recover their systems quickly enough and the fresh food spoils. What's worse, they find that not only their customer information but much of their supplier information has become corrupt in the process, and they are taking longer and longer to recover their ability to do business.

People start talking about their inability to fulfill the needs of the customer base the way that they used to, and there is a chain store not that far away that has many of the things that Ethnically Yours carried. The chain doesn't have the atmosphere that John and Mary always provided their customers, but at least it is able to fulfill orders when needed.

The disaster situation impacted the reputation, and by extension, the brand name of Ethnically Yours. They may be able to recover much of their customer base, but there will remain for a long time customer doubt that they will be able to rely on the Smiths for their supplies. Their brand has been impacted.

It is important to remember that, although the team is very important, the disaster recovery planning team is nothing more than several well-trained individuals working together toward the same goal. It is also important to remember that even a well-trained team cannot perform without adequate leadership, the direction of a captain (or coach or champion), and a game plan. Where would the Steelers, Pirates, or Penguins be without a coach, a game plan, and the desire to win to help them reach the goal? The disaster recovery team is similar to a sports team. Without team spirit, leadership, guidance, and a well-defined goal, the disaster recovery team would likely fail in their mission. What's more, having a team with ill-defined roles and unqualified members filling those roles can be equally as destructive as having no team and no plan. The remainder of this chapter provides you with a better understanding of who should be on the team, the roles of the team members, and the resources needed from a human resources perspective.

DR teams are made up of many different people in different positions, each ultimately responsible for his or her own position and knowledgeable about the ramifications of that position on the team. No person on the team can exist in a vacuum. The team has to be cognizant of what every other player on the team is doing, at least on a conceptual level, and where the goal is located.

The DR team should include, or at the very least be in contact with, the following members of the organization:

- upper management
- general information technology (IT) staff
- business members and support staff
- end users

Additionally, they'll need to work with external people, including law enforcement, firefighters, banking and finance, and others along the supply chain.

These contacts will help get the critical knowledge of the business, its external environment, and what realistically can be expected from emergency response personnel. The type and potential sources of emergency funding that may be available in case of disaster and where sources of supplies and raw materials can be acquired in an emergency situation must also be determined early in the disaster recovery planning process.

Further contact needs to be maintained with business partners, vendors, and customers as to not only the fact that disasters have been declared, but also that the organization is undertaking disaster recovery planning. The team must notify those up and down the supply chain that the initiative is underway and provide progress updates to those who want to know. This will foster goodwill between all parties, and will likely lay further groundwork for continued relations with all involved. It may also prove to be a source of information for the team on the process and on locations of emergency supplies for the organization.

Now let's look at some of the concerned parties in more detail. These people will either be key in making up the team, or will be critical in support roles to the team.

Getting Management Support

Management support, at many levels, is crucial to the success of any disaster recovery effort. Without it the efforts of the team will be of little use, and you will often find that the team will flounder. Without the support of management at the departmental level, those involved in the planning effort won't have the resources available to perform the jobs that they need to do in a DR planning session. Middle management also needs to be involved because they communicate effectively with each other and often have a better understanding of how business flows at that level, if not how information flows.

Because of the importance of disaster recovery, management should be one of the major driving forces behind the creation and efficient execution of a disaster recovery plan, and the effective running of the planning team. However, it is often difficult to get complete management buy-in to such a plan because the return on investment (ROI) associated with the cost of developing the plan and securing the necessary resources is rarely realized. The benefit to having a well-constructed plan is often never borne out in dollars and cents; however, if you have to declare a disaster, the cost to that point will easily be seen as a benefit to the organization.

Often the most efficient methods for securing management buy-in may be not to look at the return on investment, but to approach the situation from the perspective of a cost-benefit ratio comparing a properly executed disaster recovery plan to the cost of being able to continue business as an organization. You may find it much easier to determine the cost savings that can be realized in business not lost because of a properly designed and executed disaster recovery plan. This efficiently executed plan can mean the difference between organizational survival and failure or bankruptcy. Helping management see the problem in these terms may only be approaching the problem of securing their support from the negative, but at least it is approaching the problem.

Once management is on board with the project, these individuals can be looked to as a source of information on the bigger picture for the organization. They have a different perspective than most of the other players on the team.

But what about the other players?

The Need for Ongoing Departmental Support

Almost as difficult as getting management buy-in, if it really isn't their idea, may be getting support not only from department managers but from those in the organization who will be most directly involved in both the planning process and its execution. Although the idea of a road trip for the testing of the end plan often appeals to many on the DR team, the realities of putting the effort into the planning and execution of the plan is often daunting enough to chase off even the most staunch supporter. Fostering a team atmosphere where everyone is heard and where everyone's opinion appears to be valued may mean the difference between an effective and efficient team and a team that is paying lip service to get the job done.

From the perspective of departmental management, there's little in it for them to work at fostering a team attitude. A team spirit may be one of the most difficult tasks that will fall to the team leader. This is especially true due to the necessarily disparate makeup of the team. You may have to find creative ways to key people's interest, involvement, and dedication to the project. Let's face it, very few people in the organization are struggling to find things to fill their time; more likely they are trying to find time into which to fill their projects. Disaster recovery is just one more project and not one that appears to be directly related to the bottom line or overly critical in nature.

This is also one place where team-building exercises become useful. Interaction in a relaxed environment with others on the team may foster the goodwill and dedication that will be required to see the team through strained and difficult situations. Paintball games, laser tag, even just moving the meetings to a local restaurant can allow team members to relax and get to know each other on a more personalized level.

One of the first decisions to make is what exactly the team will be tasked with in both the planning and execution phases of disaster recovery. Once you have both an idea of what the business situation is for the organization and the tasks that need to be undertaken by the team, putting the correct individuals into the correct positions becomes easier. To foster the overall team interaction, getting as many of the people who will ultimately be on the team involved early will be to your benefit. Coming in after much of the groundwork has been done tends to make the new person feel like an interloper rather than a team member. The following section outlines some of the tasks that the team will face.

Team Members

The disaster recovery team, should a disaster be declared, could be chosen from nearly anyone from anywhere within the organization, or even contracted from outside of the organization. For this reason, the plan needs to be written in such a way that anyone in any position can be given the instructions on how to recover a given application successfully, and that person could walk in and perform the recovery. This is not the team that undertakes the planning for disaster recovery. However, the disaster recovery planning team that we are talking about now is the team that will be responsible for creating the disaster recovery plan and will likely be responsible for testing the disaster recovery plan and for keeping up with its ongoing maintenance.

The structure of this planning team might bear some similarity to the existing organizational chart or it might look nothing like the hierarchy of the organization. Exactly what it looks like isn't as important as having the right people in the right places. The team approach to developing the disaster recovery plan is typically used as a means for establishing checks and balances in what is attempted during the business recovery and ensuring that no department, no interested party, and no relevant information goes undiscovered.

Recovery Manager

The team itself has its own specific responsibilities and every member within the team has a responsibility to the team, the organization, and the other members of the team. Within each team, a team captain or recovery manager should either be chosen or appointed and an alternate for this position should also be appointed or designated. It is not necessarily this person's job to "manage" the team the way a department manager might manage people. Rather, the person in this position is responsible for leading the team toward its goal. It may be more advantageous to think of this position as a coach on a sports team. The recovery manager provides the leadership and direction for the team, assisting in developing the different sections of the plan and ensuring that tasks along the way are being carried out during the creation of the plan and ultimately at the time of the disaster.

The recovery manager will need to be an individual who is skilled in both managing and administration, someone accustomed to dealing with high-pressure situations and better at cheerleading than at micro-management. This person should have a broad knowledge of hardware and software, particularly the hardware and software that are relevant to the organization. This knowledge should not be limited to that which is used in the organization, but extended to that which might be employed at the disaster recovery site. The manager should have an understanding of how all the pieces of the organizational puzzle fit together and maintain a basic conceptual knowledge of how all the software applications in the organization fit together. By necessity, this position will likely be filled by an upper middle-level manager or someone on the executive committee because of the broad understanding of the company that is required.

If you are recovering a mainframe-based system, you will not likely need to be able to recover it on a Windows server; few organizations of any size run everything on a single platform. It is often the case that an organization is not going to be running its business on the newest technology available. That would be cost prohibitive and unpractical. However, recovery sites are often able to maintain only a certain number of different types of systems, and these are typically the newer models. An organization may be running its business on an IBM iSeries 800, but the recovery site may have only iSeries 520 available. This may or may not be an issue for the organization; it really depends on how backups are taken and what differences it means to the underlying data and data structures. However, it is necessary that the organization be aware of the available hardware and the differences and difficulties that it may present. The organization may be standardized on HP servers running its Windows applications, but the recovery site may be standardized on Dells. The knowledge necessary to bridge any differences and deal with the idiosyncrasies of the data, operating system, and programs on the different possible platforms will likely be necessary. This is one reason that it is necessary to include and involve technical resources with expertise in the systems and a knowledge of the underlying architecture.

Depending on the size and complexity of an organization and the degree of control necessary for the disaster recovery team, either key technical leads with access to all lower levels of expertise or all level of expertise should be allowed to provide relevant input. This input, regardless of who conveys it, will prove invaluable.

The recovery manager will need to be a problem solver because, in the event that a disaster is declared, there will be many problems to solve. These problems may or may not have been anticipated in the planning sessions but will have to be addressed. The leadership required means that the person in this position needs to have the ability and confidence to delegate responsibility to others as the need arises.

FYI *Recovery Manager and Funding*

One thing that needs to be taken into account when looking at the person filling this position is that it's important for this person to have the signature authority required to allocate funds as a part of the disaster recovery process.

2

The following sections provide information on those people who should be considered for inclusion on the disaster recovery team. Again, every organization is different and therefore every team and every team's makeup will be different. This will, however, give you a starting point for common team members.

It's important that you not only have a primary person who is assigned to each role, but that you also provide for at least one backup person for every key position on the team so that the backup can fill in if the primary person is unable to fulfill the requirements. The backups should be involved in all planning and testing scenarios and should be comfortable with stepping into the position should the need arise.

Remember that it's important to not use one person to fill two positions, regardless of how this may fit within the framework of your organization. One person will have difficulty filling two roles at once, and it's a recipe for failure. A person can be the primary person for one role and the backup for another, but care needs to be taken to ensure that key positions are filled in the event that a disaster is declared.

Facilities Coordinator

The facilities coordinator needs to have some of the same skills required of the recovery manager, but at a different level. This position requires a closer, more hands-on familiarity with the process of getting construction work scheduled when necessary and completed on time in a cost-effective manner. A further understanding of what is required to oversee the setup of the electrical, environmental, and communication requirements of a data center should also be among the bag of tricks available to the facilities coordinator.

Technical Coordinator

This position requires a strong background in the setup of interfaces between as many of the organizational platforms as possible. Although it's not possible for one individual to have complete expertise in the interfaces of all possible systems, a basic understanding of as many as possible is important. This individual will harness the required people to plan and perform the actual recovery scenarios, and will need to know who to pick and from where they need to be pulled to provide a diverse and well-constructed team.

Further, this position requires a proven ability to communicate easily with vendor representatives, technical and non-technical alike, and with engineers concerning the installation options, performance issues, resolution of problems surrounding the setup and installation of all platforms, and myriad other things that may arise in the recovery scenario. This position also requires a proven ability to effectively schedule and manage people and situations, particularly in a high-stress, time-critical situation.

Administrative Coordinator

The administrative coordinator should be skilled in the business operations of the organization, and be well acquainted with the day-to-day operations of the business as a whole and in as many departments as is possible. What's more, the administrative coordinator should be as much of a people person as possible. This person will be dealing with a significant number of highly technical individuals who may or may not have exemplary people skills. This means that this coordinator will need to deal with people at their worst, under high-stress conditions, typically with their minds elsewhere, during hard times. This person must also be familiar with purchasing procedures for the organization and access and understanding of contracts, service level agreements (SLAs), and deliverables.

Network Coordinator

The network coordinator needs to be an expert in network design and maintenance. This position requires less of a people person or an administrator, but is someone more knowledgeable about networks. The position calls for training in the diagnostics and correction of network outages and in the ability to connect and debug new additions to existing networks. An understanding of the configuration of the network as it currently exists and an ability to replicate that network, or one closely resembling it in functionality, in an unfamiliar setting with what may or may not be similar components will play an important role. Also, a basic understanding of the security issues directly connected with a network, familiar or otherwise, would be beneficial.

Applications Coordinator

The applications coordinator should, optimally, be from the existing application support group. This person should have exposure to a wide cross section of the currently used applications, although an in-depth working knowledge of all these applications is not necessary.

More extensive knowledge in the areas of the critical applications in the organization—for example, payroll, accounts payable and accounts receivable, and human resources—is desirable. This is not to say, however, that knowledge in the area of the internal systems critical to sustaining revenues should be minimized in favor of the support applications. If such an individual is unavailable, someone with the broadest available knowledge of existing technologies within the organization should be assigned to this role.

This individual will need to use all available tools on all pertinent platforms to ascertain the status of files and database objects in order to assure upper management that business is ready to commence as usual, and needs to be prepared to restore either an earlier or later version of any of the systems from backup if required. The latter is more of a judgment call situation than actually being the person who will be the hands-on individual in such situations.

This person will need to interface with other technical people and with users to verify that applications are functioning as anticipated, develop solutions to problems that may arise, and effectively interact with external support and upper management to acquire the necessary answers and support.

Computer Operations Coordinator

The computer operations coordinator must be skilled in the day-to-day operations of the systems and the system software, and have the knowledge and skills necessary to re-create production schedules for application systems or implement new schedules should the need arise. The responsibility for overseeing the setting up of a limited help desk functionality may fall to this individual. This functionality will provide information to callers on the status of all relevant systems, how to access systems temporarily, and any new procedures that will be used for submitting production applications for processing.

Table 2.1 shows a sample roster for a recovery management team. Although this is not an exhaustive list of coordinators and team leaders, it provides you with enough information to adapt the listing to your individual situation.

TABLE 2.1 Recovery management team roster.

Position	Primary	Secondary	Alternate
Recovery manager	Bill Smith	Mary Jones	Walt Williams
Facilities coordinator	Stephanie Bills	Scott Adams	Sue Smith
Technical coordinator	John Lynn	Amanda Dion	Adam Freeman
Administrative coordinator	June Thomas	William Curtis	Crystal Walters
Network coordinator	Vaughn Michaels	Deb Trooper	Robert Thomas
Applications coordinator	Kaycee Coco	Joshua Harrison	Destiny Crystals
Computer operations coordinator	Harry Thomas	Alleyse June	Harry Thomason

DR Team Sub-Teams

A team often will be made up of smaller groups, or sub-teams, of individuals, based on function. These sub-teams often work on their own within the framework of the overall team in general. The following sections provide examples of sub-teams that may be formed within the DR team in order to better facilitate the arrival at the end goal.

Management Team

In any organization, the members of the management team of the organization are critical to the everyday workings of the departments that they manage, to the areas that they oversee, and to the people who report to them. These managers or directors understand the business of the department and how that department relates to other departments in the organization. They understand the strengths and weaknesses of the people who report to them and are likely best able to judge qualified members to be placed on the disaster recovery team.

Management's role in the disaster recovery team is likely to be similar to management's role within the organization. Management team members will oversee, guide, and lead the team in an appropriate direction for the organization. They understand the inner workings of the organization as an entity; however, they are not likely to understand all the ramifications and details that need to go into the disaster recovery plan. Therefore they are not the only people who need to be members of the team.

It is important to note that although members of management are critical stakeholders and vital sources of information for the disaster recovery team, they should make up the smallest portion of the team. Other, more hands-on technical and business people should make up the bulk of the team.

Business Recovery Team

Remember that not only are you creating a disaster recovery plan, you're creating a business continuity plan. A document that will allow the business to continue in as uninterrupted fashion as possible will be one of the ultimate deliverables from the overall team. There'll be different layers and different levels within this plan based on mean time to recovery and also based on specific requirements of the organization. Very few organizations can claim to be purely technology-driven, technology-based organizations. Whatever your business is, you are fundamentally in the business of making money and providing profit to shareholders and stakeholders, and continuing to be a going proposition will allow you to continue to make money.

It's therefore important for a business recovery team to be a part of the disaster recovery team. Not only do you have to be able to recover your systems

2

and their functionality, you have to be able to carry on business logically as if you were not in a disaster situation. Members of the business recovery team are going to be the users of the systems that are being recovered. Their input into exactly how important any given system is to their being able to do their job effectively and efficiently will be invaluable in the planning process. It will allow you to better plan for exactly which systems are on the critical path.

Departmental Recovery Team

Because a disaster can happen at any level within an organization and, as we saw in Chapter 1, can be carried down to the department or location level, it is important to have sub-teams that make up a departmental recovery team. Depending on the size of the department and the department's complexity, its team may consist of two or three individuals who best know the business of the department. Optimally, each should complement the knowledge of the others. They should all understand the technology used daily and know the shortcuts that they can safely take in their jobs. This information will become highly valuable in a disaster situation. What's more, they know the way that the department functions.

Because the whole is typically at least as great as the sum of its parts (often greater), departmental recovery teams are an intricate part of the disaster recovery team and often will assist the business recovery team. They will report to the disaster recovery team on the information in and processes relevant for their own particular department.

The makeup of the departmental recovery team will be dependent on the makeup of the department. A database administration department will likely have at least one representative on the departmental recovery team from each of the database types administered and people who are well versed in different platforms on which those databases are resident. These people may be the lead database administrators (DBAs) or they may be the members of the department who have the broadest overall knowledge in their particular areas of expertise. System administration departments will have at least one representative from each of the platforms represented in the organization.

Although they may not be necessary in the initial wave of recovery, programmers will likely have not only input to the DR team, but will possibly also need to be included in a recovery situation. There is the potential need to make programming changes on the fly to allow the recovery to proceed elegantly.

A programming department may be led by either the department lead or the department manager, and the members of this team should be those people who understand the key programs in the process and how those programs relate to the process overall. You want the person who has the biggest grasp of how the application works as a whole on a departmental recovery team.

Although the department manager will likely be the lead, it is not likely that the department manager has the knowledge or wherewithal to know all the details for all the areas that need to be taken into consideration.

Computer Recovery Team

The members of the computer recovery team are most likely those first considered when looking at a disaster recovery team. They are the people who recover
the hardware and the software installations and the data in the computer system.
You may want your best and brightest from this group on the team, if only for
the purpose of the plan. You will need people who know the systems inside and
out, who have knowledge of the fastest and best way of getting things done
within the existing system, and who have extensive knowledge on how each
system interacts with other systems. They may not be the people who end up
getting called in the occasion of the disaster, but they are the people who you
want involved in writing the processes and procedures that are required for
getting the systems up and running in the eventuality of disaster.

System administrators from every different system, every different
definition of a system, or every different type of server with in the organization should be represented. For instance, your organization may have several
dozen Windows servers, each used for a different purpose and separated into
different areas of responsibility. If you are a company with an application
service provider (ASP) model you may have Windows servers that are dedicated to internal processes and different sets of servers that are dedicated to
providing services to external customers. The specifics for each server may be
very different, the required recovery time for each different type may be different, and the security requirements and other specifics connected directly to
the area of business covered by the server may be different. You want people
on the team who know the specifics of those servers that fall under their
responsibility. You would want someone from the internal server group and
someone from the external server group who have the knowledge required to
understand the ramifications of restoring each server group.

It's critical to have someone from every area of expertise included within
this group. There are processes involved in restoring a mainframe that may not
be involved in restoring a UNIX server, and entirely new set of processes for a
Windows server, ZOS server, or VMS.

Damage Assessment Team

One area that's often overlooked on the DR planning team is damage assessment. Without assessment, you don't know to what level a disaster has affected
your organization and to what level you will be required to restore. Members of
the damage assessment team may be first responders—those people trained in
emergency procedures or others who have specialized knowledge in the area.
You may find this to be one area where outsourcing for the purpose of expertise
is required. A damage assessment team need not be intimately aware of all the
processes, both business and technological, that are involved in your organization, but they need to be aware of different kinds of damage and the ramifications of the damage.

Security Team

One of the most critical sets of individuals who will be members of the overall disaster recovery team will be the security team. Often with the declaration of a disaster, simple survival means that the restoration of the ability to conduct business (regardless of how that disaster has been arrived at) is uppermost in the minds of the stakeholders. However, with the declaration of a disaster, it is even more important in critical areas to have security uppermost in everyone's mind.

If we consider natural disasters or other widespread disastrous occurrences, it is typical that the National Guard is called in to help with peacekeeping and security as a means to limit looting, vandalism, and to keep people and property safe. This is the same mindset to use when considering the disaster recovery plan for an organization. You will need to take into account internal security of the data, applications, systems, and people. You need to consider the safety and security of all the assets of the organization, both human and nonhuman.

You may have to invest in additional personnel, likely outsourced or contracted, to assist in the eventuality of an actual disaster occurring with the additional security requirements that will surround the organization. Making arrangements with firms ahead of time is beneficial because, unless it is a very localized disaster (say to your firm in particular), there will be many people competing for the same resources. Planning ahead will ensure that your contracts are honored. Security for these individuals will include rapid access to background checks, ensuring that necessary bonding is in place and that non-disclosure agreements are signed before allowing outside individuals ready access to organizational information.

The following example might help. An organization may find itself the victim of vandalism (people break in, ransack the building, break computers, steal laptops, spray paint on the walls, and start fires in the building). Additional security personnel are required for the period immediately following the break-in to secure the scene. The organization hires a local firm to help inventory the building to determine exactly what was stolen or broken so they can turn in insurance claims. Contracted cleaning companies hire local workers who are available with little notice to help with the cleanup effort. When the cleaning is complete, the organization's employees are permitted back into the building to continue work as usual. Many of these employees report missing items (Walkmans, iPods, money, CDs, confidential files, anything that might have been in their desk drawers or on their desks). Comparing the reported items to the inventory shows that many of the items were accounted for during the initial inventory. Where did they go? What assurance does the organization have that any of these additional people may have seen something that was confidential? What if this organization was a doctor's office? What medical records might have been seen by any of these people? What are the HIPAA (Health Insurance Portability and Accountability Act) ramifications? Thought needs to be given to the additional security measures necessary in an emergency situation.

Facilities Support Team

One of the most often overlooked, and often one of the most practical, areas in a disaster recovery team is that of facilities support. Although it's true that you won't have to water the grass more in a disaster, there are areas of support where the facilities team's knowledge and expertise will be invaluable. An understanding of where cleaning supplies are kept and the ability to quickly locate the shutoff valves for water and gas, and the location of breaker boxes and other utility-related accesses is often not something that anyone other than those directly connected with it will know. The information can be found, but knowing where things are rapidly is a benefit.

In a medium-sized business, there may be one cleaning person for each business location. If the business has several locations, this will mean several facilities support individuals. In the event of an emergency, if the majority of the individuals from one location have to be relocated to another location, the cleaning at the recovery location will be nearly doubled. Thought needs to be given to what this means not only to the organization as far as staffing, but how much cleaning supplies, paper towels, and bathroom tissue would have to be ordered. Those answers could easily come from someone whose job it is to maintain the organization at that level.

There are basic necessities that need to be taken care of, especially when facing a disaster situation. These necessities include, but are not limited to:

■ water service

■ refuse removal

■ basic cleaning responsibilities

Depending on how your individual recovery is handled, which is based primarily on the type and severity of the disaster, you may find that you have to relocate your business to a hotsite. If this is the case, facilities management needs to be handled by the provider of a hotsite or could potentially to be found at that location.

However, facilities management will also have to be involved in the cleanup and restoration of the primary business location so that business as usual can be restored as rapidly as possible.

Including these people on the team allows you to take into consideration their input into what may need to happen in a disaster situation and what extra steps will make the transition back into business as usual most clean.

Administrative Support Team

Ask anyone "who holds the keys to the kingdom?" and you'll get many answers. But if you ask someone who fundamentally keeps the organization running, the CEO and upper management team or the secretaries, the secretaries usually win hands down. They know where things are, how things are done, and fundamentally how the business works. They may not know how business works at a high level, but they know how their business works, and the business of their bosses.

Administrative assistants, or secretaries, are an important part of the disaster recovery team because they know how the organization works from the inside and what happens in a normal business day at a level that upper management may not understand. Not only do they know how things work, they know how to get things done in the most expeditious way. They can provide valuable input to the DR team on shortcuts that can be taken and on how things really work from their unique perspective.

Although their function may be able to be outsourced in the event of a disaster and relocated to a hotsite, what happens at their level of the organization will have to be ongoing. Having their input into how their job happens and what they do will make a transition much smoother.

Logistics Support Team

If you are a manufacturing organization, or have anything that has to be shipped from point A to point B, logistics support is important to your business and its primary location. You should infer that logistics support also will be important to your business in its backup site, particularly if that site will be utilized for an extended period of time. Depending on the type and severity of the disaster, logistics support will play a variety of functions in the ultimate eventuality of disaster. Team members' input will be important in the planning process because they typically know where in the process logistics support begins.

Organizations outsource this function, but within the organization are those who understand the inputs to the process (the raw materials, the finished product that needs to be shipped, the packing material necessary to ship the product) and the intricacies surrounding the shipping of not only products, but also secure shipping in safe delivery of dangerous goods, critical documents, and personnel.

What's more, if your organization is involved in moving dangerous goods (weapons, chemicals, flammables, or other materials with which care must be taken), this group can have significant input into the understanding of what disasters may occur surrounding this shipping. Remember, not only can your organization be involved in a disaster from the perspective of having it happen to them, but if these types of goods are involved, they can be involved in causing accidents and disasters. Recall the Exxon Valdez and the oil spill in Alaska. Exxon's computer systems were not involved and its plants and materials were not affected; however, at some level it is likely that the organization's logistics support team may have been called upon to assist in the mitigation of damages.

User Support Team

User support is an often overlooked area in disaster recovery. Although it is viewed as critical to get the computer systems up and running, it is important to remember the reason that you're getting the computer systems running. Computers don't run themselves. They rarely have the capability to input their own data and they cannot draw conclusions from the data. This is why users are involved. Whenever users are involved, they are likely to have issues and problems with their computers. For this reason the user support team will be involved.

The input the user support team provides allows you to best plan for how to support users in a disaster situation. In a disaster, users will probably be even more difficult to deal with and their tolerance for computer glitches will be lower. A fundamental understanding of how support works in a normal day-to-day business will allow for a better understanding of how support works in the days following a declared disaster.

Computer Backup Team

Without an adequate backup that is both good and proven, assurance of being able to recover from whatever the disaster may be is impossible. If you don't have a backup of your existing systems there's no media from which to recover and therefore no ability to recover from a disaster. The computer backup team will be one of the most critical on a disaster recovery team. However, they don't have to be an entity in and of themselves; they may be the members of the computer recovery team as well. This is highly dependent upon the organization and its requirements.

Preparation for the disaster recovery is not the only time you're going to need a computer backup team, however. If the eventuality of the disaster means that you have to go to a hotsite, this site will require the same diligence in backup that occurs at your primary site. You have to be able to re-recover back to the primary business site after the disaster has passed, and you have to be prepared for the eventuality of a disaster hitting the backup site.

The computer recovery team understands all that is needed in the recovery, and this makes them prime candidates for membership on the computer backup team. If they know what they need to recover from a disaster, they can better plan for backing information up in such a way that it is easily available in the eventuality of the disaster.

Offsite Storage Team

Depending on the complexity and the size of your organization, you may contract a hotsite or an offsite location for restoration, or you may have a hotsite that is real time to which you can quickly and easily switch in the event of a disaster. If you have your own sites with your own hardware where you are taking real-time duplication, this will be your offsite backup storage as well. Your data will likely be replicated either instantaneously or in very short order.

Whether or not you have the luxury of this real-time offsite storage, it is often advantageous to include physical offsite storage of backups of your system. This secure location can provide physical storage of the routine system backups that can be applied in the event of a disaster. This added level of security and comfort can mean the difference between being able to recover your business and not being able to recover at all. Although this offsite backup will likely not provide you with the ability to recover the latest transaction, it will provide you the ability to recover to close enough to current so that you can recover your business.

The people responsible for housing the data both at a hotsite and in a secure offsite location are going to be critical members of your disaster recovery team. It is their responsibility to provide you with the backups of your data in the eventuality that those backups are required. It is also their responsibility to ensure that any backups housed in their facility will be housed in a manner that allows quick and elegant access and that allows them to be safe from the disaster.

Software Recovery Team

Often, based on business requirements, an organization will have on its disaster recovery team members of what could be considered the software recovery team. Because most organizations of any size will have a significantly large list of software products and systems that are critical to the running of the day-to-day business, it may be necessary for a subgroup of people who are knowledgeable in the majority of the products used in the organization to be a part of the disaster recovery team.

Many software products are tied to specific hardware configurations or implementations, and in the case of a disaster these configurations and implementations may change radically depending on the necessity of relocation. Having individuals who are knowledgeable in these facts will prove critical in both time and money should a disaster arise.

Communications Team

Communications is often the backbone of an organization. Communications can be viewed from different levels—from voice to telecommunication to written communication or e-mail—any way that information can be conveyed from one party to another. In a disaster situation communication will be critical. People with specific expertise in the concerns and considerations surrounding communications need to be considered in the disaster recovery team.

Applications Team

The software team will be involved with getting everything organized concerning the purchased software. The applications team will be involved with the application code developed in-house. Members of this team will be programmers, systems analysts, and those involved in the support of the critical business applications. These subject matter experts, or SMEs, have an in-depth understanding of the code that they maintain and those pieces of code that are critical to the functioning of the organization.

Although it's important that the disaster recovery team have a fundamental understanding of the business at large, this team has to have a more hands-on understanding of what goes on in every application.

Computer Restoration Team

The computer restoration team most likely will be the first line of offense when it comes to disaster declaration and the ultimate recovery from that disaster. They are the ones who understand the critical path to getting the systems operational, and they are the most competent at meeting the key deadlines and getting the systems functional. Again, many on this team will be members of both the computer backup team and the computer recovery team, and it may include members from the software team and the applications team. This team has to have a fundamental understanding of everything that it will take to restore the computer and its systems to full functionality in as expedient a manner as possible.

Human Resources Team

Human resources (HR) is a valuable function in any organization, and because you have no control over the size, complexity, or duration of the disaster it's important that the eventuality of an extended disaster be addressed. The human resources systems at an organizational level will have to be addressed fairly early in the process. The human element in disasters and disaster recovery is often overlooked, and it is quite possible that the wellbeing of individuals may take second stage to the requirements of the business, particularly in the early stages of recovery. Often everyone in the organization in a disaster situation will be required to give more effort in the interest of recovering the business. However, it's important that none of those involved at any level or in any capacity have their basic fundamental rights overlooked or taken for granted.

The human resources team gives input in many different levels of the disaster recovery planning process. From the assurance that worker safety is uppermost in the minds of those involved to the remuneration of those involved to the most expedient reestablishment of all functions in the organization; HR needs to be involved so that the interests of the employees are taken into account while the interests of the organization are being addressed.

Marketing and Customer Relations Team

Although marketing and customer relations aren't likely to be the first departments considered when recovering from a disaster, both are important when trying to allay questions and concerns from clients and customers. Customers need to have a central location through which they can contact the company for information or as a place through which to conduct business.

2

These departments have their own protocols and understand not only how they conduct their own business, but also how the customer expects business to be conducted. If for no other reason than good public relations, these departments need to have their concerns and systems addressed as soon as possible.

Other Teams

Depending on the line of business and type of organization, there will be other business units and departments that have their own needs and concerns. These departments will need to have their own teams and team members. Various combinations of the previous teams are possible depending on the size and requirements of the organization. The number of members assigned to a specific team can also vary depending on need.

Now that we have seen the makeup of the team, what are some of the expected characteristics?

Characteristics of Team Members

Members of the team need to understand their particular business unit functions and how it interacts with other units. They also need to have the authority to provide the necessary actions to assist in the recovery operations. The command and control structure of the team must be flexible enough to change in response to the nature of the disaster and to place those team members best able to direct the recovery operations in the right place at the right time.

The people that you pick have to be willing to dedicate at least part of their time to meetings connected to the DR planning team process and to providing the input requested by the team. An ability to write clear and concise documentation is also valuable. The DR plan owner will tie everything together, but having a clearly written document will make everyone's job easier.

External Team Members

There are additional recovery resources that many organizations don't consider when looking at their disaster recovery plans. Although these resources are not likely to be a part of the team, they may be resources upon which you can call in the event of an emergency. The following paragraphs describe some of these resources.

Local fire departments will be called upon not only if there is a fire but also in many other situations where rescue is required. They have the facilities necessary to provide support for many emergencies.

Police departments will be called upon to keep the peace and to make sure that all concerned parties are safe and protected.

Civil defense teams can be involved in many different aspects of a disaster depending on what kind of disaster is declared. They may be involved in search and rescue, or called upon to provide clean drinking water to different localities, provide emergency equipment, or carry out rescue missions. Civil defense teams may come in the guise of the National Guard or local formal civil defense teams, depending on the location.

Ambulance services are often critical in the event of an emergency. Although it may not be a physical emergency and no direct casualties or injuries are directly connected to the disaster, stress and attempting to work too hard for too long can contribute to the necessity for emergency medical assistance.

Paper supply vendors, office equipment vendors, and copy machine vendors often need to be called upon if an organization declares a disaster, depending upon the severity and type of disaster. These vendors may need to be local to a backup hotsite or may be obtainable through the organization providing the backup site.

Computer equipment and supplies vendors are likely to be those you consider first in a disaster recovery scenario. They may, in fact, be the ones providing you with the backup site. But what if the disaster does not require you to relocate to a disaster recovery site? Are the computer equipment vendors and suppliers going to be able to supply you with the required hardware in the event of an emergency that does not require relocation? Further, are these suppliers going to be able to provide you with sufficient desktops for the adequate continuation of your ongoing business until such time as permanent replacements can be found?

Resources for freezer space/freezer trucks, again, are not often the type of vendors uppermost in most people's minds when considering disaster recovery. However, depending on the type of organization in which you are operating, they may be among the first resources that you require. If the organization's inventory requires temperature control to that extent, it may be that these resources must be closely involved in any planning, as they will be the ones to whom you turn for much of your recovery assets.

Local volunteers can often be called upon for assistance in an emergency. This may take the form of the Red Cross or other organized volunteer organization, or it may take the form of other less organized teams in any given location. Often communities have their own volunteer organizations or rely upon church resources to supply needed support. Although these organizations are often overtaxed in the event of a localized disaster, an understanding of their capabilities can be critical for an organization.

Temporary help is likely to be called upon to fill positions on a stopgap basis. It may not be practical to relocate all resources to a recovery site either from a tactical or a financial standpoint. If this is the case, temporary service may be needed to fill positions of less critical need. Cleaning services, food services, or temp agencies may be able to provide much-needed support where appropriate.

All these different people or groups can be important to the success or failure of your disaster recovery attempt. However, not one of them can assist you if you can't get in touch with them. It is therefore important that you have a notification directory or call list in order to maintain a listing of all the people who are important in the process and in what order they need to be contacted. The following section will discuss this notification directory.

Creating a Notification Directory

The ability to effectively recover from a disaster of any level depends almost entirely on the organization's ability to effectively communicate not only between team members on the DR team but also between that team and management to provide accurate and timely updates on the progress of the recovery. It is therefore critical for all team members to be able to effectively and efficiently communicate both orally and in writing.

A notification directory and, within that directory, several notification paths to each concerned individual, ensures that communication will be both timely and efficient. Because you can't rely on any one individual's dedication and availability in a declared disaster, it's critical to have more than one means by which each concerned party can be reached. A disaster by its very nature will affect communication channels, therefore notification and means by which notification is achieved needs to be planned using as many diverse methods as possible. Among these will be:

- e-mail
- telephone
- cell phone
- conference call bridge
- any other resources available so that notifications can continue

Table 2.2 shows an example of what a notification directory might look like.

Securing and Preparing Resources

Due to the nature of disasters, the requisition and provision of secure resources is key to successful disaster recovery. Having access to dedicated backup servers, secure networks, and either hotsites or redundant and independent sites before disaster strikes is a key element in recovering from that disaster. The investment in providing and securing the resources ahead of time is well paid back in recovery speed and minimal lost business.

TABLE 2.2 Sample notification directory.

Contact	Land Line	Cell Phone	Alternative Phone	Primary E-mail	Secondary E-mail
Bill Smith	(000)123-4567	(000)124-1112	(000)133-4567	bsmith@Myco.com	bsmith@Myisp.net
Stephanie Bills	(000)123-1234	(000)124-1113	(000)133-1234	sbills@Myco.com	sbills@Myisp.net
John Lynn	(000)123-1235	(000)124-1114	(000)133-1235	jlynn@Myco.com	jlynn@Myisp.net
June Thomas	(000)123-1236	(000)124-1115	(000)133-1236	jthomas@Myco.com	jthomas@Myisp.net
Vaughn Michaels	(000)123-1237	(000)124-1222	(000)133-1237	vmichaels@Myco.com	vmichael@Myisp.net
Kaycee Coco	(000)123-1238	(000)124-1223	(000)133-1238	kcoco@Myco.com	kcoco@Myisp.net
Harry Thomas	(000)123-1239	(000)124-1224	(000)133-1239	hthomas@Myco.com	hthomas@Myisp.net

There are many disaster recovery sites and disaster recovery services available to organizations both large and small. These sites can provide your organization with the ability to continue business and emergency facilities and train staff to assist you with either a testing situation or a disaster declaration situation. They provide those who contract with them access to secure information technology equipment, power supplies, communications, and environments. They provide you with critical data in a disaster and cost-effective access to a substantial amount of capital equipment that can be used not only for disaster recovery and testing of your disaster recovery plan, but also for independent software evaluations, benchmarking, upgrade testing, software development testing, temporary system overloads, hardware implementation, and load testing. They can provide you with public relations support during emergencies and can provide satisfaction of corporate governance rules and governmental requirements. And perhaps most important, they can minimize business risk, thereby resulting in greater shareholder and stakeholder confidence and goodwill.

The following sections discuss some of the disaster recovery sites available.

Alphawest

Alphawest (**http://www.alphawest.com.au**) is an Australian IT service specializing in full life-cycle services from business consulting through outsourcing services. One of the primary areas that it concentrates on is the area of infrastructure solutions, not only for disaster recovery but also for many other purposes. With locations in Sydney, Melbourne, and Brisbane, it provides Australia with the ability to house solutions in a fairly disparate set of locations. It provides for separate buildings connected via fiber channels with the ability to utilize microwave links as backups, and each site has a generator and uninterruptible power supplies (UPS). It provides a variety of platforms on wage to recover systems, from Sun and HP to Dell, Digital, or IBM. Not only does it provide hardware and heavy metal that is typically associated with disaster recovery, it also provides workstations, desks, PCs, phones, and telecommunication capability over a variety of networks.

Its different locations provide different hardware and infrastructure solutions, differing capacities, and, to some extent, differing infrastructure. All provide access control; security alarms and monitoring; physical protection in the form of smoke, fire, temperature, and humidity monitoring control; and easy access to mass transit, food, and lodging.

Affiliated Computer Services Inc. (ACS)

One company that focuses part of its offering on Disaster Recovery Services is Affiliated Computer Services, Inc. (ACS) (**http://www.acs-inc.com/**). This Dallas-based organization helps an organization focus on disaster prevention through management best practices, and provides detailed client-centric disaster recovery programs. They provide organizations with information on best-of-breed solutions and help clients partner with third party solution providers to protect its investments in information. ACS brings with it a unique ability to leverage its expertise in business processes, information technology and systems integration to help organizations define the steps necessary to meet their own organizational disaster recovery needs.

IBM

IBM (**http://www.ibm.com/**) is one of the world's premier computing companies. As one of the industry leaders, it also provides one of the largest business continuity and recovery service sites in the world. It not only can provide computer systems and networks on any communication equipment that is needed to help a contracted business recover as quickly and as efficiently as possible, it can provide the expertise that is required to recover any system running IBM or compatible hardware.

At all sites you'll find computer systems, peripherals, and network connectivity communication equipment that is needed to recover a business quickly and efficiently. Its facilities are located near hubs of mass transportation, hotels, and restaurants. IBM maintains over 100 recovery sites in over 75 countries worldwide, so it can be the recovery solution for nearly every business.

FYI *Other DR Site Providers*

There are many other Web sites that can provide you with information on disaster recovery site providers, including the following:

Recovery Point Systems: **http://www.recoverypoint.com**

Lantech: **http://www.ltoa.com**

SunGard Bi-Tech: **http://www.sungard.com**

Weyerhaeuser: **http://www.weyerhaeuser.com/disaster-recovery/about.htm**

CMHC Systems: **http://www.cmhc.com**

Team Tasks

The team needs to establish both monitoring functions, such as network intrusion detection software or severe weather notification, and notification abilities that alert the proper members to respond to the threats. Each of these aspects needs proper planning and testing on an ongoing basis to ensure proper functioning. They need to consider and plan for the eventuality of all contingencies. The following sections outline additional tasks the team must undertake. The rest of this book explores these tasks in greater detail.

Auditing Current Vulnerability

Disaster recovery planning is primarily about understanding your organization's current state of readiness in the face of a potential disaster. It is also about the steps that should be taken to mitigate risk and about planning for the ultimate recovery. An audit of the existing infrastructure, the risk surrounding that infrastructure, and a prioritization of existing systems is included in this task. The deliverable from this task (or set of tasks) is a comprehensive overview of the system as it exists now and the likely risks for the system.

Determining What Actions to Complete Now

Most organizations acknowledge that a disaster recovery plan is something that they must have, but it is also something that they hope they will never actually have to use. The next task in arriving at the DR plan is for the organization to determine what steps it can take and in what time frame in order to make the biggest impact on its ability to withstand and recover from disasters for the time and money involved in the effort. This will provide the tasks and measurements aimed at reducing vulnerability and the fastest way to recover from any disaster that may befall the organization.

Creating Recovery Teams and Test Plans

This task assigns individuals and their roles in the event that a recovery becomes necessary and in the testing situations leading up to the ability to ensure that a recovery will succeed. It is important that these key individuals understand their roles in the event of a disaster declaration. Even if exact people are not targeted, job roles need to clearly show what the position entails.

The second deliverable of this step is a comprehensive test plan. This is a living document that provides the steps necessary to recover all systems in such a manner that the organization will be able to continue to do business. As tests occur, this document is updated with things that are found to work well, and things that could have worked better. Chapter 9 walks through the tests that an organization can employ, both ones that are actually followed and the ones that involve thinking through all of the scenarios necessary to test.

Summary

Planning to plan is the successful beginning to a proper disaster recovery. Key elements are the proper identification of team members and providing those team members a chance to develop working relationships, the resources to communicate, and the proper infrastructure and support of management. With all these elements brought together it is time to plan and test the disaster recovery for the business.

We have seen in this chapter that an important place to start is with developing the team. The chapter provides examples of important team members to consider when developing the disaster recovery plan. Now that we have a basis for the team, we can begin to further explore what tasks that team will have to undertake and the process for developing the disaster recovery plan.

Test Your Skills

MULTIPLE CHOICE QUESTIONS

1. The recovery manager's role is most closely described as a _____.

    A. problem manager

    B. problem solver

    C. facilities coordinator

    D. technology manager

2. What special knowledge should the facilities coordinator have?

   A. Free access to all data

   B. Knowledge of where all files are located

   C. Understanding of what facilities are available at the DR site

   D. Familiarity with getting construction work done

3. The network coordinator should be well versed at _____.

   A. networking with subordinates

   B. networking with superiors

   C. networking with design and maintenance

   D. networking with vendors

4. The team should be made up of _____.

   A. only the primary key members

   B. key members and their backups

   C. the most intelligent people in the organization regardless of position

   D. the core members of the team, their backups, and an alternate for each position so that as many people know about the process as possible

5. The coordinator should be someone skilled in the day-to-day operations of the systems; the system software is the responsibility of the _____ coordinator.

   A. applications

   B. computer operations

   C. administrative

   D. network

6. Which of the following is not one of the reasons that human resources team is necessary for inclusion on the DR team?

   A. You might need to hire people at the recovery site

   B. The wellbeing of people is often overlooked in the recovery process

   C. To ensure people's fundamental rights

   D. To make sure that HR personnel have their voices heard early and often in the planning process

7. Which of the following is not a key characteristic of members of the DR team?

   A. Understanding of the business unit that they represent

   B. Authority to make decisions

   C. Willingness to be a part of the team

   D. The ability to recover any system in the organization

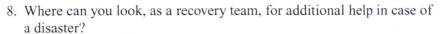

8. Where can you look, as a recovery team, for additional help in case of a disaster?

    A. Fire departments

    B. Police departments

    C. Civil defense teams

    D. Any of the above

9. How might civil defense teams help in case of a disaster?

    A. Search and rescue

    B. Provide clean drinking water

    C. Provide emergency equipment

    D. All of the above

10. Why are vendors included in additional support services?

    A. They may be a source of capital for your DR efforts.

    B. They are a source of supplies and support near the recovery site.

    C. They will be interested in the outcome of your efforts.

    D. They will know where you can find other vendors who might be helpful as well.

11. Which of the following is a difference between temporary help services and local volunteer organizations?

    A. Temporary help services will be first on site to help you.

    B. Volunteer organizations will have the most free resources in a disaster situation.

    C. Volunteer organizations will be able to fill positions on a stopgap basis.

    D. Temporary help services will be able to fill positions on a stopgap basis.

12. The notification directory serves what purpose?

    A. To enable everyone to find other team members for brainstorming ideas

    B. To ensure that everyone can be notified in the event of an emergency

    C. To allow team building to be organized during off hours

    D. So that the conference call bridge can find everyone for meetings

13. Which of the following is not a location available for disaster recovery?

    A. A site in another country

    B. A site in the same county

    C. A site in the same building

    D. Anywhere can be a recovery site

14. Which of the following is not listed as a task for the DR planning team?

    A. Recovering the systems of the organization

    B. Determining what actions to complete first

    C. Auditing current vulnerability

    D. Creating the rest of the team and the plan

15. What are the deliverables for creation of the team and test plans that are cited in the chapter? (select all that apply)

    A. A list of probable individuals for the planning team

    B. A list of roles that people will need to fill

    C. A comprehensive test plan

    D. None of the above

EXERCISES

Exercise 2.1: Recovery Manager

1. Put yourself in the position of the recovery manager.

2. Determine and list the qualities you have that would make you an excellent candidate for this position.

3. Determine and list the qualities this position demands that you lack.

4. Write a proposal for upper management on why you think you are qualified for this position.

Exercise 2.2: Facilities Coordinator

1. The facilities coordinator is a critical role. Put yourself in the position of the facilities coordinator.

2. Determine and list the qualities you have that would make you an excellent candidate for this position.

3. Determine and list the qualities this position demands that you lack.

4. Write a proposal for upper management on why you think you are qualified for this position.

Exercise 2.3: Pick a Position

There are no small or insignificant positions on the disaster recovery team. Look over the descriptions of the positions in the Team Members section of the chapter and pick a position that you think might be interesting.

1. Describe the position you chose and why you chose it.

2. Consider all the functions that the position will cover and list the functions that will prove important in a disaster situation.

3. Write why you think you would or would not be a good candidate for this position.

Exercise 2.4: Finding Additional Resources

1. Choose a disaster.

2. Decide what additional resources might be necessary for an organization given that particular disaster.

3. Report on the disaster type, additional resources that might be necessary, and where you might find these resources.

Exercise 2.5: Recovery Site

1. Look up disaster recovery sites on the Internet.

2. Find one commercial site that is not listed in the text.

3. Prepare a short report on the location, services, and amenities associated with that location. Cite your sources.

PROJECTS

Project 2.1: Small Business DR Team

1. Put yourself in the position of creating a disaster recovery planning team in a small organization with limited resources (capital and human).

2. Describe the organization's business.

3. Determine the most critical roles to fill on the team.

4. Describe how you might best combine or fill roles that you don't have the resources to fill in-house.

Project 2.2: Home Office DR Team

1. Put yourself in the position of having a home-based business. You may have one or two part-time employees, including family members. Describe the business that you have and what goods or services you provide.

2. Determine how you would best cover the key roles on a disaster recovery team.

3. Identify situations where you might lack resources or knowledge. Where would you get extra help?

4. The recovery locations in your situation may be quite different than for a large organization. What might you use as a recovery location for your home business?

5. Describe your team, your external resources, and your choice of recovery locations.

Project 2.3: Team Building

1. Launch your favorite browser.

2. Locate your search engine of choice.

3. Search for "disaster recovery team."

4. Locate other kinds of recovery teams or different positions on the disaster recovery team.

5. Describe what this team or position does and why it is important.

▶▶ Case Study

Juan was appointed as captain of ABC Company's disaster recovery team. He knows that working as a team is important and therefore is trying to figure out how to build both the team and camaraderie in the new team. Members will be from widely different departments, may have different interests, and come from different backgrounds. Discuss what positions will be most critical to fill first, what traits you would look for in each person for each position, and how you would approach building the team feeling if you were in his position.

Chapter | 3

Assessing Risk and Impact

Chapter Objectives

After reading this chapter and completing the exercises, you will be able to do the following:

- Define the risks that may impact your organization.
- Investigate different risk assessments and business impact assessments.
- Set priorities for preventive measures and the recovery from any disaster situation.
- Choose a risk assessment method to be used to identify and quantify risk in an organization.
- Perform risk assessments as they might pertain to an organization.
- Use tools such as OCTAVE to assist in risk assessment.

Introduction

Risk assessment is a critical part of disaster recovery planning. Some of the questions you'll need to answer are: What is the risk? What are the chances that something will happen? What is the business impact, and what is its relevance to disaster recovery planning? What can the disaster recovery team suggest to help the organization mitigate the risk that calamity will befall the organization?

If the planner understands what can go wrong in a particular environment (business, physical, and information technology), he or she can create a plan for almost any contingency. This chapter shows you how to evaluate risk and assess the severity of impact.

To begin, we define the vocabulary that we will be working with in this chapter.

Risk: The possibility of a person or entity suffering harm or loss because of an event.

Business impact: Impact is the magnitude of the potential loss or the seriousness of the event; by extension, business impact is the magnitude of the potential loss or the seriousness of the event to the organization or the business.

Assessment: The act or result of judging the worth or value of something or someone.

Risk is connected to the event. For example, with stocks, the risk that the stock will not go up in value is assessed. In disaster recovery planning, risk is the chance that an event (hurricane, malicious disruption, hardware failure, etc.) will occur to a given organization.

Business impact is connected to the business. In other words, with a given risk that a given event will occur, what is the impact to the business of that event? The business impact (as well as the risk) may be negligible, as may be the case if the business is a sole proprietorship accounting firm and the event is data corruption caused by a disgruntled employee. The same event may have a catastrophic business impact if the business is a multinational or global organization with thousands of employees.

Defining Risk

Risk is defined as the possibility of a person or entity suffering harm or loss. Within an organization or business, risk is viewed as the possibility that the business will lose money because of a disaster occurring. The possibility of harm or loss from any given disaster is different depending on the organization, the situation, and the severity of the disaster. It is possible to assign quantitative values to the possibility that a given event will occur, and also to the amount of damage that is likely should such an event occur. In this way, it is mathematically possible to determine what might happen and the ramifications should it happen for any organization for any given event.

In order to determine the possibilities of disaster and the resulting effects, an organization needs to undertake a *risk assessment.*

Risk Assessment

Risk assessment is a careful, systematic examination of the environment and the physical, technological, or human components that could cause harm to the organization, staff, or product. Risk assessments are conducted to determine whether sufficient precautions have been taken to protect the office, factories and warehouses, and materials and personnel, and also to prevent harm to the business and loss of revenue. Risk assessments are directed at mitigating loss of productivity: If the physical location of the business is inaccessible to the workers, they cannot continue to perform their jobs. It is important to remember, however, that loss of staff is as much a concern as loss of the physical location and materials: If no one is available to run the equipment, there will be a loss of productivity.

A risk assessment allows an organization, or a department within an organization, to determine the sensitivity of that organization or department to any given event. All potential disaster situations must be considered, even those that may at first appear to be far-fetched or inapplicable. Realistic ramifications and weights should be assigned to all events and potential outcomes.

The most important thing to remember when looking at risk assessment is to determine whether a hazard is statistically significant and whether the hazard has been sufficiently addressed with satisfactory precautions. If it is possible to determine the probability that an event will occur, then take the necessary steps to ensure that it either will not occur or that the effects will be minimal if it does occur.

For example, water can kill. Rivers flood, overflowing their banks and causing massive destruction. However, the chance of flooding in an office on the 50th floor of the USX Tower, even in downtown Pittsburgh with its three rivers, is remote. The building itself may be affected, and power to the building may be interrupted for an extended period of time (and those risks have to be addressed), but the chance of water damage attributed to a flood to that 50th floor office is remote.

In the same way, an avalanche can kill and destroy property. However, the chance of an avalanche in downtown Houston is remote. The 2004 tsunami in Indonesia was devastating. However, the chance of a tsunami hitting Kansas City, Missouri, is remote. The point is that a disaster is relative to the location of the business and must be considered in light of the geography of the business location.

A realistic assessment requires that all participants be aware of the hazards and risks that pertain to the individual business being evaluated.

FYI   *Risks vs. Hazards*

This chapter discusses both risks and hazards. Before proceeding, it is important to understand the difference between the two words. A **hazard** is anything that can cause harm. A **risk** is the chance that someone or something could be harmed by the hazard. When evaluating for risk, the given risk may be either high (more likely to occur) or low (less likely to occur).

▶▶ CONTINUED

It is important to separate the hazard from the risk that someone could be harmed by it. Although in the end the two are taken together to determine what processes need to be put in place so that the organization can withstand any event that is likely to cause significant issues, to begin the process it is important to brainstorm all the hazards that can be associated either with a location or with a line of business or particular organization.

Not every hazard needs to be considered during this process, however. Brainstorming sessions can go quickly from creative to downright silly if we do! While many events might be *conceivable*, they aren't incredibly *likely*. For example, a blizzard isn't a likely hazard that needs to taken into account if the organization is located in central Texas or south Florida. Likewise, hurricanes should not be a concern to businesses in Montana.

Once a list of all relevant hazards is developed, the risk that each hazard will happen must be determined. For example, a shop that sells fishing bait on a riverbank in a flood-prone area that lies in the path of hurricanes has a high risk of being affected by a hurricane or a flood. However, a taconite mine in northern Minnesota with a significant investment in water relocation facilities and with a large land mass with mining operations taking place at several different levels in the mine has a low risk of being affected by a flood, partly because of the practice of mining at different levels in the mine and partly due to the investment in equipment to move water from one location to another.

Risk Management

Once the potential for loss has been determined through risk assessment, then the organization can begin to manage that risk, and develop the disaster recovery and business continuity plans to address each risk. Risk management prioritizes risks in the order of severity and potential impact on the organization. For that reason, risk management is often considered to be *reactive* rather than *proactive*. In the context of disaster recovery and risk management, a reactive company will tend to wait until situations present themselves before undertaking plans to mitigate or manage the risk of disasters occurring that would impact the organization. Proactive organizations take into consideration all the alternatives that are likely to befall the organization and attempt to plan for or around those eventualities. One reason that many organizations choose a reactive approach is that it's often difficult to assign quantitative measures to the hypothetical impact of a given situation on the organization, whether in whole or in part.

IN PRACTICE: Proactive Organization vs. Reactive Organization

Organizations choose, either actively or passively, to be proactive or reactive. We need to understand the differences and the ramifications outlined below.

Proactive Organization

Clover Warehousing is a data warehousing application service provider organization specializing in data. After spending considerable time determining what hazards were likely to be relevant to the organization, it made a list of hazards and the risks associated with them. The company then decided what measures it could take to minimize the chances that the hazards would occur and to minimize the risk to the organization if they did occur.

The company determined that, although not located in a wet climate, when floods occur they are flash floods and are typically significant. It invested in pumps to relocate water should it enter the basement of the building, elevated its generators so they were sitting above the likely water level, and built diversion ditches around the building housing the servers.

The nature of Clover's business was housing data. It had no control over what kind of data its client organizations would want to warehouse; therefore it put into place a practice of offering encryption services for sensitive information. The encryption would be specific to each client, so no two client's data would be encrypted in the same manner. This would allow for no chance that one client would accidentally see another client's data.

Electronic locks placed on the server room door were biometric, so only given personnel were granted access to the physical servers. Further, enhanced security was placed on the network to help ensure that unauthorized intrusion from either internal or external sources would be minimized or detected.

Virus scan, adware scan, spyware scan, and spam scan software was installed on all servers and desktop computers, and mandatory scans ran every day at noon so they would be minimally intrusive.

The company had not been faced, actively, with any of the hazards that it examined to that point, but put in place measures to make sure that it would be impacted to a far lesser degree should any of the hazards occur.

» CONTINUED

Reactive Organization

Joe's Jerky Joint is a home-based business making homemade jerky (beef, turkey, and fish). The jerky is processed using Joe's special blend of seasonings and dried in his special smoker.

Joe was making a pretty good living with his business. He kept his recipe on an index card in the file cabinet along with a paper copy of his receipts for jerky that he sold as well as supplies that he purchased. He bought a computer to computerize his files, but never got around to putting his records on disk. He kept his files—contact information for vendors he uses and vendors who contact him, as well as a record book including his accounting files—in a shoebox in the bottom drawer of his desk that he had built in the closet in his hallway. His curing shed was built under a picturesque copse of trees on the banks of a lovely river. He always meant to buy flood insurance, but had never gotten around to it. He had been in the same location for five years.

A dam up river burst in a massive rainstorm. The water raced down the river, leveling the curing shed and flooding Joe's house and his office.

When the flood waters receded, nothing was left of the shed. The records in Joe's shoebox were sodden, the ink was washed out of the record book, and the receipts were washed clean, as was the index card on which he had written his recipe. He couldn't fill the orders he had, and he couldn't even try to subcontract the orders he had as he didn't have any record of the orders. He had no tax records, no working records of supplies bought for the current year, and no way to contact his customer base to let them know what had happened.

Joe's business suffered a great loss due to his failing to plan for what was likely an inevitable emergency. He never considered the risk of a flood, even though the likelihood of a flood given his location was great. He never took into consideration what would happen to his business if an emergency situation were to present itself. He never took even the simplest precaution (insurance and secure copies of records) to help himself reestablish his business in the event of a disaster.

Emergency Situation or Event

Risk is often associated with emergency situations, situations that people often call the event or the triggering event. The word "disaster" conjures up connotations of emergency situations, natural disasters, attack by outside sources, or other catastrophes befalling the location where the organization is found. The following situations are not the only ones that should be considered when analyzing the risks to an organization, but they are to the ones most people think of when talking about potential disasters.

Terrorist Attack   In today's world, the possibility of attack by outside agencies has increased dramatically. The attacks on the World Trade Center and the Pentagon on September 11, 2001, and the attack on the Alfred P. Murrah federal building in Oklahoma City on April 19, 1995, are prime examples of how our world has changed. The possibility of terrorist attack needs to be considered, even for those organizations that never before considered it a potential threat.

This is not to say that Joe's Repair Shop or Pinky's Wireless will be the target of a terrorist attack. It is to say that anyone in business needs to be aware of the potential threat and consider it as a possibility.

Not only can a business be affected directly by an attack on its own facilities by terrorists, it can also be affected by attacks on governmental and financial institutions, suppliers upstream, and clients downstream. With the massive networks of interconnections between organizations today, attacks against any one of them, either physically or electronically, can cause a ripple effect that can affect others. It is therefore important to consider the possibility of attack either upstream or downstream in the organization's product chain as a potential risk.

Environmental Disruption   Disruption of services due to a wide range of environmental problems ranging from minor fires to major earthquakes needs to be allowed for in any disaster recovery plan. People think about floods as disasters as they apply to their organization, but what about the flood that washes out the electric company's ability to provide service? What would happen if the only supplier that an organization used for raw materials couldn't ship product because of a blizzard in the area closing roads for two weeks? What would happen if your Houston, Texas small business's disaster recovery plan included driving out of Houston into Austin or Dallas and setting up business temporarily in a rented hotel suite, but you couldn't get out of Houston because all of the evacuation route roads were clogged and everyone was running out of gas? These interruptions in service are often *not* taken into account.

IN PRACTICE: Environmental Disruption

Data Divers is a data mining organization that specializes in scavenging historical tapes that have backups of emails for information that will either exonerate an organization involved in litigation or that an organization can use against ex-employees in similar situations.

» CONTINUED

When it was deciding where to house its servers, Data Divers looked at the locations where it wanted to lease, based on price. These locations included the first floor in a building located on the banks of a river, the basement of a building in Los Angeles, an old house built on the top of a hill in Montana, and a log cabin in the middle of the forest.

It was determined that flood was too great a risk in the first location, and there were few ways of effectively mitigating that risk. The building in Los Angeles was in an earthquake-prone location, and it would be difficult to minimize that risk. The log cabin posed too great a fire danger to be practical. But the old house on a hill in Montana was perfect. Although there is a tendency to have blizzard conditions, the addition of generators and adequate backups for the other utilities would allow the company to be self-sufficient if necessary. Because it was located on top of the hill, it would be unlikely to be in the path of an avalanche.

By doing careful research on locations that would be best for locating its new business, the company provided a careful risk analysis and was able to plan for eventualities and be able to weather the storm.

Depending on the geographic location of the organization, hurricanes, tornadoes, tsunamis, or earthquakes are often uppermost in the minds of those assisting with the disaster recovery plan. Many of these risks are geographically dependent, and contingency plans can be put into place well in advance of the event. People doing business in tornado alley or in an area prone to flooding should be aware of those tendencies and put into place plans and practices that will mean that these eventualities have the smallest impact possible and that the organization can recover as quickly as possible afterward.

Fire is a source of risk for any organization regardless of location or line of business. The risk associated with the potential of a fire and the resulting consequences of a fire will vary among lines of business. Refineries and gas stations and organizations dealing with volatile chemicals will have different risks and risk tolerances than a clothing retailer or a grocery store chain.

Proper engineering when building or renovating can diminish or prevent damage from earthquakes or hurricanes; however, the disaster recovery plan needs to provide for backup services that take these events into account. For example, even if the building is intact after an earthquake or hurricane, will there be electricity and running water? Will staff be able to get to work?

These plans can range from full real-time backups that are ready to automatically take over upon failure of the main data center, to using alternative sites that can provide all the equipment that is necessary to allow you to use your own backup tapes as a means to bring your services back online. These sites can be geographically widely separated or can simply be in a different part of town than the primary site. The selection of the proper service will depend on the organization's tolerances for lost data and lost time. The cost of one of these services can be recouped in the savings from even a single day's lost business, if recovery procedures are properly planned.

Information Security Incidents   The integrity of an organization's information has become increasingly important with the passing of time. There was a time when all an organization's information was stored on paper (and this may still be the case in many small companies today) and the recovery of that information was nearly impossible; this is not necessarily the case today. However, paper documents still have to be accounted for in every disaster recovery plan and paper still proves to be among the most difficult medium to recover. It is important to remember that many smaller organizations and businesses just starting out have a tendency to operate in a helter-skelter manner, relying on paper documents as the means to maintain records and taking chances with being able to recover these documents.

The accumulated information a business has on itself, its customers and their buying habits, and the cost of production of its products is valuable information to that organization's competitors. Therefore, the safeguarding of this information has taken on a greater importance for most organizations. Any disaster recovery plan needs to provide for the security of the information that the organization deems vital to the business functioning and thriving. This means that not only does the data have to be recoverable, but it has to be recoverable in a way that will allow for the safety of the information from being compromised.

The potential for industrial espionage is a very real threat (think of it as identity theft on a huge scale). What's more, with many of today's regulation regarding the sensitivity and security of medical information, organizations (particularly those dealing directly or tangentially with medical information of any kind) need to be aware of the potential of this information getting into the wrong hands. Medical supply houses, insurance claims processing organizations, physicians, and home healthcare organizations all need to be aware of the potential for the system to be compromised and take steps to limit the ability of anyone to compromise the system rather than to mitigate damages should compromise occur.

The theft of this information is not typically considered to be a disaster, or a triggering event for a disaster declaration, and an organization that finds itself in this kind of situation would likely not want its clients and vendors to know that their data had been compromised. This situation, however, can be classified as a disaster from the organization's perspective, and prevention, mitigation, and remediation actions need to be planned for the organization to be confident that it will continue, recover, and thrive should this disaster occur.

Equipment and System Failure Equipment failure can take on many different aspects. Individual components can fail, entire systems can crash, or key components can cause entire systems to become inaccessible, if not lost. Hard drives crash. A 240-ton production truck can take out the fiber optic network cable, disabling half of the plant. A poorly written program can be inefficient and consume massive amounts of memory, causing the Unix servers to crash. Many of these situations can be planned for and contingencies can be made for situations where these losses occur.

Data center planning, whether your data center is hosted or is wholly company owned, needs to ensure that there is no single point of failure for any system that is critical for business operations. Safeguards for immediate recovery in case of failure and notification plans for such eventualities need to be in place. Further, if high availability is critical to the organization, fault-tolerant and failover contingencies need to be provided for.

Even with modern clustering technology, disaster recovery planning needs to provide for the possibility of failure both at the single system and data center levels and have in place procedures for such losses. The rapid recovery from system loss is key to business continuation and minimizing the loss of profits.

Utility Loss The loss of utilities to a data center can be mitigated by the provision of a data center UPS or other backup system, but these measures cannot provide continuation of operations without supplementation by onsite electrical generation or onsite water purification. Consider the effects of Hurricanes Katrina and Rita in 2005 on the Louisiana and Mississippi border communities, most particularly New Orleans. These towns had more water than they could handle, but not nearly enough to use. Although the need for water purification would not be nearly as critical in most situations, there are situations where the need for access to potable water is critical. Sizing the onsite power generation properly to provide both for current needs and future growth as well as noise abatement is one key.

Another measure that can be taken to limit the single point of failure for utilities is trying to provide multiple feeds from the utility grids into the organization. This limits the chances of loss of power due to single line disruption, although it would be useless should you face grid disruption.

Malicious Disruption All businesses are vulnerable to attack both from within and outside of the organization. Both of these risks can be mitigated by the application of proper security standards to both internal and external applications. The disaster recovery plan should include provisions for dealing with security breaches ranging from denial of service attacks to the internal destruction of data by a disgruntled or terminated employee. Proper recovery operations for each type of attack need to be targeted to just the areas affected without impacting other areas of operations. Such targeting requires cooperation between functional areas to ensure minimal impact on those areas not involved in the attack.

Auditing and other detection methods can be put into place as a way to track these problems, but prevention is a much better option than detection after the fact.

IN PRACTICE: Database Auditing

Many database management systems have the facility to audit what is going on within the database. This auditing can be turned on, minimally, at the user level, at the database level, or at the object level (like tables).

This auditing can add overhead (such as storage for the audit logs) to the system, but because it is possible to discover far earlier what is happening and to determine who is accessing what in the database, it is possible to determine when someone is straying outside of their authority level and to limit their access early in the process, likely before any major problems are discovered.

Enterprise level risk assessment is not a one-time task but an ongoing process. Once an assessment methodology is decided on and put into place the practice of risk assessment needs continued refinement and improvement.

Choosing the Assessment Method

A consistent method of risk assessment needs to be applied across the business enterprise. Consistency is critical because the method will go a long way toward determining the weighted outcome and coming up with a unified result set.

Regardless of the method chosen, the assessment of various levels of risks cannot be compared to each other unless the method used to assess them is the same.

You can manage the risks to you business only if you have a method of dealing with them. Each business has a unique manner of operating and therefore needs a unique method of dealing with risk management. Input from the entire disaster recovery planning team should be sought so that an overall perspective can be built up. This can then be used to both define risks and develop plans to deal with them.

There are several different types of assessments that can provide the organization with the information needed. Each assessment comes at the situation a little differently, some from the perspective of the disaster, some from the perspective of the assets of the company that is involved, and some from the impact that a disruption could have on the organization. Combinations of these assessments are often used (for example, a disaster-based risk assessment alongside an asset-based risk or business impact assessment).

There are many methods that you can use. This chapter covers the following methods:

- Disaster-based risk assessment

- Asset-based risk assessment

- Business impact assessment

- OCTAVE risk assessment

There are likely myriad other methods—whether different methods or combinations—that you could find if you did some research on risk assessment.

Matching the Response to the Threat

Although a fire that destroys large parts of a building may require invoking the full disaster recovery plan, a denial of service attack on a Web site does not. Each threat needs a plan and a measured response spelled out in the disaster recovery (DR) plan. Each response should detail the use of resources, and assign only those resources needed to fix the problem.

Identifying Mission-Critical Processes and Systems

Each system and each process contributes to the operation of the enterprise, but there are some without which the enterprise cannot carry out the others. Identifying each of these processes and systems and then providing for their rapid recovery within the DR plan is one of the keys to successful business continuation.

Evaluating Critical Functions

Functions need to be assessed by problems that their loss will cause to the everyday operations of the business. Will the loss of a function affect the continued manufacture of the product? Will it affect the receiving of goods or their shipment? Will it affect the tracking of goods through the enterprise? Although a decision support system (DSS) such as a management dashboard may provide information to management, it may not be critical to the operation of the business. The decisions as to which functions are critical and which are not need to be made in an objective and independent manner.

Setting Priorities Based on Time Horizons

It's important to remember that everything can't be done at once. Although this may not be the solution that will please all stakeholders and upper management, it's important to maintain a realistic outlook on what can be accomplished and

3

when it can be completed. To this end it is important to set priorities for preventive measures and the recovery from any disaster situation.

One of the first things that must be accomplished when determining both the risk analysis and the resulting disaster recovery plan is a prioritized list of those processes and applications that are critical to the organization. It is often possible to divide this list into two sections, planning for recovery in phases. Typically, these chunks are based on time horizons defined in service level agreements (SLAs) with external or internal clients.

For example, many processes must be recovered within 36 to 48 hours. This time may be stretched to 72 hours based on organizational requirements. These preliminary systems may include order processing, payment processing, or other customer-related processes so that the organization can restore relations with customers and vendors as quickly as possible.

A second tier of processes may include the ability of the organization to write checks, process payroll, and provide important although less critical systems to the organization and its vendors, partners, and customers. These processes may need to be brought online within the first 2 weeks or months after a disaster. Depending on the time horizons identified, the ability for accounting to close the books and provide financial information to interested parties may fall within this time frame.

A third tier may include those processes that provide functionality to the organization but which are not critical or highly important to the day-to-day processing or week-to-week functioning of the organization. These processes may include time tracking, operational reporting, and printing and mailing reports to external organizations.

Implementing Disaster Avoidance

The best disaster is the one you don't have to recover from. The time and money invested in planning and implementing programs to avoid threats and risks will pay for themselves in continued operations.

One of the primary outcomes of the risk assessment exercise will be a list of things that can be done, preliminarily, within your organization to help you to avoid disaster rather than having to recover from it. Although not all disasters, hazards, or vulnerabilities will be avoidable, avoiding the ones that you can will be key to limiting the impact that all disasters have on your organization and limiting the scope of what you have to recover from.

Avoiding Disasters through Effective Preventive Planning

Identifying risks to the enterprise's operations allows you to effectively plan the ways that you can avoid the possibility of exploitation of the risks. Finding and nullifying risks to critical processes by doing things like providing multiple suppliers for critical parts or providing security for critical computer applications is part of any good DR plan. If you can prevent something from failing, you nullify the need for recovery.

Although there are many types of disaster and hazard threats that cannot be avoided, the risk assessment process will point out those areas where new or altered processes or security measures can help to avoid the potential loss of data or unscheduled downtime. If the risk assessment is successful, you will easily be able to see those areas where you can put into place measures that will allow you to avoid as many of the threats as possible.

Some measures may be as simple as changing passwords from the defaults and on a regularly scheduled basis, or enforcing organizational statutes. It may mean rearranging seating within your organization so that only those who require access to the servers have that privilege. It may mean adding security hardware to the infrastructure to limit access to the assets should inappropriate individuals attempt to physically access the hardware.

Creating Contingency Plans for Unavoidable Threats

Even if you can prevent most of the risks from being exploited, there will be some risks that are unavoidable. Planning to mitigate the effects of these risks is both necessary and prudent. However, the amount of time and resources invested in that planning should be dependant on the probability of the event occurring. You would not spend much time planning for an earthquake in upstate Vermont, but a lot of time looking at the possibility of snow causing a roof collapse.

People in the World Trade Center and in the Pentagon likely never foresaw the eventuality of September 11, 2001. Even if they had foreseen the potential for terrorist attacks via airline crash, the ability to put into place any means to nullify the threats would have been futile and likely would have fostered a false sense of security in those involved.

The remainder of this chapter covers each risk assessment method previously described in greater detail. Some are less complicated than others, some deeper and broader. As with everything, the tools that you choose (in this case the assessment methods) are often are the ones that fit the situation. They may be the ones that you are told you have to use. Whatever the tools, however, the methodologies are similar.

Disaster-based Risk Assessment

The premise of this type of assessment is that the decisions relating to risk management and disaster recovery should be made based on awareness of existing risk factors rather than out of habit or based on what may prove to be unfounded fears. Leaders, particularly those who are in charge of the disaster

recovery team, should act with keen appreciation for the essential factors that make each risk situation unique. They should understand it as it relates to the organization and undertake it in that manner, rather than simply on conditioned responses and as a means to get to the next step. Management needs to be able to rely on support personnel internally, or find those individuals on a contractual basis to fill the gaps should these people be required and are unavailable. They should be able to rely upon those contracts to be carried out in the best interest of the organization and to a degree that will allow the organization to continue in the event of an emergency situation.

Hazards exist. It's a fact of life. However, hazards (or the reactions to hazards) do not have to be so great that the organization is stifled or smothered. The purpose of the risk assessment and resultant risk management and disaster recovery process is to ensure that not only are the risks identified but also that any of those risks that may exist can have proven means of remediation or recovery. Hazards and the associated risks cannot be avoided, but they can be mitigated and planned for. In many cases, this is the best we can do.

One of the most common structured approaches to risk assessment is the disaster-based risk assessment process. This process breaks down the overall process of risk assessment into small, discrete chunks, or more delineated tasks that provide the user with an overall understanding of how those tasks relate to each other. This section will discuss the disaster-based process in more detail and provide information on its use.

Table 3.1 shows an example of a broad tracking document to determine exactly where the organization is in its disaster recovery process. Each department is listed, and progress on the goals is tracked in the columns. Remember, this is often an interactive process, with corrections being made

TABLE 3.1 Departmental risk assessment steps.

| Disaster Recovery Planning Process | Risk Assessment Steps | | | | |
	Step 1 Identify hazards	Step 2 Assess hazards	Step 3 Develop controls and make risk decisions	Step 4 Implement controls	Step 5 Test and evaluate
Accounting	X	X			
Systems Administration	X	X	X	X	
Human Resources	X				
Marketing					
Sales	X	X	X	X	X

to the process and to the plans based on both the implementation process and the results of testing. For more detail, various components of each step also can be listed, and each of those tasks checked off the list as they are completed. This document should be reviewed frequently at update meetings, and managers can offer encouragement and incentives to get the various tasks completed.

This process is broken down into five steps:

1. Identify hazards.
2. Assess hazards.
3. Develop controls and make risk decisions.
4. Implement controls.
5. Test and evaluate.

The following sections explain each step in greater detail.

Identify Hazards or Risks

Creating a list of all possible risks may seem like a daunting task. There are many events and conditions that can be considered a risk to the organization, from a fire to a meteor hitting the building. However, only a portion of the list will apply with any significance to a particular business, and the chances of some (like the meteor) are so remote as to be negligible. The DR team needs to examine each business unit and each department and determine which risks apply to that group.

Each department or business unit should work on its own list independently. This will allow the tasks to be done in parallel and will allow each business unit or department to get a better feel for what events will actually affect it and, by extension, the organization as a whole.

There will emerge, from this exercise, a list of the most common risks to the organization as well as a better idea of the interdependencies between the various business units. These risks and interdependencies will then allow not only the disaster recovery team but also the organization as a whole to come up with a complete picture of the risks affecting the business as a whole. It will also be the basis from which the overall disaster recovery plan will be derived.

Hazards are actual or potential conditions that can occur:

- Injury, illness, or death of key personnel due to bio-terrorism
- Damage to or loss of plant equipment due to hurricane
- Damage to or loss of plant equipment due to tornado
- Damage to or loss of plant equipment due to fire

3

- Damage to or loss of plant equipment due to flood
- Damage to or loss of property due to hurricane
- Damage to or loss of property due to tornado
- Damage to or loss of property due to fire
- Damage to or loss of property due to flood
- Losing or having compromised intellectual property due to network hacking
- System degradation due to extensive adware and spyware
- System inaccessibility due to denial of service attack
- Inability for users to communicate with the system due to network failure
- Loss of system, in part or all, due to disk or other hardware failure

The hazards, risks, or sources of danger can be attributed to enemy, adversary, environmental, or any condition that causes undo loss or strife upon an organization. In this case, the hazards are the hardware failure, tornado, denial of service attack, or other events. Hazards are found in every area, in every region of the country and of the world, and are capable of wreaking havoc to one degree or another upon an organization. Some hazards are unique to an area and others can be categorically ruled out for another area. Hurricanes don't hit Denver, Colorado; blizzards rarely hit Bangalore, India. Adding the information on what can transpire should the event occur will give you a better idea as to the organizational ramifications connected with the hazard. More information that you can use will be presented later, but this information is not necessary at this point in the process.

Accurately identifying hazards to the organization is key to the organization's ability to recover from these disasters. Also, hazards often change rapidly. Things that you consider to be of little risk at one point in time can quickly become major threats based on a given set of circumstances. That is why vigilance and risk assessment are typically ongoing activities. Complacency, ignoring the fact that existing controls may or may not continue to provide the hazard control that they have in the past, and ignorance of rapidly changing situations can together be considered to be a hazard in themselves.

The leaders of the team first have to analyze the current goals of the disaster recovery team and the goals of the organization, both stated and implied. This has to be done with the understanding about what needs to be accomplished and with an eye on setting intermediate milestones along the way for the team.

Risk assessment is often a difficult and complicated undertaking. This is particularly true if it is being undertaken as a whole rather than in stages. It is often easier for the team or for individuals connected to the risk assessment to complete the undertaking in bite-sized pieces. This may be an hour at a time, twice a week, or until a good understanding of the risks can be accomplished.

Goals that are too complicated or goals that are too lofty allow (and encourage) inaccuracies in the process. Actual risks can be missed in the process of trying to meet impossible deadlines, and perceptions of risk where risk does not exist can lead to misplaced effort.

Remember that hazard identification and the whole risk assessment process will end up being a different scale, a different scope, depending on the size of the organization that is performing the assessment. Many of the events that are hazards for a multinational organization are also hazards for small businesses, but many are unique to the location, the size, and the complexity of the organization.

Team members should constantly consider their enemies, which may be human, technological, or environmental. Also, they should remain conscious of the capabilities that the enemies have to disrupt your organization. Table 3.2 is an example of a small business' hazard identification list. This business is a family-owned specialty grocery store located on a hill in western Pennsylvania. In this list the organization in question has determined the hazards that are most likely to affect the organization. There are many hazards that are particularly relevant to small businesses. These include, but are not limited to, flood of the business itself, flood of access routes to the business, fire, arson, computer virus, utility outage, illness of key personnel, theft, and power surge.

Large businesses are affected by many of the same things; however, there are some differences that are more relevant to larger businesses than to smaller ones. These include, but again are not limited to, denial of service attacks, hackers,

TABLE 3.2 Weighted list of hazards identified by a small business.

Hazard	Weight (1 to 5 scale)
Flood of business	2
Flood of access routes	4
Fire	4
Arson	3
Virus	2
Electrical outage	4
Catastrophic illness of owner	5
Theft	4
Power surge	3

spam, adware, interruption of supply chain, interruption of shipping channels, fire, flood, earthquake, hurricane, tornado, other natural disasters, multiple disk crashes, massive power failure at multiple key locations, data corruption, programming logic errors, malicious data alteration or deletion, and many more.

Assess and Prioritize Risks

After the risks have been identified, each of the listed risks needs to be assessed and each hazard given a weight of how likely that hazard is to affect the organization and the potential impact of that hazard on the organization. The recovery team needs to determine what the chances are of each hazard occurring, as well as determine the ramifications to the business, in a worst-case scenario, should that hazard occur. The assessment and prioritization will be a more subjective rather than objective assessment, but it's important that careful thought be given to the realistic ramifications of a disaster to the overall organization's operation and that intelligent and realistic measurements be assigned to each. Although the tendency may be to either take an overly optimistic or overly pessimistic view of what the ramifications may be, care must be taken to judge the real risk rather than either of the extremes. If you do need to choose between the two extremes, however, planning for the worst case allows you to plan for the most severe ramifications and be pleasantly surprised if that isn't the extent to which the event impacts the organization.

Once you have determined the hazards and the ramifications, you need to make a prioritized list of those hazards that are most likely to occur in your unique circumstances and which have the most serious ramifications should they occur. Using this list you can then determine the best disaster avoidance strategy to keep the hazard from affecting your organization and the best disaster recovery strategy to use in each situation. Use this list as a means to help you to work your way to a point where you determine that the cost of continuing to put avoidance and recovery strategies in place is not cost effective. Putting in fire alarms in any situation will be cost effective. Preparing for a hurricane in Minneapolis would not be.

Table 3.2 showed an example of a prioritized weighted list of risks associated with small businesses. Table 3.3 shows a similarly organized list for larger organizations.

When performing this part of the exercise you need to look at who could be hurt, and how and to what extent the injuries can impact the individual or the organization. Remember, it isn't just a cliché that your most valuable assets are people. They are the ones who know how to get the company back on its feet and who know the inherent meaning of the data. Their safety needs to be paramount in the decisions on how to limit the impact of, and recover from, any potential risks.

Also, you need to determine how to make the best use of the resources available and how to most quickly limit the impacts of any risks that you

TABLE 3.3 Partial weighed list of hazards identified by a large business.

Risk	Weight (scale 1 to 10)
Denial of service attack	8
Hackers	7
Spam	7
Adware	7
Interruption of supply chain	5
Fire	9
Flood	8
Earthquake	6
Hurricane	7
Tornado	7
Tsunami	2
Power failure at one or more locations	6
Avalanche	5
Disk crash	7
Data corruption	8
Virus	7
Interruption of outbound transport of product	6
Network failure	8
Hardware failure	8
Data deletion	8
Programming logic errors	9

determine to be significant. Any company has only a finite amount of resources and therefore needs to make intelligent decisions as to what it can reasonably accomplish with the plans and what it can't.

IN PRACTICE: The Reality of Risk

It is important that all major hazards and risks that are relevant to an organization be examined. An exhaustive analysis of every hazard that might be relevant in any way, regardless of how rare the event may actually be, might be overkill. This exercise needs to be approached in

▶▶ CONTINUED ON NEXT PAGE

3

a complete manner, but with an eye on the reality of the organization and location situation. It isn't really necessary to consider snowfall as a serious risk in Houston or Miami. Although it might occasionally snow, the risk to a business from extensive snowfall is negligible.

It is always interesting when there are individuals with a sense of humor on the team. They can lighten the mood and make the meetings more interesting. They may come up with hazards like a herd of hungry rabbits attacking the data center, or the computers developing a personality and taking over the process themselves. The levity can be particularly useful when the team has decided that they will at least examine every hazard that is brought to the table. Although these ideas are far-fetched, and the people with interesting senses of humor know this as well as the rest of the team does, they can introduce a level of reality necessary when looking at potentially bad situations for extended periods of time.

Develop Controls and Make Risk Decisions

It is important to make intelligent decisions once you have completed your risk assessment. When you have determined the primary risks—the hazards and events that will have the worst ramifications and that will be most likely to occur—you need to decide what you are going to do with that information and what you can do to limit the impact or mitigate the damages.

At this point you need decide what kinds of controls you can most easily put into place that will address the largest number of hazards and events, particularly the most significant ones. Many of these controls will likely be procedural (changing passwords at the organizational level at least every 90 days, mandating that work stations be locked when users walk away from them, or allowing access to sensitive data and locations only by those with a need-to-access basis). Others will necessarily have to be physical (fire prevention and elimination in the computer room, sump systems in the basements of buildings in likely flood-prone areas, or the implementation of an automated early response system to alert all personnel in the case of an event occurring).

Additional people will need to be involved at this point in the process. Because of the nature of the decisions financial intervention on the part of the organization will often be required, and key people with the ability to make these decisions, or at least those who can assist in influencing these decisions, need to be brought into the process. It is no good determining that you need to install a fire suppression system in the server room if funding will not be provided for such a decision. These people will want hard facts, for example, the relative cost effectiveness of installing Halon over carbon dioxide over nitrogen over simple water over dry chemical as a means to suppress a fire that may occur in a computer room. Direct (the cost of the system) as well as indirect (the cost of replacing water-soaked components should the suppression system either deliberately or inadvertently be triggered) costs need to be provided to the decision makers.

Once the decisions are made, it is time to implement a plan for managing the risks to the organization and for putting the controls in place that will minimize the impact of the hazards. It is also time to put into place the meat of the DR planning.

Implement a Risk-Handling Plan and Controls

The next step in the process is to implement the risk-handling plan (the prevention steps and the recovery plan) and to put into place the controls that will, hopefully, make those plans unnecessary.

Now is when you put into place those measures and controls that will help mitigate the damages and limit the impact that any event may have on the organization. It is also the time when you determine how best to bring back the company's systems and get it back into a functional state in the quickest way possible given any constraints on the organization.

In this step you will determine the frequency of backups required for your organization to meet its SLAs and to remain a going concern. You will determine how best to test those backups, because without knowing that you can recover backups they are useless. You will also determine what systems are critical to recover and in what order they need to be recovered. This prioritization of systems will be covered to a greater extent in Chapter 4.

Now is the time that money starts to play a bigger role in the planning. This is when you purchase the redundant hardware and put controls in place that limit access to data to those who need it. You put the new rules and regulations in place in the organization and impress upon the organization the importance of adhering to those rules.

This is also when you begin the process of testing your DR plan for effectiveness. Testing will prove to you and to all stakeholders that your plans are sound and that you can recover the business to the point where you can continue as an organization regardless of the eventualities that may befall the organization.

Evaluate, Track, and Report

Finally, you need to evaluate the measures that you have put into place, track the successes and failures in your measures and in your testing, and report back to the organization as a whole on the effectiveness. These last steps will be iterative. It will never be as simple as putting measures in place to limit your exposure to emergency situations and then feeling that you are safe forever. The organization needs to periodically reevaluate the steps it has taken to control the risk that it faces from disaster situations and determine if what is in place is still sufficient or relevant to the situation and make adjustments as necessary. There was a time that simply putting a sign on the door to a server room was sufficient to keep people from inappropriate access to the servers and the data; it then became necessary to adjust the security measures and lock unauthorized people out of the server room. Eventually, it became necessary to alter the network access to keep people from accessing the servers inappropriately from remote locations. Because technology changes, and society changes, it is important to realize that preventive measures have to change and the evaluation process needs to continue indefinitely. You must consider what has been learned, what can be done differently to do better the next time, and then test these new scenarios.

Not only is it important that you report the successes, it is even more important that you report your failures and learn lessons from what didn't work. These lessons will prove to be invaluable in the next iteration of testing and will likely prove to be just as valuable if and when the time comes that an actual disaster is declared.

During the testing phase, make notes of where you found places that you could take shortcuts, what didn't work, or what didn't work the way that you thought it should. It may even be worthwhile to add the position of scribe to the disaster recovery team roster and have someone designated to take notes during the process and own those notes until they are incorporated into the plan later.

IN PRACTICE: Not Resting on Your Laurels

It is important to note that this is an iterative process. You can't just do it once and never address it again. Although many of the hazards and risks won't change to any great degree, the steps that the organization puts in place will change over time.

At one point, limiting access to a building at Lawrence Data Archiving meant simply giving everyone who was allowed to be there a key. Once in the building, everyone was free to come and go as they liked. That was when there were 5 employees.

As the business grew, security had to grow as well. The organization identified the free and easy access to the servers as a potential security risk. Further, it was determined that providing keys to all employees to come into the building was a maintenance issue as far as tracking keys and replacing keys for people who lost theirs. An ex-employee (who had had her key replaced several times while employed) was found in the building using the bathrooms with her children. Not all keys had been turned over when the employee left.

> ▶ CONTINUED
>
> The organization decided that, to mitigate the risk, it would provide those who needed access to the servers with an electronic key card. Further, all employees were given a key card, and security to where the employee was permitted to go was tied to that card. If the card was reported lost or a replacement was requested, the security to the lost card was terminated. That way, anyone who needed access to the servers would be given a card and only those with cards could get in. This was when there were 50 employees.
>
> Over time, employees began to leave their cards in their desk drawers, hanging on lanyards on their cube walls, or just laying on their desk. There was an incident when someone who was not officially given access to the server room was found inside, having appropriated someone else's key card to gain access. It was time to reevaluate the risk mitigation methods that were in place. There were now 150 employees.
>
> The organization decided that biometric options were the way to go. Fingerprint scanners allowed people into the building and into most locations where they were permitted to be. Access to the server room had pupil scan added to the fingerprint scanner as an added measure of security. This way, employees could not lose their access method, nor was it easy for someone to use someone else's security. When an employee was no longer employed by the organization, the computerized access was revoked. This was when the organization had 500 employees.
>
> As you can see, reevaluation based on needs of the organization, over time, needs to take place. This is true of any organization and any hazard and risk combination. Needs change. Technology changes. The organization needs to change along with it.

Asset-based Risk Assessment

A second five-step approach to risk assessment is *asset-based risk assessment.* It attacks the problem more from the perspective of the assets rather than from the perspective of the disaster. Under this approach, you assess all assets, threats, vulnerabilities, and risks to come up with appropriate countermeasures for each. The following sections describe these steps in greater detail.

Asset Assessment

The first step in this particular risk assessment methodology is asset assessment. Disaster recovery team members and the asset owners identify and rank the assets that are most critical to the mission-critical operations, followed by the next levels of operation, and finally the least critical operations. By identifying and prioritizing these assets the organization can take the first steps toward focusing its disaster recovery resources on those assets that are most important to the organization.

Typically, assets are the tangible things in the organization (people, servers, networks, or other equipment). However, these are not the only assets of an organization. The often-overlooked, more intangible assets include information and data; the processes that are particular to the organization; the reputation of the organization in the marketplace; and the goodwill that is associated with that organization by its vendors, its customers, and its partners. It may well be that the information and associated automated processes are the organization's most important assets. Tangibles are often replaceable, particularly commodity hardware and software, but the intangibles may be irreplaceable.

Organizations, from a security perspective, need to protect sensitive and proprietary information, and may face HIPAA ramifications if proper security measures are not taken. HIPAA, the Health Insurance Portability and Accountability Act, provides for the privacy of an individual's medical information. Disaster-impacted organizations need to not only maintain and protect the sensitive and proprietary information, but also protect information about the functions of the organization and its employees, the critical processes that are centrally unique to the organization, and information connected to the disaster itself.

For each asset that the company identifies, it needs to identify all the events that could impact each of the assets. This needs to include the damage or destruction of the asset, or damage that could impact the information or functionally provided by the asset. An estimation of what the effect of the loss of the asset would be to the organization, both short term and long term, needs to be provided.

A worksheet is typically used to record the results of this assessment. An example of this can be seen in Table 3.4. Because it is the foundation of the remainder of the assessment, the asset assessment is the most important step in this process. The rest of the steps build upon its foundation.

Threat Assessment

The threat assessment step focuses on the adversaries or events that can in any way adversely affect the identified assets of the organization. In this step, it's important to find a means to quantitatively assign a value to what may appear to be a qualitative judgment of the department or the individual involved in the assessment. This quantitative measure can be inferred from the data and information gleaned from the research and interviews done. A threat is usually considered in terms of other adversaries or events. It's important to remember that in order to be an adversary, one must possess both the ability and the intent to cause unwanted events. Natural threats to the organization, such as hurricanes, tornadoes, or fire, do not possess intent that has the capability to cause great harm.

Caution

HIPAA

It is critical for an organization with health-related information to protect access to data during a disaster, throughout the recovery, and even while testing its systems. Records may be accessible to unauthorized personnel, locks may be circumvented, and alarm systems may be inoperable. HIPAA-impacted organizations must be extra cautious when its information is housed offsite, as it may be accessible to people who are not authorized to view it. These situations can leave you open to violations simply due to poor planning.

TABLE 3.4 Asset assessment list.

Asset	Location
mysrvoracle1	Denver
mysrvoracle2	Denver
mysrvoracle3	Austin
mysrvoracle4	Austin
mysrvoracle5	Pittsburgh
mainframe	Denver
mysqlserver1	Pittsburgh
mysqlserver2	Pittsburgh
myfileserver1	Austin
myfileserver2	Austin
mymailserver1	Denver
mymailserver2	Austin
mywebserver1	Denver
mywebserver2	Austin

IN PRACTICE: Serious Threat

Freeman was a developer on a Windows system at Westin Walker Company. The developers in this company had access to all development servers but no one was supposed to have access to move programs into the production servers. Freeman was angry at the idea that he was not able to move one program in because the administrators didn't think it had been tested thoroughly.

He decided that he had done a complete job with the testing and he would circumvent the system to get his changes into production because he knew better than the administrators what was important to the users and that his code would not affect any of the data other than what was intended.

Freeman copied his program into the production server that he had access to that no one knew about. No one knew about the change until a week later when extensive data corruption in the database was discovered. It took several weeks to recover the data back to the original state and reapply the changes. The damage that was done to the organization's reputation was immeasurable.

The intent was not to cause data corruption, but the malicious intent to put into place something that was not authorized did cause data corruption.

In order to determine whether adversaries pose a serious threat to the organization, you must determine if they have both the intent and the capability to cause the unwanted events. Further, you must determine or infer their history by a track record of successful attacks against assets similar to those found in the asset assessment. Similar steps can be made for events rather than adversaries because you can determine whether a given event has a historical track record for causing detrimental effects to assets and organizations similar to those involved in the assessment.

What's more, there are certain events—most particularly connected to viruses, denial of service attacks, and other cyber events—that may be treated as independent threats rather than adversaries. Because you cannot track the ability of the attacker or determine the history of the attacker to cause adverse effects for an organization, you may need to handle these threats somewhat differently than threats that can be viewed historically.

Again, all assets must be considered, including information and automated processes. Organizations that rely heavily on critical networks connected to the Internet must be cognizant of different events in the larger environment than organizations that don't rely as heavily on these features.

Again, an effective way to handle threat assessment is to make use of a worksheet. By expanding on the asset assessment worksheet, and including the relevant additional information, Table 3.5 shows an example of what might be

TABLE 3.5 Threat assessment worksheet.

Asset	Threat
mysrvoracle1	hacking
	destructive statement
	crashed database
	crashed server
mysrvoracle2	hacking
	destructive statement
	crashed database
	crashed server
mainframe	hardware failure
	server room fire
	destructive program
	hacking
mysqlserver1	hacking
	destructive statement

» CONTINUED ON NEXT PAGE

▶ CONTINUED

Asset	Threat
	crashed database
	crashed server
mysqlserver2	hacking
	destructive statement
	crashed database
	crashed server
myfileserver1	hacking
	virus
	spyware
	hardware failure
myfileserver2	hacking
	virus
	spyware
	hardware failure
mymailserver1	hacking
	spam
	virus
	hardware failure
mymailserver2	hacking
	spam
	virus
	hardware failure
mywebserver1	denial of service attack
	virus attack
	hacking
	hardware failure
mywebserver2	denial of service attack
	virus attack
	hacking
	hardware failure

found in a threat assessment worksheet. The worksheet lists the assets along with the undesirable events that could adversely affect the performance of the assets without making concrete reference to particular adversaries. Included in this worksheet should be information that might be known about adversaries' capabilities to cause undesirable events. In the case of an event rather than an adversary, you can make use of information relevant to the chance that an undesired event will occur and infer the ramifications of the event occurring to the assets.

The deliverables from this step will be an overall threat level for each asset for each adversary, with the worksheet allowing the assets and threats to be efficiently and effectively organized and documented, and all information later to be organized integrated into a single complete analysis.

It is often advantageous, particularly for smaller organizations where financing for extensive software or external assistance is not available, to store this information in a spreadsheet workbook or in a word processor document so that it is portable, inexpensive, and so that a couple of different types of backups are available in the case of a disaster.

Vulnerability Assessment

The next step in the analysis is the vulnerability assessment. This is similar to what might be conducted in a traditional security survey in that the team members identify and characterize vulnerabilities in the organization related to the specific assets and undesirable events. It is important to address these vulnerabilities as a combination of factors. For instance, you cannot simply say that people are vulnerable to death; in fact, 100 percent of people are likely to die at some point. Although this is accurate in relationship to the risk assessment and disaster recovery plan, it's important to assess the combination of the person and the event. For example, people are 20 percent more likely to die in a tornado in Tornado Alley during June, July, and August. It's important during this assessment to look for the exploitable situations in an organization that are created by a lack of adequate security measures, personal behaviors, or commercial construction.

Vulnerabilities will likely include the absence of adequate security personnel; poor access controls, software controls, or contractor access to systems; and often unscreened or unsupervised visitors in secure areas.

Again, it's important to look at the combination of threats and assets and determine the vulnerabilities that are directly associated or able to be associated with each combination. In this way you can more appropriately assign discrete and measurable controls to each combination and make the end task of protecting the organization or recovering from an attack more defined and easier to implement.

It's also important at this level to look at each asset and threat not only from an internal view looking out at what you perceive to be the dangers, but with an eye toward how an adversary or external event might view the same asset-threat combination. Those involved in this assessment should ask themselves, "If I wanted to physically harm this asset, I would . . .", "If I were <insert natural disaster> I would affect this asset by . . ." or "If I were a <hacker, virus, worm, or other attacker> I would attempt to break into this asset by . . ." In this way you can put yourself more into the position of the adversary and find different ways that an asset may be compromised.

During the vulnerability assessment, it's important that you take into account the *severity* of each vulnerability. Compiling this information gives the team more complete information, so combinations of threats can be analyzed.

Risk Assessment

The risk assessment step is the point in the process where all previous assessments, assets, threats, and vulnerabilities are combined and evaluated. By looking at all previous worksheets and asking the following questions you can determine the weighted lists of assets, threats, and vulnerabilities to use as a basis for identifying necessary controls:

- What's the likely effect to the organization if this asset is harmed by one of its relevant unwanted events?

- How likely is it that this adversary or adversaries can and will attack one of the assets to which they are associated?

- What vulnerabilities is this adversary or adversaries most likely to take advantage of connected to this asset?

The purpose of this step, and the end result of proceeding with this step, is an evaluation of how all the ratings interact to arrive at an overall level of risk for each asset. Using the risk analysis worksheet is extremely helpful in this step as it will assist you with organizing the information and presenting it in a readable and understandable format.

By making effective use of this worksheet, you should be able to determine the major vulnerabilities and threats in the organization, where they will lay, and what assets they affect that compare the overall risk across the spectrum of assets. You will then be able to determine the physical and cyber risks as well as which of the risks will require the most immediate attention and controls.

Initially, the terms used to describe the ratings of severity for each component may be qualitative and imprecise. Verbal ratings such as medium are often subjective and hard to combine to get an overall understanding of complete risk to the organization. However, users and subject matter experts may be more comfortable in using brief, subjective terms rather than attempting to objectively assign a number to the process.

In situations where subjective measures are being used, it is typically preferable to assign a numeric value to each subjective measure. For example, you may be able to assign a numeric rating scale of 1 to 10 or 1 to 5 that can then be used to combine all weights in an analysis to come up with an overall weighted scale.

In order to arrive at the weighted scale you need to compute the following equation with the values derived from each table. The equation for deriving risk in the case of this analysis follows:

$$Risk = consequence * threat * vulnerability$$

What you come up with is the overall weighted scale. After this step is completed, the disaster recovery team leaders or managers will determine the threshold where the cost of further analysis and controls becomes more costly than the benefits that are derived from it. For example, although the threat of a hurricane to a server in some situations is severe, the benefit of ensuring that a server in Montana is hurricane proof is not likely cost effective because hurricanes don't typically occur in the state of Montana.

Some of the analysis will end at this point. However, in many cases countermeasures must be put into place to mitigate the risk to the organization of the threats and vulnerabilities to the assets. By determining the point at which diminishing returns occur, and the point at which the organization is no longer willing to fund the mitigation of the risk, the final step in the risk assessment process can be taken.

Controls

You can now identify the countermeasures that may be necessary in order to provide the organization with the steps to follow after a disaster. Using the worksheets as a guide you can determine the most significant vulnerabilities, threats, and consequences that need to be addressed and the assets to which these are attached. You can find the most cost-effective options for mitigating the risks associated with the combination. You may want to consider planning for more than one contingency for each combination, based on differing severities and consequences.

The completion of this step is the basis for decision makers to develop an appropriate disaster recovery plan. Keep in mind, however, that the process must be continual not just a one-time exercise. Threats change, assets change, and processes and abilities within the organization change. It's important to remember that this is an ongoing process, one that needs to be revisited periodically to ensure that the organization is both secure and covered in the event of a disaster.

New threats will emerge from new sources. Threats may appear quickly and may require the organization to do a "quick and dirty" version of the risk assessment to determine how to handle the new threats. Organizations that use a process of continual assessment will be better able to adapt to unanticipated threats as they occur.

The Business Impact Analysis

Another risk assessment process is the business impact analysis (BIA). In this process, rather than identifying the assets and driving the process from that perspective, you address the whole organization from the perspective of the perceived threats. We will start out by taking a more in-depth look at what we mean by business impact, and then look at an outline of how this assessment process works.

Business Impact

All disasters and emergencies—regardless of size or severity—have a business impact. The level of impact, however, will vary. Assessing the level of harm that may occur from any given threat or risk is essential to designing a disaster recovery plan. The response to any level of emergency, disaster, or event needs to fit the type of disaster or emergency, and the danger that event presents to the business.

The potential impact is assessed using several criteria. The following sections address many of these criteria and will provide you with a better idea of how different people play their parts in the overall assessment.

Service Level Agreements   One of the first considerations is the service level agreements (SLAs) that the organization has to meet. When formal (or even informal) agreements are in place with internal or external customers, those have to be taken into consideration early in the disaster recovery planning effort.

An SLA is defined as "a contract that spells out the terms of service that an outsourcer will provide." **(http://guide.darwinmag.com/technology/ outsourcing/sla/)** In setting SLAs, two things need to be uppermost in the minds of the negotiators:

- Can the SLA be reasonably fulfilled?
- Can the SLA be reasonably enforced?

An SLA that does not meet both of these criteria will result in problems for both parties at some point in the agreement's lifetime. If the provider does not have a full understanding of how the SLA is to be fulfilled, it may not be able to provide the service in a timely manner. Further, if the criteria can't reasonably be fulfilled, the consumer may be accused of knowing beforehand that it could not be fulfilled and taking advantage of the provider. If it is not reasonably enforceable, it is possible that there could be lengthy court battles over exactly what is to be expected and how the parties are to work together to achieve the goal. Consumers may not understand their role in the success of the contract and providers may not fully understand what is expected of them in the event that their services are required. This can also lead to the inability of the organization to recover from a disaster.

SLAs, as well as being established between the organization and each of its vendors, should also be set between the IS department of the organization and with each of the business units. These agreements define the guidelines that will allow the planning of disaster recovery by allowing timelines to be built upon the various SLAs; Each step along the line will be taken in order of its necessary completion depending on the disaster that invokes the plan.

SLAs need to be constructed with input from all business units on the needs that each unit must have met and from all the functional areas on what services they are able to provide.

3

IN PRACTICE: Service Level Agreements

Conceptually, service level agreements are fairly easily defined—a contract that spells out the terms of service that one party can expect from another party. But in an organization, this can mean a lot of things and, unless it is spelled out, can remain a great definition but one that is not practical.

One company claims that they need to have "five nines" availability of its systems to its customers (internal customers as well as external customers) for their tier 1 production systems. Five nines is 99.999 percent, or about 315 seconds of downtime a year. This is not in writing anywhere, and when pressed they claim that the 99.999 percent is only for the time when they don't schedule outages for maintenance. That means that the five nines that they demand in availability is only for unplanned outages, but nowhere is this defined or written down. Further, when pressed to provide SLAs on any of its systems, it relies on rough estimation to determine how much downtime it can withstand and when the appropriate people are called in. It calls in upper-level support after a system has been down about an hour or so. It can withstand downtime of about 2 or 3 hours. There is no way to hold anyone, internal or external vendors, to such broad generalizations.

Another company has SLAs that say that it will have maintenance done on nonproduction systems within a 48-hour window. It requires at least 48 hours notice of an upcoming window and a written statement of work to be done in those 48 hours. There are hourly financial ramifications (typically $1000 an hour for every hour it exceeds 48, charged on the quarter hour) for missing the SLAs unless the reason for the delay is attributed to the customer not providing adequate feedback in a timely manner. This is spelled out in writing in every contract (internal as well as external) that the company maintains. Any deviation from the normal contract is written, especially for the client, and is flagged as different whenever maintenance begins so that all involved know the timelines and the ramifications for missing them.

Functional Area Input   The role that each area in the organization plays in the overall functioning of the business needs to be carefully assessed. Each functional area needs to be able to define its own place in the organization as well as be able to elaborate to the disaster recovery team what it believes it will take to recover its systems. The people in these areas will know best what systems they use regularly, which systems they use during different periods of the month or the year, and what systems can be allowed to be pushed out into later in the recovery efforts. This not only helps with the definition of the organization as a whole, but allows each of these units within the organization to realize its worth to the organization and to the disaster recovery effort.

By allowing each area to have input to the total process you allow them both to take ownership of their part of the plan and to buy into the overall plan and the cooperation necessary to successfully complete the steps outlined in the plan. How each functional area fits together to fashion the whole recovery plan needs to be coordinated by the head of the planning team. Encouraging the functional areas to be a part of the planning and testing will foster a feeling that the team is working to actually allow them the ability to do their job the way that they are used to and will encourage them to tell you things that they may have otherwise forgotten.

How the Assessment Works

The purpose of the business impact analysis process is to assist the organization and its management with understanding the impacts associated with all possible threats to the organization. It also assists with the use of that information to calculate the maximum tolerable downtime for the organization based on the time-critical services and resources that the organization relies upon. For most organizations, the resources involved in the time-critical assets include the following:

- Personnel
- Facilities
- Technology, including all computer systems
- Software
- Data
- Networks and network equipment associated with data communication
- Networks and network equipment associated with voice communication
- Paper document records and electronic records
- Plant and equipment
- Inventory, for both internal use and external sale

It is important to note that with the business impact analysis, as with all the analyses, the approach that is taken by the organization is customizable to both organization and situation. Because the needs and resources of a small business are often exceptionally different from the needs of a large organization, even though many of the underlying basic needs are similar, flexibility must be considered at all levels of the disaster recovery planning process.

There are many ways to conduct the information gathering that's required in BIA, including one-on-one interviews with subject matter experts and brainstorming with individuals across the organization. It's helpful to meet with a cross-section of people, as each offers a unique perspective on the organization, its processes, its assets, and data. The information can be gathered face to face, or through the use of electronic data transfer such as emails or central Web sites. The use of a formal or semiformal questionnaire in these cases is often useful, so similar answers can be compared to each other rather than trying to glean information from a freeform discussion. In a group setting these questionnaires can be discussed at length while allowing for the same questions to be answered in all arenas, and again the answers can be compared with each other on equal footing.

In constructing the questionnaire remember that custom questions can be created based on the needs of the organization and the scope of the business and the analysis.

Quantitative questions can be used to assess the economic impact of potential organizational disruption. These are often measured in monetary terms and can be extrapolated from other man-hour type information or forecast loss of business for the duration of an outage. An estimation of the impacts at this level will assist the organization with understanding fully the potential loss not only in terms of loss of income but also increased incurred expenses. Loss in terms of quantitative categories may include the following:

- Lost revenue

- Lost sales

- Lost trade discounts

- Lost accounts payable discounts

- Incurred accounts payable penalties

- Interest paid on borrowed money

- Interest lost on loans

- Contractual fines and penalties for missed SLAs

- Unavailability of funds to the organization

- Penalties due to late deliveries

- Canceled orders due to late deliveries

- Added expense of relying on outside services

- Cost of temporary employees
- Cost of rental or lease equipment
- Need for emergency purchases, often priced at a premium
- Salaries paid to idle staff
- Cost incurred for temporary relocation of employees
- Transportation costs for backup to an auxiliary site
- Replacement cost of key employees

Although this is not an exhaustive list, it gives you an idea of the types of costs that can be incurred in the event of an outage. These are only the immediate quantitative costs directly associated with the disaster and the time immediately following the disaster. The financial ramifications can often be long reaching in the event of a disaster lasting longer or having greater impact than anticipated.

Although the economic aspects of a disaster can be easily understood, and can be measured in terms of dollars and cents either lost or incurred, it's important to also ask qualitative questions to estimate the potential loss impact in terms of emotional understanding and feelings. Although in today's business uncertainty is a daily fact, extended uncertainty and the feelings associated with and surrounding a disaster situation can often provide convincing arguments to the organization's management and a disaster recovery team for shorter recovery windows than may be provided for otherwise. Typically, qualitative questions include the loss of customer service capability, the loss of customer confidence, the loss of vendor confidence, and the loss of employee confidence in the organization.

Questionnaires should also make use of specialized questions, if such questions are relevant to the organization. For example, one question for accounting might be: If you had to process invoices manually, rather than through the system, how much longer would it take you to accomplish this than it does now? Or how would the necessity of having to process invoices manually for several days at month end affect your comfort level in doing your job? If the questions are couched as a means to weigh the relative importance of a system rather than a judgment on a person's ability to perform his or her job in a different manner, valuable information can be gathered not only on the relative importance of systems, but the comfort level that people have when faced with high stress change.

Once the questions are compiled to create questionnaires, the organizational chart for the organization will drive the questioning process. In an organization of any significant size, representatives from all levels of the organization must be involved to obtain the broadest picture of the situation. It's important to not rely entirely on the formalized management structure as the only means of gleaning information because much valuable information is found at lower levels of the organization, and much of this information never flows to the top management. The people who work with the system day to day provide valuable information on how the data relates to each other and how the systems function within the organization; they may also have valuable information on how to quickly recover from problems. These may be situations and solutions that upper management has not thought of.

Identifying the Threat   The first thing that BIA does is to identify the threats rather than the assets. By looking at the threat first you can limit the number of assets to those that are directly affected by the given threat. Although this may lead to certain assets not being addressed, the most vulnerable assets should quickly rise to the top of the list. These are going to be the assets that need to be addressed first. The lesser important assets will be discovered through the process.

The deliverable from this step will end up being a list of all realistic potential threats to the organization. This list should remain realistic and not reflect reactionary attitudes. Again, there's not much chance of a hurricane in Minnesota, and there's not much chance of an avalanche in Houston. Once you have the list, you can then proceed to the next step in the process, which is assessing the risk of the threats to the organization.

Assessing the Risk to the Organization   Once you have the list of threats to the organization, you can then proceed with determining the risk that those threats pose. This will give you both the statistical chance that the risk will occur as well as the ramifications to the organization should the risk occur. If you can come up with a weighted list of both the chances that the disaster will befall the area or the organization and a weighted list of the ramifications or consequences to the organization, you can provide an overall ordered list for each scenario.

You can then proceed with the most likely and most serious threats and vulnerabilities and address those with respect to avoidance or mitigation.

Identifying Business-Critical Activities   Now that you've determined the threats to the organization and the weighted list of the ramifications of those threats, you can determine the business critical activities performed by the organization and assign those activities and their associated assets to the weighted list and come up with an overall process, assets, threat, and ramifications list that will allow you to further prioritize your avoidance and mitigation plan.

Providing Required Support from Information and Communications
At this point in the process you can start assigning people from the disaster recovery team connected to information and communications systems to addressing the

disaster recovery plan as it relates to the most serious concerns. This will be an iterative process as you address the most serious concerns remaining and apply the solutions to all relevant processes and assets.

OCTAVE Risk Assessment

There is one more assessment process that we should address. Created through Carnegie Mellon University, the OCTAVE risk assessment process is a flexible and simple process that is easily adaptable to an organization of any size, type, and complexity. It can provide an overview that is relevant and valuable not only for disaster recovery planning purposes, but also for internal security audits and revelations.

OCTAVE (Operationally Critical Threat, Asset, and Vulnerability Evaluation) is a risk-based strategic assessment and planning technique used primarily for security but which can also be used for disaster recovery planning purposes. Because it addresses threats, assets, and vulnerabilities, it is similar to the other evaluations; however, it is less focused on information technology and more targeted on the ability of small teams from an operational and business perspective to work with the IT department to address the needs of the organization. This small team identifies, based on the knowledge of many employees, the current state of the organization with respect to security and its risk sensitivity and in relation to critical assets within the organization.

This highly flexible assessment strategy can be tailored to nearly any organization and can be very effective in identifying those areas where the organization is most likely to be affected by a disaster situation. Because it focuses on the organizational risk rather than just the technological risk, and is targeted toward balancing operational risk, security practices, and technology, it is often a better fit for many organizations.

OCTAVE is driven by operational risk and security practices. Technology is addressed only as it applies in relationship to the security practices and operational risk. This enables the organization to not only gain a better understanding of current risk and security practices, but to examine how breaches in these can affect the organization as a whole. Because disaster recovery is, at its source, a breach of security (whether by human instigation or natural intervention) at some level, this approach can be systematically used to determine an organization's vulnerability to security breach and thus to disaster.

By making use of this alternative approach, an organization can make information protection decisions that are based almost entirely on the risks to the confidentiality, integrity, and availability of critical information-related assets. Again, physical assets are less important because they are easily replaceable, whereas less tangible assets are often irreplaceable. All aspects of risk are factored

3

into the process and by extension into the decision-making process. This allows an organization to adapt its security and protection practices in real time. These aspects include the assets, threats, vulnerabilities, and organizational impacts that have played a part in all these analyses.

Where other evaluations typically look at systems and approach the problem from that perspective, OCTAVE provides a framework in which to perform organizational evaluations. It focuses on the security practices surrounding the data and data-related assets rather than focusing strictly on the technology and adds components of data and security where necessary. Other approaches often are seen as tactical (self-directed) rather than strategic (directed by external entities) in nature, and they may have a lack of subject matter experts who can provide the necessary skill.

One of the reasons why this approach is often more successful than others is because interdisciplinary teams lead the evaluation and make critical determinations regarding the assets and discretionary measures that need to be taken. These teams include people from both the business units and the IT departments because, to effectively address business process recovery and continuity planning, both perspectives are critical when addressing and observing the global, local, organizational, and departmental security risks and vulnerabilities.

Because OCTAVE is an asset-driven approach, the analysis teams identify those information-related assets that are critical to the organization (for example, the information in the systems on which those permissions reside), focus the risk analysis activities on those assets that are judged by the teams to be most critical to the organization, and consider all relationships among the critical assets as well as the threats to those assets and vulnerabilities (organizational, human, technological, and environmental) that can expose those assets, threats, and vulnerabilities. The team further evaluates the risks as they exist in the operational context. They look at how the assets are used to conduct the organization or business, and with the exposure to risks are existing and potential security threats. As a result, the team creates a concrete, practice-based strategy for improving the organization's security and risk management.

OCTAVE requires three steps, thereby enabling the organizational personnel to quickly and efficiently assemble comprehensive pictures of the organization's information security. Following are the phases on which OCTAVE is based.

Phase 1: Create a Threat Profile

Phase 1 is to create an asset-based threat profile for the organization. This is very similar to phase 1 in the previous five-phase processes, in that it identifies the assets of the organization. It then addresses what is currently being done by the organization to protect those assets. The team then selects those assets that are most important within the organization, or that are considered critical, and provides the existing or suggested security requirements for each asset. Finally, it's the team's responsibility to create a threat profile for each asset.

Phase 1 is typically subdivided into three processes.

1. **Identify senior management knowledge.** Identification of important assets, security requirements, threats, and organizational strengths and vulnerabilities from a representative set of upper management and documentation of the findings are relevant outcomes of this phase. These can then be combined with the information gathered in subsequent processes.

2. **Identify the operational area knowledge by collecting information about the important assets, security requirements, threats, and current organizational strength from lower-level managers in selected operational areas.** This information is combined with the information gathered in process 1 and should be gathered from managers across the organization in all mission-critical areas of business.

3. **Identify staff knowledge about the important assets, threats, and security requirements, as well as organizational strengths, weaknesses, and vulnerabilities from staff of the business areas and IT staff members in the organization.** These inputs are combined with the information from the previous processes to create the threat profiles. The analysis team selects the top critical information–related assets and defines for those assets the threat profiles for the organization.

It is interesting to discover the differences pointed out by senior management, middle management, and the IT and operational staff. They may well see the company's important assets very differently. Phase 1 is often educational to all involved because of these differences as much as it is in learning information about the different critical processes and information assets in the organization.

Phase 2: Identify Infrastructure Vulnerabilities

Phase 2 involves identifying infrastructure vulnerabilities. In this phase, an evaluation of the information infrastructure is conducted. The analysis team examines the network, assesses patterns to the information deemed critical to the organization and classes of IT components that are directly or closely related to each asset. It is then determined to what extent each cluster of components is resistant to threats against the physical assets and those associated with the informational assets.

Phase 2 is subdivided into two processes. The first process identifies the key components. The set of key components that either support or process the critical information–related assets are identified and a means by which these physical assets can be evaluated is defined. Once the key components and physical assets are defined, the evaluation of the selected components can begin. Evaluation needs to be done at this point on the selected components as far as threats and vulnerabilities to these assets and the ramifications to the organization continuing should physical assets be compromised.

Phase 3: Develop a Security Strategy

During Phase 3, the team identifies those risks to the organization's critical assets that are most likely to affect the organization, and determines the processes that will limit the impact of the potential hazards and help recover from those hazards that are realized. The protection strategy and mitigation plans address the risks to the critical assets and the vulnerabilities to the threats based on the analysis of the information that was gathered.

Phase 3 can be broken down into two processes:

1. **Conduct a risk analysis.** The deliverable from this analysis is a set of impact evaluation criteria that is defined by the organization and the team to establish a common basis for determining the impact value—high, medium, or low—that is attributable to threats against the mission-critical assets. Any and all realistic risks are evaluated for impact. Probability can also be assigned at this point to further refine the process and determine the probability of the high impact, highly likely threats and vulnerabilities to the organization.

2. **Develop the protection strategy for the organization.** The strategy focuses on improving organization-wide security practices and provides a plan for mitigating the impact of the risks to the critical assets.

Further information, including detailed processes and analyses used in the OCTAVE analysis method, can be found at **http://www.cert.org/octave**. Much of the documentation is included on the companion Web site.

Summary

This chapter explains how to assess an organization to determine its vulnerabilities, what hazards are risks to its continuation, and how to begin to mitigate the risks and plan for recovery should an event occur to interrupt operations.

We have further seen that an important place to start is with developing the team. The chapter provides examples of important team members to consider when developing the disaster recovery plan. Now that we have a basis for the team we can begin to explore further what tasks that team will need to undertake and the process of developing the disaster recovery plan.

Test Your Skills

MULTIPLE CHOICE QUESTIONS

1. What two features of disasters impact the response that the organization has to an emergency?

    A. Type of disaster and location of the organization

    B. Location of the organization and time of the emergency

    C. Time of the emergency and extent of impact presented

    D. Type of disaster and extent of impact presented

2. What two considerations need to be taken into account when establishing service level agreements?

    A. Can the agreement reasonably last a lifetime and can the agreement be reasonably fulfilled?

    B. Can the agreement be reasonably fulfilled and can the agreement be reasonably enforced?

    C. Can the parties reasonably agree and can the agreement reasonably last a lifetime?

    D. Can the agreement be reasonably enforced and can the parties reasonably agree?

3. What of the following is not a result of gathering functional area input?

    A. Helps with the definition of the organizational emergency

    B. Allows each business unit to realize its worth to the organization

    C. Allows the functional area to take ownership of its part of the DR plan

    D. Helps the functional area to buy into the plan

4. What is the definition of risk used in this chapter?

    A. The possibility of a person or entity suffering harm or loss

    B. The amount that an insurance company stands to lose

    C. The variability of returns from investment

    D. The chance of nonpayment of a debt

5. Why are risk assessments done?

    A. They are the first step in the DR plan

    B. To determine if enough precautions have been taken to protect the organization from harm or loss of revenue

    C. To find out what emergencies might befall an organization

    D. To give the DR team something constructive to do

6. What is the most important thing to look at in a risk assessment?

   A. Who is doing it

   B. If the area is prone to flooding

   C. If a hazard is statistically significant

   D. The cost associated with the assessment

7. What is a hazard?

   A. A risk associated with an event

   B. The chance that something can cause harm

   C. A disturbance in operational flow

   D. Anything that can cause harm

8. What is not an emergency situation cited in the text?

   A. Terrorist attack

   B. Bankruptcy

   C. Environmental disruption

   D. Fire

9. Which of the following is not considered to be a disaster?

   A. Terrorist attack

   B. Hurricane

   C. Theft of information

   D. Fire

10. Which of the following is an example of malicious disruption?

    A. Earthquake

    B. Denial of service attack

    C. Electrical fire

    D. Loss of utilities to a data center

11. What is the first step in a five-step risk assessment?

    A. Identify hazards

    B. Identify people to do the assessment

    C. Identify controls to put into place

    D. Test and evaluate

12. The most valuable assets in any organization are the _____.

    A. people

    B. revenue streams

    C. physical assets

    D. data

13. What are OCTAVE's primary drivers?

    A. Operational risk and security practices

    B. Organizations and hazards

    C. Technology and environments

    D. Data and hardware

14. Which of the following is not one of the phases of threat profile in OCTAVE?

    A. Identify key components

    B. Identify staff knowledge

    C. Identify operational area knowledge

    D. Identify senior management knowledge

15. What are the two processes in the security strategy of OCTAVE?

    A. Risk analysis and asset analysis

    B. Asset analysis and evaluation of selected components

    C. Protection strategy and risk analysis

    D. Evaluation of selected components and risk analysis

EXERCISES

Exercise 3.1: Equipment and System Failure

1. Search for information on system and equipment failure on your favorite search engine.

2. List what might be done to provide fault tolerance for a single system.

3. List what might be done to provide fault tolerance at a data center level.

Exercise 3.2: Utility Loss

1. Make a list of utilities required by a data center.

2. Consider and list what events might occur to interrupt each of these utilities.

3. Consider and list what might be done to mitigate each loss.

Exercise 3.3: Risk Assessment

1. Using the risk assessment method associated with Table 3.1, put yourself in the position of assessment analyst.

2. Choose one department in an organization.

3. Complete the table based on that position.

Exercise 3.4: Small Business Hazards

1. Look at the list of small business hazards in Table 3.2.

2. Expand the list by an additional five hazards.

3. Write a description of each of the five additional hazards.

Exercise 3.5: Large Business Hazards

1. Look at the list of large business hazards in Table 3.3.

2. Expand the list by an additional five hazards.

3. Write a description of each of the five additional hazards.

Exercise 3.6: Asset Assessment

1. Look at your personal computer system or at a system in the computer lab.

2. Perform an asset assessment for all the assets.

3. Write a detailed description of the assessment.

PROJECTS

Project 3.1: Functional Area Input

1. Decide on a functional area of an organization.

2. Put yourself in the position of the manager of that functional area.

3. Consider what you may see as your department's most important functions in the organization.

4. List these functions.

5. Determine what level of risk can be attributed to these functions and the kind of events that may impact the functional area.

Project 3.2: Localized Hazards

1. Pick a location in the world.

2. Write an introduction to this location.

3. Research the hazards that are inherent with the location, natural as well as man-made.

4. Determine the risk that each hazard may happen.

5. Order the risks and hazards from most likely to least likely in the location chosen.

Project 3.3: Security

Security is of paramount importance in the information industry. This project will look at the hazards and risks through the lens of security.

1. Choose a type of disaster.

2. Describe the disaster.

3. Determine if there may be potential security issues associated with the disaster.

4. Describe the issues and the potential risks associated with the disaster and security issues.

5. Provide information on what might be done to mitigate the risk.

Case Study

You are responsible for performing a risk assessment. Choose one of the types of assessments in the chapter or find another type of risk assessment and describe that new assessment type. Perform a risk assessment using the chosen type of risk assessment for a home office. Detail all the hardware, software, and information assets that might be affected.

Chapter | 4

Prioritizing Systems and Functions for Recovery

Chapter Objectives

After reading this chapter and completing the exercises, you will be able to do the following:

- Identify all assets and functions in the organization.
- Prioritize disaster recovery efforts based on assets and functions.
- Differentiate between tier 1, tier 2, and tier 3 recovery targets to prioritize systems that must be recovered in the event of a disaster.
- Determine dependencies between different data, functions, and assets.
- Distinguish between an inconvenient situation and a true disaster using disaster declaration threshold criteria.

Introduction

It can be overwhelming to be faced with a sea of servers, an ocean of PCs, a network of cables that could make an immense spider web, and more job descriptions than you probably ever knew existed. Knowing where to start, what to start with in the eventuality that your plan has to actually be more than a plan, and what pieces rely on other pieces to make the puzzle complete can not only be confusing and overwhelming, it can be daunting even for experienced disaster recovery professionals.

Although the impact of where to start is easier for someone faced with a smaller network of systems and therefore a smaller impact, it can still be difficult to make progress without knowing what all has to be handled.

In this chapter you will learn how to prioritize your systems and figure out how to get your systems restored in the right manner and in the right time frame. You will learn to identify dependencies between different systems and how data flows in the system can be affected by not identifying these dependencies.

Identifying and Prioritizing Assets and Functions

Identifying assets and functions is something most organizations struggle with, even when not connected to disaster recovery planning. Although most organizations have some sort of asset tracking system, it is important to remember that just because an organization can account for assets, it may not be able to readily physically locate all those assets. Also, when it does locate the assets, they may not be in the location of record.

Identifying Critical Assets

Before we can go about identifying assets, it is probably best if we can define exactly what an asset is. The Web site Answers.com (**http://www.answers.com**) defines assets as "the entries on a balance sheet showing all properties, both tangible and intangible, and claims against others that may be applied to cover the liabilities of a person or business." This is typically the definition an organization uses when making reference to its assets, and is therefore the definition that we will use. The following sections identify the critical assets you'll need to consider.

Hardware   The first assets people tend to consider in disaster recovery are the hardware assets, things that if you swung a hammer you could hit. Thus this is where disaster planning often begins. This is neither good nor bad, it is only simply something you should be aware when you start your career dealing with disaster recovery.

Take an inventory of what hardware is associated with the organization. Inventory all hardware—large and small, the obvious and the fairly well hidden. Don't overlook anything. Go to everyone in the department, one department at a time. Ask what hardware they use and what hardware they know about. Don't be surprised at what you uncover that your accounting system might not have record of or about which your hardware support people might not know.

For example, you may find that you have a depreciated server that is no longer under support and that is only used by accounting to run an old depreciated version of the software that the department relies on for half of its processing. This will be something that may or may not be being backed up regularly and that may not be included in any recovery site contracts that you may have in place. You may no longer be able to obtain either the operating system on which it runs or the installation media necessary to install it. These are all critical notes to take when you are going through this kind of discovery.

Once you have discovered these assets, however, it is important to remember that you have to keep track of them, or this can lead to recovery document maintenance difficulties. Many larger organizations have at least one position dedicated almost entirely to asset discovery and tracking.

Tracking assets is an activity that can have many different solutions. Often brute force discovery, and even rediscovery, can be the most effective way to approach the issue. Going office to office, location to location, is an effective way to ensure that an organization is missing as few physical assets as possible. This does not preclude the fact that some assets will eventually be marked as missing, but it does allow for an inventory, matching assets to locations, that is as accurate as possible.

One method often employed in hardware tracking, similar to that used in retail establishments to track their inventories, is bar coding and the use of barcode readers. Whenever hardware enters the organization, it is affixed with a barcode. Whenever this hardware is allocated, distributed, installed, or moved, the barcode is read and the associated metadata is entered into a database. This provides a simple mechanism for determining what hardware is located in what location. It is also one more system that has to be backed up and maintained and added to the disaster recovery documentation.

FYI | *Asset Tracking Software*

A simple search for "computer hardware PC audit inventory" or some derivation yields a tremendous amount of information about potential sources of inventory tracking software. There are many different titles and a wide range of prices to match the needs and budgets of most organizations.

For those needing only a simple method, a single-user database or a spreadsheet can help track the necessary information. Figure 4.1 shows a simple database used by a small business to track hardware and software assets. Because many software products interface with other products (and across manufacturers), these designs can be expanded when necessary. Figure 4.2 shows similar information for hardware in spreadsheet format and Figure 4.3 shows software information in a similar format. Notice that the software spreadsheet can associate the software with a particular hardware asset, if necessary.

continued

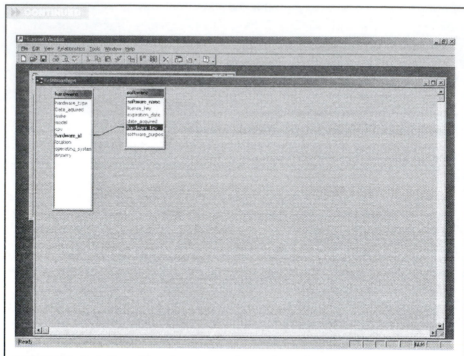

FIGURE 4.1 Small business database for asset tracking.

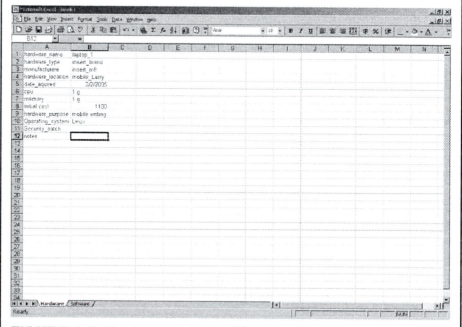

FIGURE 4.2 Hardware asset tracking spreadsheet.

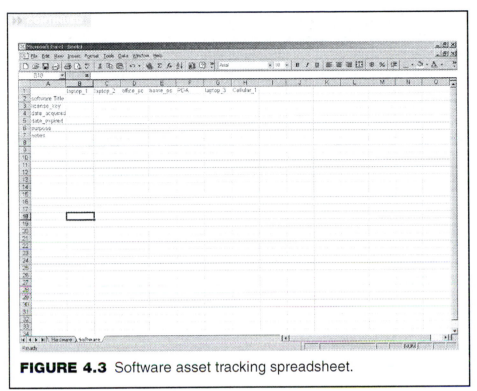

FIGURE 4.3 Software asset tracking spreadsheet.

Unfortunately, hardware tracking still requires some manual effort on the part of the organization, regardless of which method an organization chooses to track the assets. Often the amount of manual effort required is directly related to the method of asset tracking used. Again, larger organizations likely have one or more persons dedicated at least part time to tracking hardware. What about smaller organizations? Often the entire dedicated staff available to a small organization consists of the only person in the organization for some businesses, or all the IT duties end up falling to one person in larger businesses. It is often difficult in these situations to assign a high priority to maintaining an inventory of the hardware assets, their configuration, and relative importance when there are so many other pressing concerns that need to be addressed.

For example, Kim is an organization of one who provides independent contracting programming services to clients; she also provides technical writing and teaching on the side. Consider the time that she needs just to maintain the business. She may have one or two servers that she develops on, several desktop computers that are used routinely, multiple laptops that are dedicated to different aspects of the different lines of business, a personal digital assistant (PDA), one or more cellular phones, multiple printers, and one or more desk phones. The hardware associated with running the business begins to mount quickly. Much of it needs to be depreciated and that depreciation information needs to be maintained as information associated with the hardware.

Many small businesses don't have an accurate idea of what hardware they have associated with their business, let alone the configuration, location, and value of the different pieces.

It is a vital early step in the disaster planning process to gather together the information on all these assets. This is labor intensive and time consuming, but it will pay off later when the organization has to fill out insurance paperwork accounting for all the assets or when contracts are signed to provide temporary or permanent replacement hardware in the event that a disaster occurs. Even if all that has to happen is that the small business needs to go out and replace the affected systems, it will need to know what comparable or compatible systems need to be acquired.

It is important to note that many hardware vendors provide (often at additional cost) software that will collect inventory data on their own hardware platform and maintain that inventory for you. This is good if an organization has standardized on a particular hardware vendor or on a few select vendors. If the organization gets too many of these products, it can be difficult to keep up with the software products and it may become necessary to rely on the manual method again.

Software   When people inventory software they usually think of all the big things that need to be considered: the operating system, the enterprise database management systems, the email product used, and the word processing and spreadsheet software that are used every day and that are ***commercial off-the-shelf (COTS)*** products. But what about customizations that you may have made to the product and its functionality? Will that be maintained or can it be easily recreated? Although you may be able to get copies, in a pinch, of most of the products that are used by the organization on an almost hourly or minute-by-minute basis, what about the tweaking that the internal users or programmers have done to extend the functionality?

Further, what about the software that has been built internally? Where is the source code for that kept, and where is the installation media stored? Is it all on disk and being backed up with the rest of the data on the server? Are you sure that it is in the backup set for the server? What happens if you have to recreate that application?

Although it is understood that most organizations don't endorse the use and installation of "unauthorized" software, it is often the case that what they don't readily know about they don't condemn, but they also don't support. Many times there are free software programs on which different people in the organization rely heavily. PostScript readers, Visio or Project readers, and old versions of Microsoft Access used for one or two specialized programs may be relied on heavily by users. Will you be able to gather these applications together later, at the disaster recovery site, or whenever life can return to normal at you primary location? Having a record of these software products will help immensely in your endeavors and will become an invaluable tool when looking

at what to store with your offsite backups for the disaster recovery project and for the restoration of your primary site.

A good inventory of the software that is installed and used will not only give you a better idea of what you will need to account for in a disaster recovery situation, it will allow you to have a better understanding of what your exposure is to failing a software audit and being exposed to an extensive fine. Maintaining an accurate inventory of what software is installed in an organization can often mean the difference between fines being levied on the organization during a software audit and not having fines levied. However, knowing what software is installed on many computers is difficult at best, particularly in larger organizations.

Employees often forget that their computers are company property and they install software from home or that they have downloaded. Many times this software will cause issues on the computer because of incompatibility. Rarely, unless there is an issue that needs to be resolved by the company help desk, will users remember to tell anyone that they have the software installed. This software often becomes a relied upon tool that enables the user to perform his or her daily job. If the software becomes required and relied upon, it will be expected to be available after a disaster.

Having a well documented and publicized policy on company software and hardware standards can help with this. Software that is not on the standards list will *not* be recovered. If software is necessary for a particular job, it needs to go through the process of getting put on this list and the company needs to provide this process. Once the software product is justified, it can be documented as to where to access the software and how to recover it, and the licensing particulars can be added to the standards list and the recovery plans. Although this does not guarantee that employees won't install their own software (it is difficult at best to ensure this), it can discourage them from the installation of unauthorized software.

FYI *Users*

Users will often forget that they never told anyone that they have installed and are relying upon unsupported and often unlicensed software. If questioned later, they will assure the questioner that they have indeed informed the proper people and therefore their software needs to be recovered, and whoever is responsible for maintaining the records must simply have forgotten to record the software. Maintaining good working relationships with everyone in the organization is important to everyone on the disaster recovery team and the disaster recovery planning team. During recovery is neither the time to worry about what is fair or unfair, nor to explain the importance of maintaining both accurate records and legally licensed software in the organization. The task at hand is the disaster recovery effort.

Small organizations—organizations with few hardware assets, such as home offices or home-based businesses—can often get by with maintaining their hardware asset lists in a spreadsheet file or even on paper, as long as that paper is stored in a safe place where it can be easily accessible in the event of a declared emergency. Often people store this kind of information in a safety deposit box or even secured with someone in another city.

Data   It may seem odd to consider taking inventory of data, considering that data itself is voluminous and that data about data (metadata) can be even more so, but it really isn't that you need to know for every file and every table that you have x number of data elements and that element 'a' has this meaning and element 'b' has that meaning. This kind of data inventory has more to do with knowing what kind of data you have, what systems you have, and which systems interface with which systems (internally as well as externally).

You should know what the databases are and generally what is in them. You should also know what any files are that are in your system (not in people's private data directories necessarily, but in the overall system in general). Again, this is something that either should have already been done at an organizational level or at least at a departmental level, but don't be unduly surprised if this is not the case.

Because most systems are fluid in nature, and very few organizations go for extended periods of time without some kind of software implementation or development of new applications or programs, keeping up with what new data is resident on the system is also a challenge. If there is a resident data architect, periodically discussing with him or her new additions allows the disaster recovery team to better keep up with the new data that has become part of the system. This allows them to better maintain their records, and allows for better tracking and less repeating efforts on a routine basis to rediscover data that both has been resident and which has joined the systems.

Remember that most of the work that the disaster recovery team does is likely to be in addition to their regular jobs in the organization, and is often done either when they can adjust their schedules or on their own time. Doing the same job over and over, duplicating their efforts repeatedly, will soon become difficult and tiring for all concerned.

Human   Human assets are often the most overlooked assets in an organization. Simply looking at an organizational chart or global email address book can give you an idea about who works in your organization, but this does not help you to identify key personnel or places where there is little or no overlap in human capital. This is not only because the cost of human capital is generally one of the biggest costs that an organization faces, but often because the idea of cross-training has not occurred to anyone.

It may initially appear that identification of human assets will be a simple task. In reality this is little easier than the identification and tracking of nonhuman assets. Identifying the existence of people within the organization is usually easy enough; acquiring a listing of active employees from the payroll system should provide an accurate listing of people employed by the organization. However, they may or may not be accurately portrayed as to their physical location (for example, they may work remotely from home, or they may have had to change their physical location to another office in another city for a period of time and that might not be reflected in the payroll or human resources systems). Their job responsibilities may no longer include those to which you have them assigned in the DR documents.

There will likely also be people external to the organization who need to be included in the disaster recovery documents. Vendors change addresses, organizations change vendors, contact information for external support personnel change, and even support organizations change. All this information should be tracked so that the disaster recovery effort can be as effective as possible.

People, unlike hardware and software, are able to help keep track of themselves if reminded periodically, so this might be a track that an organization takes in order to keep its DR documents up to date. Update the documents any time there is a new vendor or vendor change and send out periodic emails to people requesting updated contact information so that the documentation can be kept up to date.

Other   Depending on the business or the organization, there may be many other kinds of assets that are relevant to the disaster recovery planning process. Manufacturing facilities often have plans and materials that they will need to recover the business. These idiosyncrasies are industry specific and often company specific and will need to be taken into account when looking at the recovery planning process.

Identifying Functions and Processes

People have an easier time putting their fingers on what assets are. Even data, to some extent, can be seen if not truly touched, and the value that is inherent in it can be gathered; but what about functions? Functions are just as critical to an organization's success as its assets, but they are far less often recognized as such when it comes to disaster recovery planning. Functions often go hand in hand with processes, but each is unique in definition and practice.

Functions   A business function is an action that is easily identifiable and that is related to a requirement of the business organization. Examples of functions might include, but are not limited to, the following:

- Selling products in a retail store
- Delivering products to the end customer
- Processing payments in the accounting department of an organization
- Providing technical help desk support for the end users of a system

■ Securing the data integrity for an organization or a department within an organization

■ Developing the tactical and strategic plans for an organization

■ A mixture of all the above for a small business

These are all examples of those tasks that are either key to a business' ability to meet its operational requirements or that are among the many stand-alone areas of a business.

Processes   Business processes are the implementation of labor, technology, time, or any resources related to the successful completion of a business function. Functions cannot be successful without their processes, and processes without a function attached are wasted resources.

Taking into account the list of functions in the previous section, processes that are associated with these functions may include, but are not limited to, the following:

■ Display of product in preparation for sales

■ Inventory tracking of product to facilitate sales

■ Packaging product for shipping

■ Delivery of product to the buyer

■ Tracking revenues and expenses

■ Maintenance of the help desk system

■ Management and leadership of the security system for the organization

As an organization's disaster recovery team prepares the disaster recovery plan for the organization, the team must properly identify *all* the functions and processes that are associated with the particular organization and then select those functions and processes that are *critical* to meeting the requirements of the business to function during a disaster (these are tier 1 functions and processes). Once the critical processes and functions are identified, the next level (tier 2 functions and processes) can be determined. These are the functions and processes that are important to the organization, but which are not critical. Finally, tier 3 processes and functions can be identified. Tier 3 includes those functions and processes that may not necessarily contribute to an organization's core competencies or its key processes, but without which the organization may find itself unable to continue for the longer period of time. These tiers are discussed in more detail later in this chapter.

Some of an organization's critical functions are externally driven business requirements. These requirements will typically include regulatory compliance issues, contractual issues related to labor or environmental commitments, or requirements that are set forth by certification organizations (such as SAS 70 or ISO). These external requirements, along with their corresponding internal requirements for production, delivery, customer commitments, and management mandates, help us to define the line between inconvenience and disaster and helps determine what might be an inconvenience for one organization and a disaster for another. Not only does this add shades of gray to the determination process, it also means that the analysis process must include a consideration of both the internal and external requirements and their roles in the critical, important, and auxiliary functions and processes. Regardless of the source of the business drivers, however, they are requirements and have to be taken into account in disaster recovery planning.

Driver discovery includes an analysis of the organization's operations, the functions and processes involved in those operations, and the assets that are involved in their support. This process will help determine what needs to be done in order to not only protect the assets but also to ensure the continuation of the functions and their processes. This is one of the first responsibilities of the disaster recovery team.

Identification of the organization's critical functions and processes and their underlying support assets is the result of this analysis. At first glance, an analyst might conclude that everything an organization does, every day, is critical. And in essence, this is true. Most organizations today don't operate with much fluff in the system, but they do have differing shades of importance in the processes and functions. Some departmental managers may consider their department to be the provider of the most critical function or process to the company. No manager is going to look you straight in the eye and say, "No, our department provides no noticeable value to the organization."

FYI | *An Auxiliary Benefit to the Process*

An auxiliary benefit to the process of looking at the processes and functions in an organization and the underlying assets that support them is the ability to find the places where you can leverage economies of scale and scope, where you can eliminate duplication of software licensing, or where you can combine functions to achieve less waste in the processes.

That said, care must be taken to make sure that no one is made to feel that their function or the processes in which they are involved are being considered as candidates for elimination. This process must always be undertaken with political finesse.

Obviously, an organization needs each of its departments in order to function over an extended period of time. This means that no department, regardless of the determination of the disaster recovery team, should be made to feel that its worth to the organization is in any way reflected in the position in which it find itself in the ultimate plan. Everyone needs to understand that, during a disaster, the functions and processes of some departments become more critical than other departments. For instance, payroll seems to be a very important function of an organization. All the employees want and need to be paid, and salary will become a driver for everyone depending on the severity of the disaster. However, if payroll is processed once a month at month end, and a disaster occurs during the first or second week of the month and it is determined that it is expected to last a few days to a week (as might be the case in a category 1 or 2 hurricane somewhat in from the coast), then restoring the payroll system is not a critical process during the initial stages of the disaster. It may not play a part in the disaster recovery at all if the disaster is localized. However, situations can change fairly rapidly, and where it may have seemed as if the disaster was going to be over in a matter of hours or days, it may actually stretch on for far longer. Thus any plan, implemented or still in the paper and ink stage, needs to be flexible in order to handle the changing needs of the organization. Accordingly, if the disaster occurs during the last week of the month and is expected to last more than a week, it now becomes necessary to restore the payroll system to an operational condition sooner during the disaster. Depending on these different scenarios, the payroll function may or may not be a critical process for consideration during a disaster; however, it will remain a critical process for the organization.

So then, how does the disaster recovery team assist in the identification of the critical business functions and processes and the assets that underly these functions and processes? First, the DR team members must identify the organization's business requirements, the core competencies of the organization. These are the essential requirements for the organization to continue to function during the disaster. The critical processes and functions contribute in one of two specific ways to support these requirements. The first is that the process or function must generate revenue such as:

- Retail operations
- Phone orders system
- Web-based e-store system
- Product delivery system
- Vendor support
- Accounts receivable

It is important to note that marketing and sales don't necessarily, by themselves, generate revenue. They may be important to the organization's continued competitive success, but in the event of a disaster, they may not necessarily be one of the business drivers.

The second way a process or function supports the organization is by protecting its assets (data, hardware, software, etc.) from physical loss or from the loss of integrity or reliability such as:

- Data backup and verification

- Data storage

- Data retrieval and verification

- Operating system support

- Hardware support

- Network support

Identifying the Key Personnel Required for Operations   Before an organization can declare a disaster, it is important that you identify those individuals (either specifically or by title) who will be critical and instrumental in the recovery effort. Although specific people are often put into the plan by name, specifying individuals by title or by job classification allows for less rewriting of the plan in the event that people change job positions or leave the company.

Larger organizations maintain a significant staff for the data center whose job it is to maintain and be responsible for the hardware, operating system software, and any and all application software for the organization. Depending on the size and complexity of the organization, this staff can be significant and cross many departments. In smaller organizations, the operational staff may consist of only one or two individuals. Still others may consist of one person, and that person may have other duties as well.

The IT staff complete most day-to-day operations, including backup and recovery, maintaining the health and wellbeing of the systems, and providing for the advancement of code through the system and assurance that such code will not break what is already there. Departmental staff members in the departments that are supported by these IT departments are required to validate the restored systems to make sure that they are operational and functioning properly.

Chapter 1 stressed the importance of including members from a variety of departments on the disaster recovery team to help identify critical *and* secondary processes and functions. The team also identifies staffing requirements necessary to travel to the recovery site for system restoration and recovery, or to work with the IT staff locally, to reestablish services after a disaster.

In order to achieve a successful restoration and recovery, the departmental staff members must also help to identify the testing criteria for system and data analysis during and after the recovery and to assist in determination of the criteria necessary to declare a disaster.

Prioritizing Disaster Recovery Planning Efforts

Once you have determined the assets, processes, and functions of an organization, it is time to determine what priority is assigned to each of the different aspects so that the organization can recover its business as logically and organized as possible.

Processes or Functions that Create Assets

Every organization has products and/or services that generate revenue or that increase the organization's financial value. Retail stores sell products to customers. Application service providers (ASPs) sell the use of applications to their customers. Plumbers sell their abilities to solve your problems.

For retail sales to occur, remote stores must have connectivity to the main office, regardless of whether that main office is in the back room of the store or in an entirely different city. They need this connectivity for tracking employee hours, recording sales, maintaining inventory records, and many other purposes. The interconnectivity—be it a local area network (LAN), a wide area network (WAN), or simply telephony—is used by retail stores to provide the communication back to the main office. Many retail stores, regardless of size, use e-commerce solutions as an additional (or sole) method of transacting sales with customers. In this case, the communication channel is even more important, but so is the ability to ship the product to the customer after the order has been placed. Adding to the complexity of chain stores, which often have a main office in one place and remote retail locations in many others, consideration has to be given to the continuation of the retail locations should the disaster befall the central home office. The ability in these cases to store and generate their own information and the necessity of the resynchronization of the data with that of the main office has to be counted among the processes and functions in this identification process.

Phone systems or broadband connections create the communication link between clients and ASP companies. Cellular and wireless communication is employed more frequently by even small businesses that sell their services directly to the end client (such as plumbers, electricians, handyman companies, and lawn services). These external processes and functions need to be identified and accounted for in the eventuality that the disaster recovery plan needs to be implemented.

It is important not only to have this documentation, but also to keep it current and up to date. Conducting an annual review of the documentation for accuracy should be a standard practice for the organization. This will keep the information fresh not only in the documentation, but also in the minds of those involved with the disaster recovery team effort.

IN PRACTICE: The Big Blue Burger Barn Chain—Processes and Functions

The Big Blue Burger Barn operates several dozen restaurants in several cities across multiple states. As with many other organizations, the chain's in-store computer systems are tied to the main headquarters' central computing system. Every night after each store closes, the in-store system transmits all the data collected from the point-of-sale systems. All sales transactions and the associated inventory ramifications are transmitted; wasted product information, cleaning product used, revenues collected, and payroll information are also among the information that is transmitted at the end of every day.

This information, when collected from all the stores and compiled with that of the main office, presents a financial snapshot of the organization. Management can then use this financial data to view a picture of the organization at many different granularities. They can view the profitability of one store, of all the stores in an area, or the overall profitability of the organization on any given day or over a period of time. What's more, the collected data is used to automatically generate restocking orders based on the inventory reduction for each store.

Recently, a data communications problem between a restaurant and the main office resulted in the loss of data transmission from the restaurant. The main office didn't report the missing information to the restaurant management; therefore management of the local store assumed that everything was as it should be. The first indication to the local management that anything had been amiss was when the delivery truck arrived with the week's supplies and they did not receive large drink cups. The data transmitted indicated that their supply was low, but since the inventory system did not receive the transactions accurately, the low inventory level of drink cups went unnoticed. The result was that the restaurant had to go several days without large drink cups.

Although this was not a disaster to either the local establishment or to the overall organization, the effect on the employees who had to repeat many times each day that they were sorry they could not upgrade drinks to a large size was taxing. Many customers were disappointed at not being able to get a large drink. The long-term effect of customer impressions of the large organization's inability to manage inventory may never be known.

The brand name, in this case, may have been damaged to some considerable extent locally, which could impact the organization in that market. This can be considered a minor disaster.

Processes or Functions that Protect Assets

Protecting an organization's assets is just as important as generating assets. Frequently, this is achieved through the creation of a secure or redundant system for the assets. A process such as data backup usually accomplishes the task of creating a redundant set of data assets. However, simply creating a backup of information is not enough. Verification of the data on the backup media is important to ensure that the original data's integrity still exists. If the data is transmitted offsite, the integrity of the information is equally important, and must also be verified. Continued use of the same media beyond its recommended life increases the potential for a loss of data integrity. The information that the organization has to secure may include data that goes beyond its financial information. Client information, vendor and employee information, and patent and other proprietary information are equally critical. In some cases, an organization is required by industry practices or laws to maintain this information, typically for a specific period of time.

In addition to creating the data that represents an organization's assets, the DR team must consider the impact from any gaps in the data that may occur between the time of the backup and the end of local processing. There are backup strategies (including periodic incremental backups between more complete backups, creating archives of interim snapshots of the data, and running databases in a mode that will allow you to recover to any point in time) that can limit an organization's exposure to these gaps, but there will always be gaps to some extent.

Eliminating these gaps completely isn't likely to be practical, but knowledge of the gaps is crucial to the organization's continuation. Recovering this data may be as simple as re-inputting the data into the systems in question. It may also be as complex as setting up failsafe systems as interim points in an e-business solution that captures the data offsite and then forwards that data to the primary processing system. In this way, you are far less likely to lose data, but as with anything there are costs associated with the security.

Now that you have determined what your assets, processes, and functions are, you will need to determine what you need to recover, and in what order that should occur.

Determining What to Recover When

Now that we have a prioritized list of what all the organization has, how do we determine exactly what to recover and when it needs to be recovered? It isn't possible to recover everything all at once; as with everything, there is a limited supply of resources that can be used to recover the business, and there is a limited supply of hours in a day and human power that can be used as a way to recover the business.

Although tier 1, tier 2, and tier 3 are not overly descriptive terms, they do describe the kind of systems that are involved. Think of a multi-tier cake. The most decorated, and often considered the most important part of the cake, is the top layer, tier 1. Tier 1 comes first as you cut the cake. Tier 2 comes immediately after tier 1 cutting down through the cake, and tier 3 follows tier 2. Similar thought can go into systems. Tier 1 is the most important, the one that most people care about, the one that has the biggest impact systems. Tier 2 will be the next most important, and tier 3 will follow that.

Tier 1

Tier 1 systems are considered critical to the continuation of the business. They are the mission-critical functions that *have* to be recovered within minutes or hours of the disaster. This time frame, naturally, needs to be determined by the organization and the service level agreements that are in place. For example, you may have a guarantee to your customers that you will have your critical systems available to them within 72 hours. This means that you have the luxury to ensure that the tier 1 systems are recovered and available not in minutes or hours but in 3 days. This may seem like a long time, but consider the aftermath of hurricane Katrina in New Orleans, and the fact that many people were not found within the first 3 days.

Each organization's tier 1 systems are as unique to the organization as the organization is in the community. This is not to say that there will not be any commonalities. It is likely that any organization will find that its ability to process payments and invoices will need to be among the earliest to be recovered. The ability to buy supplies and sell product will be necessary for the continuation of any organization that is involved in manufacturing, and the ability to process purchases will be important to most organizations during their disaster recovery process.

It is critical to include those areas that either generate revenue for the organization or process revenue for it in tier 1 systems as well as those areas that support the functions and processes that generate and process revenue. Accounts receivable will process the payments generated from sales. This means that accounts receivable functionality needs to be restored, as well as the computer systems departments that directly and indirectly support accounts receivable.

One function that is often overlooked is backup and recovery. Even at the recovery site, you still have to take into account backup and recovery. There is always a potential of loss and disaster at the secondary location as well, and the ability to recover from this kind of disaster is just as important as it is in the primary business location.

Further is the need for security, perhaps even more so at the backup location than at a primary site. Security systems, processes, and functions should be paramount in your mind as you plan for your recovery scenarios.

It is also important that any system that is necessary to support the disaster recovery personnel be either recovered or an alternative system be identified and secured ahead of time. This can mean that cellular telephones be employed for the means of communication between members of the recovery team or between team members and members of management and others in the organization of relief personnel in the field. Alternative email paths can be identified and utilized for similar purposes. It isn't likely that the email system or telephony will be identified as one of an organization's tier 1 systems, but it is likely that, to many within the organization, its functionality be maintained as a means of communication.

Gmail, Yahoo! mail, or other, alternative email systems can be used for emergency communication. Cellular service may be spotty or nonexistent to the disaster location, depending on the severity and scope of the disaster, but may be more available in the recovery location. Land line phone service can be rerouted by the phone company to a temporary alternative location for the support of customers and internal people.

FYI *If Something Can Fail, It Will*

It is important to remember that in disaster recovery—as in every aspect of business and life—if something can go wrong, it will, and at the least convenient time. You will be recovering these systems on different hardware, on different networks, and often with different installations of the software and the operating system. Introducing this many variables will likely mean that programs will perform slightly differently than they do on their native machines, even if all precautions are taken to ensure that everything remains the same.

Tier 2

Tier 2 assets, functions, and processes are considered important functions and processes. They need to be recovered within the next incremental time period (for example, within a day of the disaster). They may not be critically necessary for the continuation of a business, but they are important for the business to continue as a successful and profitable venture.

The payroll system will likely fall into this category. It is not, strictly speaking, necessary for the continuation of the business to have payroll up and running all the time. Even if it is a couple of days late, the process can be run to allow people to get paid. In cases like this, people don't often care if their pay is a little late, as long as it is processed in a reasonable amount of time.

Again, recall that there are systems that will be somewhat fuzzy as to what tier they belong, and they can belong to different tiers based on the time of month that a disaster is declared, or even the time of week or year. Fiscal year end may drive many systems into tier 1 that would otherwise be relegated to tier 2.

Because it is important to get the right systems into the right tiers, and often the right tiers at the right times, it is important to make judicious use of time that you can spend with upper management on fact-finding interviews. Determine when critical processes are done and put that information into the disaster recovery documents. Make note if something cannot be run until the very first day of the month and determine if it is possible to adjust recovery scenarios to fit the timing of declared disasters.

Tier 3

Tier 3 systems, processes, and functions are those that are nonessential and can be recovered in the days or weeks following the disaster. These are the processes that might be seen as nice to have, or support systems. Help desk functionality may fall into this category, depending on what the organization does and how long the users can function without it. However, it is more likely that this "support" function will end up being tier 2. An example of a Tier 3 system is a time tracking system, particularly in an organization where the predominance of the employees are salaried and the tracking of time is a formality. Another system that might be categorized as a Tier 3 is an internal reporting system that provides historical information for budgeting for department managers. This information may not be critical for an organization to continue business in an emergency, but it will be valuable over a longer period of time.

More of what we are talking about here is the set of functions and processes that an organization can do without for more than a week to 10 days. Most organizations balk at the thought that they may have processes and functions that can be done without for the span of up to half a month, but with careful consideration, many can determine (particularly if the concept of disaster timing is taken into account) that there are systems that can be put into this category.

It may help to point out that there are cost-benefit trade-offs to having all systems recovered at a backup site. If the disaster scope is small enough, many of these systems will not be necessary to the organization during the disaster.

The incremental costs associated with including systems in tier 2 include the cost of re-backing up and re-recovery, the man hours necessary for recovery to begin, and the additional cost associated with the processing at the recovery site. It is usually easier to determine what an organization can live without if recovering everything is put into monetary terms.

All the reporting systems that users rely on for nearly everything, when it comes right down to it, can be lived without if they and management realize that recovering them will mean that something more critical to the continuation of the organization needs to be recovered later or if they learn that the recovery means that it will cost an additional significant amount to recover that functionality in a short duration recovery situation.

There are other processes and functions that can be put off nearly indefinitely. Custodial services, some levels of secretarial support, and maintenance can be put off until the organization can be recovered at its primary location. Again, it is not that these positions are not important to the organization, but when you are working in a lean and stressful situation, you need to not only be willing to work under less-than-optimal conditions, but to allow some less critical positions to be foregone for a time.

Conducting Dependency Analysis

Once all the systems are identified and put into their relative positions in the recovery plan (tier 1, tier 2, or tier 3) the real work begins. Now we have to take this information and figure out what pieces depend on the data from other pieces and use that information as the basis for revising where the different pieces go in the puzzle. It is likely that some of your tier 2 and tier 3 systems will, because of these dependencies, have to move from one level to another.

It is almost always the case that no system resides in a vacuum. No system is a stand-alone system; it is either the source of information for another system, a consumer of information from other systems, or both. The identification of the relationship between these different and often disparate systems is often captured in the metadata (the data about the data and about the systems). If the disaster recovery team cannot find this information, then it has to be uncovered as a part of the DR planning process. Determination of the sources of files for systems and where output files go is often something that you can learn from programmers and developers. They usually know where the input to their programs comes from (they have, after all, had to find data with which to test the programs, and therefore know where to get that information). Asking pointed questions to these developers will allow you to learn this information.

In this way, you will find that the disaster recovery documents will become a source of information for many different departments in the organization. The disaster recovery team, and the disaster recovery document, will become the all-knowing source of information for many different systems.

IN PRACTICE: The Big Blue Burger Barn Chain Saga Continues

Looking back at the saga of the Big Blue Burger Barn chain, we can see that the dependency of the data transmission relies on the communication channel between the local restaurants and the main office. By extension, the ability of the local store to sell product,

CONTINUED ON NEXT PAGE

regardless of the product, relies on its ability to receive the product or the containers for that product from the warehouse, which is driven by the inventory system.

This is an example of dependency. The inventory system depends on the valid transmission of the data from the stores and the stores depend on the inventory system providing them with the necessary supplies.

The organization realized the dependence that it had from an organizational perspective on the communication channel. Without accurate transmission of the information, management would be unable to determine profitability or the way to alter sales and product for each individual store. They did not, however, realize how much each store relied upon the accurate transmission of data to the inventory system. This dependency was news to them. This is the kind of dependency that the process of creating the disaster recovery document will help you to uncover.

How do you determine what will go in each tier or what might not go in any tier at all? This is where subject matter experts (SMEs) are helpful. They, of course, can't be relied upon without question, because they are dedicated to their particular subject matter, and it is likely that they will often believe it to be more important than it necessarily is. However, they can be relied upon to help you.

When in doubt, call in upper management. Although they will likely not know which system (from a hardware or software perspective) is more critical, they will have a better understanding of the big picture and will be able to tell you which processes and functions are most important (they may even give you a weighted scale) to the organization. This is when your map of processes and functions to assets comes most into play.

Finally, what we need to determine is the criteria for disaster declaration, and the ramifications of the timing.

Defining Disaster Declaration Threshold Criteria

It is important to remember that the difference between a situation that may simply be an inconvenience and one that is an actual disaster often depends on the point of view of those affected. Although there are situations that we can agree on as being disasters (hurricanes, the 9/11 terrorist attacks, fire, flood, massive power outages), there are grey areas that are less clear cut. Being stuck in a traffic jam may be very annoying, but few people would consider it to be a disaster. But in the prelude to Hurricane Rita in 2005, trying to get out of Houston and sitting in your delivery truck with a load of perishable goods for 14 hours or more, and finding that you have run out of fuel, may qualify as a disaster.

Recall that each of an organization's critical functions and services are requirements for that organization to produce its products or provide its services to its customers in an ongoing manner. However, understand also that, depending on the situation, the unavailability of some of these functions and processes for a limited period of time will not seriously compromise the organization. The lack of some services for a short period may result in an inconvenient situation, but not constitute a disaster.

So when exactly does an inconvenient situation become a disaster for an organization? Formally declaring a disaster, mobilizing the resources necessary to accommodate that declaration and its resulting recovery situation, and formally notifying the customer or client base is a step that an organization should not be ready to take lightly. It is a point that can have long-reaching ramifications to the goodwill of the customer and the willingness of a significant portion of the customer base to continue to do business with the organization. It will have significant monetary ramifications to the organization and will have an impact on how the employees perceive the organization over time.

The point of declaring a disaster is a threshold that, when crossed, significantly impacts the organization's ability to meet its tactical and strategic operational goals without immediate intervention to restore critical processes and functions.

Every organization has to be responsible for determining that threshold. Every company, every division, and every group has to determine its own sensitivity to situations (even from one situation to another). Some of the factors that go into making such a decision are internal whereas others are external.

In addition to the organization's critical processes and functions, other internal and external factors may drive the need to declare or not declare a disaster. Service level agreements (SLA) within the organization or between the organization and its partners, clients, and vendors may be instrumental in the identification of a threshold for a disaster declaration. Internally, there may be levels of service defined between the information technology/information systems department and various other departments in the organization. These can be instrumental in determining the different tiers of recovery and in the determination of critical processes and functions in the planning stages. They are also to be considered carefully when determining whether to declare a disaster. If the responsible parties in the IT department feel that a situation can be remedied internally without needing to go to the extremes of formally declaring an internal disaster, that will be their call to make. Services included under these SLAs might include data access, email, telephony, Internet/intranet access, printing services, and other IT-related services. Human resources (HR) may offer access to benefits information, payroll deduction modifications, and other resources for employees on the company intranet. If HR establishes an SLA with its IT support group that assures that it can maintain the intranet Web site with a guaranteed uptime of 99.8 percent availability during established working hours and a 95 percent availability during nights and weekends, then the support organization has a fiduciary responsibility to ensure that these thresholds are met.

Legal contracts for on-time delivery of parts or product and binding labor union commitments can also become factors that can affect critical processes and functions. Additional external influences may come from a competitive marketplace or legislative or regulatory obligations.

External situations can play a part in the decision to declare an emergency or disaster. It may be that governmental agencies in a particular location declare that a situation is unsafe and mandate that evacuation is required. This was the case for many during Hurricane Rita in the summer of 2005 in Houston, Texas. Although the disaster never manifested in that location, and the duration of the situation was short lived, it was mandated that evacuation be undertaken. Many companies were affected in this situation, and many had to implement disaster recovery situations as a result.

IN PRACTICE: Events vs. Disasters

Not every "event" impacting an organization can be considered a disaster. Consider the following scenario. In 15 minutes, Joe is supposed to present a report to the Board of Directors of Company X. Joe has worked for two weeks developing the perfect explanation of a critical point in the project plan, a point that has been contentious to the team and the organization for a long time and that has caused significant delays in the project thus far.

As Joe reviews the report one final time, he realizes that he incorrectly used the word "you" instead of "your" in the very first sentence of the report. In order to make the best possible presentation, he opens the report on his computer, adds the missing letter, and attempts to print 24 copies of the final draft of the report for the board members. After walking to the laser printer and finding 24 blank copies of his report, he realizes that the printer is out of toner. No one is around to help Joe locate another toner cartridge for the printer. The board meeting is now in 5 minutes.

Although this series of events may seem to Joe to be a disaster, to the company as a whole it is simply an inconvenient situation. Alternatives for the target printer can be found relatively easily in another department or the meeting can be postponed for an additional

▶▶ CONTINUED ON NEXT PAGE

▶▶ CONTINUED

10 minutes. The inability to print on this printer does not prevent a critical function or process to the organization to occur.

Now contrast Joe's situation to the following scenario. Gwendolyn normally arrives in the parking lot at work at 5:00 A.M. to perform minor maintenance on the accounting system before the majority of the users arrive. This morning as she turns onto the street on which the building is located, she notices several large fire trucks, a dozen or more police cars, and an ambulance surrounding the building where she needs to go to perform her maintenance. This is the only building in the city with direct access to the systems she needs to access.

Gwendolyn soon realizes that there has been an arson fire in the building, and most of the computer systems have been vandalized. The main servers, located in another city, are unharmed, but her ability to access these systems in a timely manner has been cut off. This means that the accounting system that she was supposed to be performing maintenance on will not be fully functional when the accountants in the headquarters building show up for work.

This situation can be classified as a disaster (albeit a minor one) as it affects the ability of the organization's key functions and processes from efficiently being accomplished.

Summary

Prioritization of critical functions and processes requires the DR team to evaluate the requirements of the organization. These requirements are met through the successful completion of critical functions and processes. Internal and external factors contribute to establishing the critical nature of processes and functions, including the time frame that an organization can continue to operate without them operating normally. At some point, referred to as a disaster threshold, the loss of critical functions and processes creates a situation that impairs the organization's ability to meet these requirements. This inability to conduct business under normal operating conditions is the time to declare a *disaster.* The loss of critical functions or processes may have secondary functions and processes that, under normal conditions, are less critical to the operation of the organization. However, during a disaster, these secondary items may exacerbate an already bad situation.

The restoration of the critical business processes and functions requires key personnel to establish, test, and verify that the disaster recovery is successful. These individuals participate in the identification of the dependencies and interactions between the critical processes and functions and assist the DR team in the analysis of the potential impact on business due to a disaster.

Test Your Skills

MULTIPLE CHOICE QUESTIONS

1. The assets that you can touch and feel are known as _____ assets.

   A. software

   B. hardware

   C. physical

   D. technology

2. To take an inventory of hardware, you should _____.

   A. inventory the obvious and expensive hardware

   B. inventory the mission-critical hardware

   C. inventory important departments

   D. inventory all hardware, including large and small as well as the obvious and the fairly well hidden

3. When conducting an inventory, you may find that _____.

   A. generally all your hardware will appear on the accounting system

   B. generally all servers are current and backed up regularly

   C. you might not have a record of all the hardware that your support people know about

   D. your departments will have a list of servers and backup schedules for all systems under their control

4. When inventorying software, you should include the _____.

   A. operating system

   B. enterprise database management systems

   C. email product used

   D. all of the above

5. Which of the following is an example of free software that might be found on a computer system in your organization?

   A. Windows

   B. PostScript reader

   C. Visio

   D. Microsoft Office

6. What is often the most overlooked asset in the organization?

   A. Human

   B. Data

   C. Function

   D. Process

7. An action that is easily identifiable and that is related to a requirement of the business organization is known as a(n) _____.

   A. asset

   B. function

   C. process

   D. action

8. The implementation of labor, technology, time, or any resources to the successful completion of a business function is known as a(n) _____.

   A. asset

   B. procedure

   C. process

   D. action

9. Functions and processes that are critical to meeting the requirements of the business to function during a disaster are known as _____ functions and processes.

   A. tier 1

   B. tier 2

   C. tier 3

   D. tier 4

10. The disaster recovery team assists in the identification of the critical business functions and processes by first identifying the _____ of the organization.

   A. core support

   B. core competencies

   C. data structure

   D. data competencies

11. Phone systems or broadband connections create the _____ link between clients and ASP companies.

    A. data

    B. human

    C. communication

    D. infrastructure

12. Functions and processes that are considered to be important functions and processes to the organization are known as _____ functions and processes.

    A. tier 1

    B. tier 2

    C. tier 3

    D. tier 4

13. The identification of the relationship between different and often disparate systems is often captured in the _____.

    A. data mining

    B. descriptive data

    C. corporate description

    D. metadata

14. It is important to remember that the difference between a situation that may simply be an inconvenience and one that is an actual disaster often depends on the _____.

    A. point of view of those affected

    B. business position

    C. location of the situation

    D. number of people affected

15. _____ within the organization or between the organization and its partners, clients, and vendors may be instrumental in the identification of a threshold for a disaster declaration.

    A. Service license agreements (SLAs)

    B. Service limiting agreements (SLAs)

    C. Service launching agreements (SLAs)

    D. Service level agreements (SLAs)

16. Before an organization can declare a disaster, it is important that you identify _____ will be critical and instrumental in the recovery effort.

    A. resources that

    B. time tables that

    C. those individuals who

    D. assets that

EXERCISES

Exercise 4.1: Identifying Technology Assets

1. You are part of a disaster recovery team charged with completing the asset inventory at a small business that primarily sells a small selection of products to the public.

2. Establish a sample hardware asset list for this company and classify those assets as tier 1, 2, or 3 assets.

3. Develop a list of the software needed to restore operations of the small business.

Exercise 4.2: Functions, Functions, So Many Functions

1. Pick a public-interacting unit of your institution, such as registration, the bursar's office, or the library.

2. Complete a reasonable business function inventory for that business unit.

3. If a comparable unit exists in another business, such as a department store, perform the same exercise.

4. Compare and contrast the inventories.

Exercise 4.3: Processing Your Process

1. Find a small business in the area and offer that business a process inventory for the business function of its choice. If an external interaction is not desired, students may select from a list of businesses, such as real estate office, public attorney, medical doctor, or shipping company.

2. Exchange your inventory with another student that has a different type of small business and write a comparison of your inventories.

Exercise 4.4: Human Inventories

1. Complete a personnel inventory of the registrar's office for your institution or an institution that publishes personnel information on the Internet.

2. From that list of personnel, decide which people would be necessary for a recovery of that business unit, assuming a complete disaster. Justify why each person is critical and what role they should play in the recovery.

PROJECTS

Project 4.1: Develop a Complete Asset Inventory

1. Assume you have a large data center consisting of over 300 systems with multiple operating systems. Assume that the data center houses 30 personnel during normal operations and the entire IT infrastructure for the company.

2. Develop a complete asset inventory overview and create a detailed inventory for the tier 1 and tier 2 assets.

Project 4.2: Bench Testing Your Inventory

1. Develop a strategy for testing the inventory collected in Project 4.1.

2. Your testing should cover at least the following troublesome area of asset classification: the "official" hardware inventory does not match a sampled inventory of the data center. For example, the official inventory of rack 15 shows 10 servers running Linux, but the actual rack contains 30 servers running a variety of operating systems.

▶▶ Case Study

A large multinational organization has hundreds of thousands of assets. Write a paper discussing various strategies the organization can use to manage such an inventory. In this case, the inventory specifically addresses hardware and software assets. As a bonus, explore some methods for helping the organization with the harder to manage assets, such as functions and processes.

Chapter | 5

Identify Data Storage and Recovery Sites

Chapter Objectives

After reading this chapter and completing the exercises, you will be able to do the following:

- Determine the best way or ways to back up your data so that it can be recovered later.
- Evaluate your offsite storage options.
- Acknowledge information as well as hardware and software as an asset.
- Determine recovery site options.
- Examine recovery site types.
- Develop recovery site selection criteria.
- Outline a recovery solution.

Introduction

Once you have determined what you need to restore, you need to have an idea of where you will be able to restore it. Depending on your particular hardware configuration, this decision may be more difficult or easier than you anticipate. This chapter will help to determine the alternatives and the wisest choice for your situation.

Data Backup

Backing up the data—how, when, and how often—is one of the first consider-ations that come into play in a disaster recovery plan. Many decisions need to be taken into account when you are looking at a backup strategy, more than can be covered here. However, we can look at the main points to take into consideration.

It is important when doing your disaster recovery testing that you test with a normal backup. Don't schedule a special backup just for the purpose of using it for DR drills because you believe that you can restore from it. It is important to use ordinary backups for testing.

How to Back Up Your Data

There are many ways to back up data. You can opt to invest in enough storage to maintain a backup online, on a hard disk. You can look at burning data to a DVD or CD, depending on the amount of data to be backed up and the recovery method that you end up choosing (although that choice is often made based on the type of backup rather than vice versa). Or you can follow the time-honored tradition of backing up to tape. Let's look at these different options in the light of recovery and recovery ability.

If you back up to disk, and the restoration is to the same server from which the backup was taken, recovery is simple, elegant, and quick. Disk-to-disk recovery is the quickest method because your access times do not include the time that it takes to transfer data from another medium. Looked at through the lens of disaster recovery, however, if you store your backups at the same loca-tion as the data that was backed up, and a disaster makes this site inaccessible, then your backups are inaccessible as well. Further, if there is a hardware failure or a catastrophe that destroys the hardware on which the backups are stored, then there is no way to recover.

If you back up to tape, you have a backup methodology that has been proven over time. The restore time is longer than for disk-stored recovery because the tape drive needs to access the media, and you have to unspin the tape to retrieve the data from it. Restoring an entire tape, as would likely be the case in a disaster situation, is less labor and time intensive than recovering a single deleted file. This calls into play the definition of disaster that you are using in each case. If the loss of a partial file system constitutes a disaster, but not a disaster that requires restoration in an alternative location, then there are different concepts to take into account.

Please note that the types of backup methods as well as how they are deployed are covered later in this chapter.

> ## IN PRACTICE: Storing the Backups
>
> Another consideration to understand with the use of tape backups is tied, to a great extent, to the location where the backups are taken and stored.
>
> A company in Texas found itself unable to guarantee that it could restore from tape backup because the company that it contracted with to transport its tapes from its data center to the secure offsite location where the backups were stored hired new people and found that one of their carriers, rather than delivering tapes to the secure, climate-controlled location, was carrying the tapes in the trunk of his car in July and August.
>
> A company in New Orleans chose to back up to tape and to store the tapes offsite with a company that chose to store the media in the basement. Drying the tapes out after that company experienced a flood caused by a broken water pipe was a time-intensive job, and one that no one was sure was not going to destroy the tape's ability to be read and restored from.

Another option is to make backups to CD or DVD. This media has faster seek times than tape, historically is less volatile and prone to degradation than tape, and is more portable than a SAN or a drive array. The disadvantage, however, is the amount of data that can be stored to the media. The DVDs we are referring to have much higher capacity than those that you write to from your home computer (9.4 GB compared to the 4.7 GB that you likely find with DVDs created for home use), but when backing up terabytes, petabytes, or exebytes of data on large systems it will still take a considerable number of DVDs (but then, it would take a large amount of anything to hold that much data).

DVDs are good for backing up the data for home offices or small businesses. It is important, however, to note that they are not nearly large enough to back up large amounts of data. Tape backups are still the most common method of backing up large amounts of data. Network-attached storage is also a method that is growing in popularity. Although network-attached storage doesn't necessarily meet the needs of an offsite recovery effort, it is still the backup method of choice for many large organizations.

Backups that are taken to disaster recovery testing should be the same backups that are done for the purpose of production recovery, not special backups taken for the purpose of recovery testing.

When to Back Up Your Data

When you schedule your backups (either manually or automatically) is a matter of complying with company requirements and with what you are doing and how. If you need to shut down all the systems on your server in order to take an adequate backup, then scheduling the backups for a Tuesday afternoon would probably not be a good idea. However, if you can leave all systems up, active, and available while you are taking your backups, this may be a viable time to perform the backups. It would be advisable, however, to schedule them when the system is less active and has fewer processes running and fewer users accessing the data.

Although it is always a best practice to perform backups when servers are least active (typically after hours), in a truly global organization there is often not enough slow time for the server to allow for this. Research on server load for most servers in the organization is advised so that backups can take place during the lowest average load.

Keeping all this in mind, it is also important to remember that there are some systems that either cannot be backed up when the files are open and being accessed by the applications or that must have special processing in order to have the backups be consistent and in a manner that allows for a successful restoration of the system.

The most obvious example of this is when working with databases. Many database management systems are structured in such a way that the database has to be shut down in order for backup and subsequent recovery to be successful. Either the database has to be shut down or special settings have to be set in the database to allow for accurate backups. If these procedures are not followed, the database likely will not recover to a point where it can be opened.

Various techniques can be used to back up data that is in use, or to minimize the downtime to seconds or minutes to facilitate the backup, including snapshots or third-party utilities.

How Often to Back Up Your Data

How often you end up taking your backups ends up being a combination of math and company policy. Many companies have a records retention policy that dictates how long you must retain records and be able to recreate those records. Many governmental regulations come into play with these policies. To take into account all factors when making these determinations, you should consider the following parameters:

- The *recovery point objective (RPO)* is the point in time to which systems and data must be recovered after an outage as determined by the business unit. Your backup methodology must take into account the need to lose no more than an hour's worth of data, or exactly no data loss in case of disaster or the ability of the organization to recreate a week's worth of data after the systems are fully functional.

- The *recovery time objective (RTO)* is the period of time within which your systems, applications, or functions must be recovered (either because of contractual obligations or because of organizational requirements to withstand the loss of productivity) after an outage (e.g., one business day, 72 hours, or 2 hours). RTOs are often used in combination with service level agreements (SLAs) as the basis for the development of recovery strategies, and as a means of determining whether to implement the recovery strategies during a disaster situation. This parameter ties in closely with SLAs and with the expectations of the organization. If you must have your business fully functional within 72 hours, then you can't rely on a backup methodology that takes 60 hours to restore because that leaves you only 12 hours to get both personnel and media to the recovery location and for troubleshooting and problem resolution.

- The *maximum allowable downtime* is the absolute maximum time that the system can be unavailable without ramifications to the organization, either directly or indirectly.

Where to Store Backups

This is one of the most important decisions surrounding backups that you will make. Considerations need to include the accessibility to the backups when needed; the time it takes to retrieve the backups; and the climate, geography, and topography of both the primary business and backup storage locations (whether or not these are the same location).

On Site   Storing your backups on site makes for easy access to the organization. This has advantages and disadvantages. Having the backups handy means that you can restore a single file whenever someone needs it to be restored. It means that, in the case of failure, you don't have to factor in the retrieval time for the media from an alternative storage location. You can simply retrieve the files whenever necessary.

However, there are two disadvantages to this scenario. First, storing the media on site means that you have added security precautions to take into consideration, as you need to store the backups in a location that is inaccessible to most people in the organization. Retrieval of the media for any reason other than to rotate or destroy the backups at the end of the retention time needs to go through the process of getting permission from the disaster recovery team captain or whoever is responsible in your organization for such a sign-off. In this way, you can ensure that no one retrieves the backups for nefarious purposes. Second, storing the media on site means that whatever disaster may befall the organization is likely to befall the backups as well. Although this may not be true for a Denial of Service (DoS) attack, virus, malicious data tampering, or hardware failure (by far the most common "disasters" that you will have to deal with), in the event of a fire, flood, or other physically disruptive disaster you will likely be no more able to access the backups than you are to access the primary system.

Often, organizations use climate-controlled fireproof, waterproof, and even tornado-proof safes or shelter structures to store tapes on site. This lessens the risk of the tapes being damaged in a disaster and still allows for rapid access by the organization when necessary. It also allows the organization to guarantee the chain of custody and minimize the points of access to the data that is contained on those tapes. This can be of particular interest for legally sensitive data.

Offsite   Offsite storage, on the other hand, is more expensive because you have to pay rental and service fees for the offsite location, as well as any services associated with that storage. There are many levels of offsite storage to consider. Depending on the size, budget, and complexity of your organization, one of these solutions should be optimal for you.

Owned offsite storage, depending on the complexity of the organization and its requirements, could be as little as storing the backups at the home of a responsible individual or at a rented storage locker. Each option brings with it advantages as well as disadvantages. Storing the backups for an organization at the home of a responsible employee has the advantage of very limited cost, but it also means that this person has to be available should a disaster occur, and also that the backups are stored in such a way that a disaster at that individual's house cannot destroy the organization's tapes.

If the organization has more than one physical site, even separate physical sites within the same town, the tapes can be stored in a vault at the secondary site. In some cases a site may have another building at the same complex, one that is an acceptable distance from the primary site or main server building, that could serve as an alternate site. The organization needs to determine the acceptable distance between server locations and the offsite location. It is important to note that this can also be tied to the RTOs and the SLAs previously mentioned.

Depending on the criticality of the data and the need for assurance of both safety and accessibility, greater distance may be required (1 mile, 5 miles, 500 yards, half a state away). Only the organization can make that kind of decision, and then only after careful consideration. These decisions need to be made on a case-by-case basis.

IN PRACTICE: It Is All a Matter of Location

Depending on the organization's location or the resources available to it, it is possible that there may be opportunities to own the offsite storage location for the backups. In many locations there are old, abandoned mines that are sufficiently climate-controlled. These include limestone, coal, iron ore, and salt mines.

Underground storage initially became attractive as secure storage of documents and people during the Cold War when people were more interested in the end results of nuclear attack. The fear of bombs has lessened, but the massive underground structures live on. They have since been transformed into locations for tape and other records storage.

These facilities, 200 or more feet underground, are highly secure and access is easily controlled, with only one way in and one way out, and they are virtually immune from nearly any natural disaster (fire, flood, hurricane, or civil disorder). This makes them very attractive as storage locations (either owned or contracted), and organizations choosing these locations can rest assured that their backups will be safe from nearly any eventuality.

FYI *Contracted*

One thing to remain aware of with the hiring of an offsite vendor is that the vendor must be able to assure you that it will be around when the time comes for you to declare an emergency, and that it can deliver what is promised in the timely fashion that you need it.

Don't just rely on vendors telling you that they can. See if you can get references from other people who have used them in the past. See if there is proof, one way or another, of their ability to deliver. And above all, get it in writing that is legally binding.

The contracted organization needs to be in the business of data archival and retrieval or the contract will likely not work in the end. SLAs need to be established with the vendor to ensure the organization's RTOs can be met successfully and in a timely manner.

Information as an Asset

This is all well and good, when you are looking at hardware as an asset, but it is important to remember that people and information are also assets of a company, and that companies often overlook these critical assets in DR planning. They consider, at great length, what it means to have duplicates of their data, but it is not always the hardware that fails.

Often it is software that fails, and software failures often go undetected for extended periods of time. Where hardware failure is very apparent and gets noticed by virtually the entire company, bugs in software can cause insidious corruption that may go unnoticed for days, weeks, or even longer.

IN PRACTICE: Homegrown Applications

Software often is not designed by an external company (such as IBM, Oracle, or Microsoft) but is designed and implemented internally. Sometimes, although precautions are taken and testing is done, the inevitable happens, and a set of circumstances come together that causes a calamity to the business.

For example, a very large organization had a homegrown purchasing and accounting system. This system processed purchase orders, receipts, and invoices daily. The system, with few changes, had been in place for over a decade. Receipts were processed every night, via files handed off from each division to headquarters. These files went through several COBOL programs before they were added to the database and before the costs for the receipts of purchases were attributed to the different plants.

One of the plants was in Northern Minnesota, and due to connectivity issues several days passed during which no files were handed off. When they finally were, an extremely large file was in the batch to be processed. Mainframe processing often bases the size of output files on the average file size for a given period of time. When the allocated file size grows larger than the allocated file, the program running abends (abnormally ends), and the operators restart processing after adding additional space to the output file. Ordinarily processes are put into place to account for the restarting of programs and the condition would be handled efficiently.

This time, however, the file was big enough that the program had to be restarted several times, and there were no precautions in the program to skip the already processed receipts and move ahead to where the program abended.

The run started, ran for several thousand receipts, and stopped. Operations added space to the file and restarted the program. The first several thousand receipts processed again and then several more thousand receipts processed before the program broke again. Operations added more space and restarted the program. The first several thousand receipts processed a third time, the second several thousand processed for a second time, and the batch finally ran to completion.

A sequence number that was generated whenever the program ran is the only thing that made these receipts unique.

No one noticed that the database and resulting files were incorrect for over a week, because the accounting departments at the

> plants were understandably concerned when their anticipated and realized costs were radically different.
>
> Recovery in this case couldn't be to restore the system and reprocess—too much time had passed and too much processing had been involved. New programs had to be written to determine how to back out the duplicate and triplicate receipts and not affect any other part of the system.
>
> Not only was this a lesson in recovery and the differences in recovery, but the differences in the types of disaster from which you have to recover (in this case, internally programmed software failure) and the ways in which you can recover. Further, it was a lesson in the fact that, no matter the size of the company and the amount of effort put into disaster recovery and the effectiveness of backups, there is always something that you can learn about your system.

It is important to remember that part of the information that many organizations forget to bring to the disaster recovery site is the information that will be necessary for restoring systems and data. It is easy to remember that you need the backups of the data, but you may need information on the licenses that you have purchased for software or software-hardware combinations. This is particularly true for systems like IBM mainframes, where the license is tied almost directly to the hardware and alteration of where the operating system or other software is installed will mean that the software cannot be used. These vendors fully understand the need for disaster recovery and disaster recovery testing and will work with you to provide temporary licenses for new hardware configurations, but having your existing license key available at the DR site will mean that you can more effectively and efficiently work with your vendors to expedite the process. Time is critical in a disaster situation, and the time that you save could mean the difference between meeting and missing SLAs, and the cost can be extensive.

Metadata is just as important as licensing information. The company must determine what data is important and how important each different piece of information is. Wasting time early in the recovery process recovering information that isn't as critical as other information is a less than effective use of resources. Apply your efforts where they are going to make the most difference, especially early in the recovery process (whether it is a real disaster or a drill). Part of the planning process should include attention to which information has to be available and in what order to have the data ready for the users.

Critical data is data that has to be retained and recovered for legal reasons and for the restoration of minimum work levels. Within this definition of data, it is important to note that the critical data necessary to restore minimum work levels is the data that should be concentrated upon. You have to be able to access the data that needs to be retained for legal reasons, but that data does not necessarily have to be among the first recovered. The definition of minimum work levels is situation specific, but among this information would likely be accounting information and access to purchasing, receiving, invoice processing, and payment processing functionality.

Vital data is information that has to be retained and recovered to maintain normal business activities. This information and data represents a substantial investment by the company in time and effort, and the recreation of the data may be difficult or impossible. This data may or may not be necessary in a disaster recovery situation. This is determined situation by situation (the data in question, the criticality of the restoration, and the duration of the disaster all play a part).

Sensitive data is the data or documentation that is necessary for normal daily operations of the organization but for which there are alternative sources of the same data or data that can be easily reconstructed from other data that is readily available (critical or vital data may be sources for this data).

Noncritical data is data that can easily be reconstructed at minimal cost or that has its source in critical, vital, or sensitive data but that has less stringent security requirements.

Recovery Site Alternatives

Every organization is faced with many alternatives, not only from a backup and recovery storage perspective, but also when dealing with the determination of recovery site alternatives.

Function

Disaster recovery sites function as a scaled back office for your key functions so that your company can continue its business until either its primary site can be restored to operational functionality or until your company can come up with a viable alternative for long-term functionality. A disaster recovery site is a stopgap location so that you can keep from having to close the business while the long-term solution can be accomplished.

That means that when you are looking at the different options and the different locations, you need to keep your business and its functions and needs in mind. Make sure that what you are looking at will meet the needs of the company for at least a couple of months. If you are back up and running as usual in a shorter time, that is wonderful, but you should look at everything with realistic expectations.

Hot Backup Sites   A hot backup site is a location, other than your typical business site, where a duplicate of your data is stored, ready for access in a moment's notice. Real-time data transfer occurs between the primary and the hot backup site, which means that the site has to be contracted continuously or that the company has to own both the primary and the hot backup site.

The advantage of a hot backup site is that the company can guarantee that there will be at most a certain period of data loss (for example five minutes) that can account for the lag between the two sites. This can be a core competency or a selling point for an organization to its clients.

The disadvantage, of course, is cost. Not only do you have the cost of either contracting or acquiring the backup location, but also the cost of the network traffic that is required to keep the two environments continuously in sync.

Warm Backup Sites   A warm backup site is a facility that is already stocked with all the hardware that it takes to create a reasonable facsimile of what you have in your primary data center.

In order to restore the organization's service, the latest backups from your offsite storage facility must be retrieved and then delivered to the backup site. Once this is accomplished a bare metal restoration of the underlying operating system and network must be completed before recovery work can be done.

The advantage to the warm backup site is that it can be gotten to and a restoration accomplished in a reasonable amount of time. The disadvantage is that there is still a continued cost associated with the warm backup site because you have to make sure that you maintain a contract with the facility to keep hardware up-to-date with that which is found in the organization's data center. This is the only way to ensure that the backups can be read when the time comes and the only way to be sure that the restorations can be accomplished successfully.

The warm backup site is the compromise between the hot backup site and the cold backup site.

Cold Backup Sites   A cold backup site is a building space that can be leased or located (if you are very lucky) when a disaster occurs. Everything that will be required to restore your organization to productivity will have to be procured and delivered to this site when the disaster has been declared. Only after the physical resources have been acquired can the process of actual recovery begin.

The advantage of a cold backup site is that the cost is minimal. Even if the organization chooses to contract the floor space long term, the cost is far less than that associated with the others.

The disadvantage of a cold backup site is that the organization can find itself unable to recover operations for an extended period of time, particularly if the organization relies on resources that are difficult to obtain or that require extended lead times to be configured. If an organization chooses to rely on a cold backup site, and it is not reliant on commodity hardware, that organization may fail to recover in a timely enough fashion to remain a profitable business and may fail.

Reciprocal Agreements   Reciprocal agreements are often a viable and useful alternative to a warm recovery site, but you have to make sure that the company you are working for and the company that you are anticipating entering into such an agreement with are not only aware of the advantages and disadvantages of such an agreement, but that the company that you work for is a good fit for the agreement long term. A company that is not a good fit long term may still use a reciprocal agreement as a short-term solution to the disaster recovery scenario, but all parties have to acknowledge that the solution is, indeed, short term.

A reciprocal agreement is the agreement of two (or more, but this is less frequent) companies to join together and act as partners in disaster recovery. One kind of business that can make use of this kind of agreement particularly well is the home office or startup business. These businesses often have shoe-string budgets and can little afford to be without access to their information for extended periods of time, and can afford even less the outlay of money for the purpose of making sure that there is a place where they can recover their information should a disaster or unplanned event prevent them from using their own resources. Two or more of these companies can enter into a simple agreement so that they can share the cost of resources over the duration of the agreement.

For example, Larry is a freelance author. He is working nearly full time at writing while also holding down another full-time job to pay the bills and provide insurance and support to his family until he feels able to get into writing as a single full-time profession. Adam is a tax accountant who is just starting to venture out on his own. He, too, is working at another job until he can build his client list to such a degree that he can see his way clear to make his own business his only profession. Amandya runs a home crafting business making custom scrapbooks for customers' weddings, their children, or other significant life events. This is her only official job. Finally, Joy has an established, though limited, enterprise that provides housekeeping services to a given set of clients. All these people have their own set of information that is relevant to their particular businesses and their own needs from a hardware and software perspective. However, many of the needs overlap or are exceeded by the needs of another (one application has greater hardware requirements that others may be able to take advantage of even if the need is not present) and can therefore be easily met. Some, such as the tax accountant, have specialized software requirements that the others don't have. These four organizations can enter into a reciprocal agreement that can include the cooperative effort to purchase a backup system that is stored in a central location (another person's home, or in a storage locker somewhere) that can be used by one or more of the organizations (at one of the four offices in question, or at another agreed upon location) for the purpose of disaster recovery. For this to work well, the parties involved cannot reside in very close proximity to each other (for example, the same street or the same housing area, and likely not even the same town) so that there is a good chance of recoverability should a hurricane affect Amandya's location or a forest fire affect Larry's access to his home office.

Such an agreement is typically made up of two parts, agreed upon by all parties. The first is a letter of understanding that lays out, ahead of time, any costs associated with the agreement and a general agreement of what responses each company expects to offer and receive during an outage. This letter of understanding should also provide information on proposed recovery sites for each party in the event of a disaster. For example, should Joy need to recover on the backup system, she would have a certain amount of time to either inform or request from any other party (Larry, Adam, or Amandya) that she is in need of temporary recovery facilities, and office space could be made available to her at one of the alternative locations. The second part of the agreement is a completed configuration questionnaire that covers current and anticipated hardware and software requirements, and an anticipated schedule for updating the software and hardware and making the associated changes to ensure that all parties' needs will be met and that all parties will be able to use the systems in question in the event of a disaster.

At some point, the parties involved may find this to not be an adequate solution or they may find that their needs and the needs of the others begin to diverge to an extent that the agreement is no longer anticipated to be beneficial. In this case, it is important that the agreement be equitably dissolved and the parties that choose not to remain in the agreement find other recovery solutions.

Another interesting situation where reciprocal agreements are profitable is when key personnel in the organization have their own resources at home from which they can perform many of their ordinary work duties temporarily. The use of these resources as auxiliary disaster recovery resources can be contracted as a reciprocal agreement with the reimbursement for the personal computer and supplies needed to be part of the disaster team. The benefit to the employee would be financial; the benefit to the company would be the readily available resources should they prove to be in short supply at some point.

Two Data Centers   This alternative can be seen as a logical extension of either hot or warm backup solutions; however, it can be defined differently when the organization in question isn't sufficiently large to contract either for a hot or warm backup site or to own a hot backup site in another location. If this is the case some organizations, typically smaller ones, can equip a limited second data center.

For smaller organizations second data centers can mean (if the company is small enough) a couple of laptops equipped with sufficient hardware resources and the proper software necessary to conduct business. It can mean a duplicate set of hardware (if a couple of laptops are not sufficient for the amount of resources or if laptops are not robust enough to provide sufficient power for the organization's need) set up with software stored in an offsite location, such as a storage locker or a rented space in a warehouse.

This solution is limited in cost, but can be sufficient. If space is required temporarily to recover the business, office space is easily contracted on a limited time basis either from official locations or, in a pinch, from a hotel in a safer location.

Consortium Arrangement   If we consider a consortium to be a group of organizations that have formed some kind of association or formal combination with the purpose of engaging in a mutually beneficial venture, then we can extend that to a disaster recovery consortium arrangement and see that the venture would be to provide disaster recovery facilities to the other members of the consortium. This isn't totally unlike a reciprocal agreement, but as the group is often formally joined together, the venture ends up being more formalized and longer lasting than the reciprocal agreement.

Since it is unlikely that any of the members of the consortium are in the group for the sole purpose of providing the other members with backup facilities, it is more likely that each member would provide a given amount of space on existing hardware to other members for the purpose of all or part of their temporary recovery efforts.

Because few organizations, especially in today's business environment, can afford to dedicate significant chunks of their resources to remaining available for use in a disaster situation for one of the other members of the consortium, this type of agreement is not typically used.

5

Vendor-Supplied Equipment   Agreements are often made with vendors to be able to provide emergency equipment to organizations in the event of a declared disaster. Space and the utilities to make a functional representation of the organization are often easier to come by in alternative locations, and often are contracted for extended periods of time, but the hardware on which the systems run is contracted only to be made available in the event of a disaster.

This is much easier to do if you are requiring the use of commodity type equipment rather than custom equipment. For example, PCs, even several dozen or several hundred, are far easier to come by than two or three PDP-11s. With the increasing popularity of Linux as a reliable operating system for industry, this commodity kind of hardware is becoming more prevalent, but the reliance on mainframes has not diminished and it may be the fact that, depending on the extent and severity of the disaster, some equipment may not be as readily available, even to fulfill vender contracts, as it could be.

Caution should be taken when entering into this type of agreement to make sure that the vendors in question will be able to fulfill a need such as this in a timely enough fashion for the organization.

Combinations   In disaster recovery, as in many areas of business, exactly what happens and how is not always cut and dried, not always black and white. In a lot of cases, one solution does not fit every aspect of a company's disaster recovery needs. In these cases combinations of solutions are created to custom fit the needs of the organization.

IN PRACTICE: Custom Solutions for Solutions Reference

Solutions Reference is a research company that assists companies with marketing research and with research and development based on that marketing research. It has determined that, in different situations, it needs to employ different recovery methodologies.

In the event of a natural disaster that affects the locations where it has its primary computers, the company will take its daily backups to an offsite recovery location in a different state so it can recover while its primary location is being brought back online.

The company has determined, however, that (because it is in a hurricane prone location) it can opt to head off the effects of a disaster by temporarily relocating the servers for a period of time to the servers in the winter home of one of the company managers in California. The manager simply needs to fly himself (and potentially his family so he has that piece of mind) to California, attach his system via the extended network to the network at work, and make a copy of the system. The switch over can occur at that time, meaning that there is literally no downtime for the servers and the clients are unaware of any potential for disruption.

Written Agreements

Written agreements for the specific recovery alternatives selected should be prepared, and should include the following special considerations.

Contract Duration   The duration of the contract needs to be set and agreed upon by all parties. Close attention should be paid to when the end dates are approaching so that renegotiation of the agreement can occur and the parties in question are not left stranded without an agreement and a disaster pending.

This is one reason why a single owner of the disaster recovery plan and all associated materials is usually critical to an organization. One person (with a backup, of course) owning all disaster recovery material means that that person is responsible for keeping up with agreements, licenses, and contracts and that the organization can rest assured that it will not be left without an agreement should it need to rely upon it.

It is particularly convenient if agreements and contracts can be written so that they all expire at nearly the same time, so that all negotiations can occur around the same time. This will make remembering easier for the responsible parties.

Termination Conditions   All contracts and agreements should have termination conditions that allow either party to terminate the agreement, although there are usually financial repercussions for whoever decides to terminate before the expiration date of the contract.

Conditions for termination include the insolubility of one of the parties or the occurrence of too many declared disasters without justified cause in too short a period of time. Although some disasters are unavoidable, such as floods and tornadoes, others are often preventable in part or completely by taking reasonable precautions.

One example is the case of Crystal Dogs. The Crystal Dogs company was a dot-com startup that sold crystal dogs online. It was a home business retailing crystal dog figurines and Christmas ornaments, an Internet-only business whose founders ran the Web site and all associated systems. These owners contracted with another service provider (DR_Cheap.com) to be their backup for a nominal fee so that, in the event of an emergency, the business could be up and running again without having to resort to spending a lot of money on a backup site.

Crystal Dogs, however, failed to take the minimal necessary precautions to secure its network and install firewalls and filters on its systems, and it fell victim several times within a 6-month period to DoS attacks and viruses and had to rely on the services of DR_Cheap.com an inordinate amount of time.

DR_Cheap.com felt that they were losing money on the proposition (kind of like an insurance company when you have an unusually large amount of accidents in a short amount of time) and dropped the contract with Crystal Dogs because it felt that Crystal Dogs wasn't taking the necessary precautions to prevent declarable disasters.

Testing   Any agreement should have, as a part of the services provided, the facility to allow your organization the ability to test your disaster recovery plan. It is important to note that, unless you have fully tested the plan and are confident in your ability to recover from a disaster with the given plan, you really can't say that you have a disaster recovery plan. You can say that one is in process, but without knowing that you can rely on the plan in case of a declared disaster, you can't say that you can actually recover.

Costs   Another critical feature of the written agreement needs to be the provision for all costs associated with the agreement. The contract needs to detail anything that isn't covered by the agreement, and you need to make sure that it includes anything that you think ought to be covered. Usually hardware is covered, but are there any software costs that you think ought to be covered that aren't apparent in the agreement?

Although this may not seem to be overly important for many software products (such as Microsoft Office), there are times when not having the correct license key can mean the difference between being able to recover during a test or declared disaster and not being able to.

For example, there are keys associated with VMS and ZOS operating systems without which you cannot install the operating system. These keys are costly and often associate a given version of the operating system with a given configuration of hardware. Deviation at any level from the original configuration can invalidate the keys. Special keys may need to be acquired in the event of a test or a declared emergency, and it is best to know upfront if you are to be responsible for acquiring these or if there will be additional costs associated with the acquisition of them should the contracted company be required to acquire them.

Special Security Procedures   In many cases, the agreement will have a clause or clauses concerning security measures that are required or being provided. It is important to make note of these measures and procedures as they may or may not be sufficient in your organization's given situation, and special provisions may need to be made to ensure the safety of all parties and the security of property and information in the event of a test or of a declared disaster.

Notification of Systems Changes   There should be a process set forth in the agreement documents providing a process or procedure by which you can change the configurations of your systems covered by the agreement. There will likely be charges associated with these changes; however, as a means to protect your organization's interests in being able to upgrade and stay current on systems, it is worth the extra money to have written into the agreement the clauses that will allow you to make such changes.

Hours of Operation   What happens if you have to declare a disaster at 3 A.M. on a Sunday morning? Will you be able to reach anyone at the DR company to let you in and help you get set up? Will you be able to find someone to call? Will you even be able to get into the site before 9 A.M. on Monday morning? What will it do to your company if you are unable to start your disaster recovery efforts until 30 hours after the disaster happens? Will you be able to access your backup tapes in that time frame, or will you have to wait until Monday morning for that, too? The hours of availability for all agreements should be spelled out so that you can be sure you have access to the resources required when they are needed, not necessarily just when it is convenient.

Specific Hardware and Other Equipment Required for Processing   Does your organization have special hardware needs? Are you running on a PDP-11 (a DEC computer from the early 1970s and still in use in many companies today) and you need to have that available to meet your disaster recovery efforts? If you have such a need, it should be spelled out in detail in any agreement. This extends to any odd tape devices required for recovery, printers that are programmed for in your application (do you only print your reports on certain-sized paper, do you need a special printer to handle your check or invoice printing requirements, or is your application set up to send commands to a DEC Laser printer or an HP printer and the company with whom you have a contract has standardized on something else?), or any other quirky hardware that may be difficult to obtain on short notice.

Personnel Requirements Many companies will contract to provide hardware and even software to another company in the event of a declared disaster or for the purposes of testing a disaster recovery plan, but what happens when you need people to do the job? First, is your disaster recovery plan sufficient that it would allow someone walking in off the street to do the job for you? Then, what are the security requirements for the people performing the recovery if they are not employed by your organization? Finally, where are you going to get these people, how much are you going to have to pay for them if the need arises (the Year 2000 "scare" taught many people, COBOL programmers in particular, the real facts about supply and demand, and looking for people who can fill roles with no warning in a disaster may mean paying an extreme premium for the service), and how much notice is going to be needed to get qualified people to perform the recovery or the tests? These questions should be spelled out in any agreements that you have that could be impacted by the answers to the questions.

Circumstances Constituting an Emergency Arguably one of the most important parts of the agreement is the definition of situations that may arise that constitute an emergency. One company's total fiasco might only be a bump in the road to success for another. Planning far enough in advance for what your company might see as a sufficient disaster or emergency not only allows you to plan but also those organizations with whom you sign agreements to plan for such a contingency.

It is important to outline what constitutes an emergency. Although you don't actually have to detail everything that might happen, you should at least make sure that you find a way to quantitatively detail what the impact to your organization needs to be in order for you to declare a disaster and therefore make use of the agreement.

Process to Negotiate Extension of Service Because any agreement is limited in duration, the process for renegotiation of services needs to be outlined in the agreement or in auxiliary documents to the agreement. This is important so that both sides of the negotiation know what to anticipate and when to anticipate it.

Nonmainframe- or Nonserver-related Resource Requirements
Although many people, and indeed many companies, think of mainframes and midrange computers or Linux and Windows servers when they think about disaster recovery (some even take the printers into account), many don't think about the smaller and less glamorous resources such as desktop computers, laptop computers, phone systems, and other devices that allow people to actually do their jobs.

Because many disaster recovery service providers don't provide for the computers that the users will need in order to get back to work so that the company can continue with business as usual, those facilities need to be planned for as well.

For example, IBM doesn't necessarily have the facilities at their Boulder location to house a hundred or more people sitting at desktop computers without special arrangements being made to make the facilities available. However, it likely would be possible to find, in the same general location, office space or warehouse space that could be made ready fairly quickly so that users could be brought to the area of the disaster recovery site for the duration of the recovery efforts and until the main office site could be made safe for business again.

Priorities   Recall that in Chapter 1 we looked at breaking necessary functions into groups of prioritized jobs for the purpose of making the recovery and the recovery planning more efficient and organized. These priorities can be translated into the agreement. The resources necessary for a tier 3 recovery need not be available at the same time as those that are necessary for a tier 1 recovery. In the best-case scenario, those resources may never be required because the organization's main office may be available by that time.

If the resources required can be put off, then cost can be spread out over the duration of the recovery effort and concentration can be paid to the job at hand rather than worrying about the extra hardware that may be around the area.

If there is hardware around, someone in IT will often try to recover everything available rather than concentrating on the job at hand. If there are spare cycles, a technologist tends to try to apply those cycles to any job at hand. It is better, in this case, to pay close attention to the job at hand.

Other Contractual Issues   There are likely other issues that need to be put in writing. Legal assistance should be sought with this as with any legal agreement. If you are with a large organization, there will likely be legal council already associated with the organization. If you are with a smaller company or you own the company, you may need to find legal assistance for the purpose of these agreements.

Alternative Site Selection Criteria

Whenever you are selecting possible sites for your disaster recovery site, you will be faced with many alternatives. It would be helpful to have a list of prioritized features that you are looking for in a recovery site. This section provides you with some of the criteria that are commonly used in the determination of provider and site selection criteria.

Number of Sites Available

Although you will likely want to recover to the closest location available to limit the cost of travel and the time needed to get to the recovery site, a single disaster may affect more than one location, and different disasters may happen in different locations at the same time. The availability of more than one location can mean that you have choices in the event of a declared disaster. You may have to agree on a primary recovery site so that the provider can plan ahead for the eventuality of your needing to recover at this location.

Many companies can't offer a wide selection of recovery sites, but they will be able to give you at least two or three different locations to which you can relocate your functions.

Distance from Site

Keeping in mind what your company will need in order to recover and get back up and running in a timely manner, and the time frame that you have committed to be able to do just that, you will need to determine the best places to find a recovery site. If you are in Minnesota and you have 72 hours to have your recovery done, it isn't likely that you will want to use a recovery site in Australia. Colorado may be a viable alternative, or even Atlanta.

Another reason to look at distance from the site is that if the site is too close to your business, you may find the recovery site affected by the same emergency that is affecting your business's primary location. If a hurricane were to affect Tampa, choosing a disaster recovery location in Tallahassee may not be an optimal solution. Houston or even New Orleans may not even be good solutions. Pittsburgh, however, may be a solution for you or New York or Delaware.

Balancing the need to stay far enough away to allow you to escape the disaster and being close enough to make getting to the site in a timely manner practical can take on the air of an art rather than a science.

For example, if you are recovering a business located in Amarillo, Texas, or Hibbing, Minnesota, you may need to take into account that there are a limited number of locations to which you can fly directly, even though there are international airports available. You may have to plan in time to get from your location to another location, stopping at interim airports with an indeterminate layover at any of them.

In narrowing your choices, look at current flight schedules and notice not the shortest time from point A to point B but the longest time it could take you to get there given the schedules. Then double that time to account for possible delays or cancellations. It is better to have a realistic idea than to suggest the best possible picture to the team and to upper management and be proven wrong at the expense of the company. The tighter the timeline required and the tighter the budget for the recovery effort, the more important it is to err on the side of pessimism.

Facilities

Look at the complete picture of the recovery site and the surrounding location. How hard is it going to be to get what you need while you are there? Don't just consider what will be needed immediately for the recovery proper. What will be needed for the period of time after the recovery for employees to get back to work and be productive? Computers are a given, but what about notebooks, pens, and envelopes? And people can't work 24 hours a day. What is the local environment like? Let's look at some of these considerations.

Office Supplies   One of the most overlooked things in a disaster recovery plan and in the selection of the disaster recovery site location selection is the ability to acquire office supplies. Although in a perfect world we could exist in a paperless society, in reality, this really isn't much of an option. People still prefer to take notes on paper with a pen. Even a stylus and a PDA don't usually offer people much compensation for being able to write with a paper and pencil.

Printer paper and toner may or may not be included in the cost of the recovery site. You should know upfront what is and isn't provided and you should take into account where you can purchase, locally or quickly, the products that you will need.

Meals   You have people; they have to eat. If you are looking at being at this location for an extended period of time (a month or more), having everyone subsist on vending machine food isn't practical or healthy. Paying attention to the restaurants and supermarkets in the proposed disaster recovery site area means that you can prepare for the fact that you will have many people who will need to be fed and in turn can prepare those going to the recovery site for what they will find there.

One company I know of created a disaster recovery journal. It is a three-ring binder with menus from local restaurants, maps to the restaurants from the DR site, and maps to local shopping establishments (malls, Wal-Mart, grocery stores) so that anyone who ends up at the disaster recovery site (for testing or for a declared disaster) can go to a central location and find information on what they need to know. Every time there is a DR test, one person on the testing team is designated to go to all the local establishments and get a new menu for the journal. This may not be a part of the true disaster recovery, but it is something that will make those involved more at ease.

Living Quarters   Look at the proximity of hotels, motels, and short-term housing to the disaster recovery site. A site is less practical if it has only long-term housing (a one or more year lease) close to it.

Again, making an up-to-date list every time there is a DR plan or having someone maintain a list of these local residences will allow those traveling to have a starting point both for the testing and for a declared disaster.

Postal Services   If your organization is going to have to send and receive mail (bills, invoices, payments), having ready access to postal services will be a must. If you are going to be at the backup location for more than a few days, you will likely find yourself having to rely on the postal service in the recovery location. Knowing where it is and how to access it and creating a working relationship with the people there will go a long way toward easing pains should disaster declaration become necessary. Knowing where to access and how to locate these facilities should be part of the criteria what you base your decision for the choice of location.

Recreational Facilities   Okay, so maybe it isn't one of the things that people think of first when looking at disaster recovery sites, but when you are dealing with people who are a long way from home, under stress, and probably working long hours, in order to keep tempers from flaring, and so that you can make the most productive use of the hours that you do have, having recreational outlets for people will go a long way toward maintaining morale.

Whether it is a gym, park, golf course, or other outlet, knowing that there are places central to where the recovery site is located to give people a place to work off stress should be on your list of things to look for when looking at recovery sites. The company is going to have the company as its top priority. This is a given. But in order for the people involved to be as productive as possible, providing them with this outlet will do more for the bottom line than anyone could anticipate.

Cost

In the long run, it frequently comes down to cost. This may not be the only deciding factor, but it will likely be one of the primary factors leading to the decision.

Site Cost   The site, regardless of where it is or what it provides, is going to require a significant outlay of money. But the organization needs to look at this more as an insurance policy than as a sunk cost. An insurance policy is something that you buy and pay for on a regular basis, something that you hope you never have to use but that you know is there in case you do. The same holds true for the disaster recovery site. Although you may make use of it on occasion for testing (kind of like health insurance, you use it for physicals), you hope you never need it for anything really serious.

Travel Cost   Travel cost may be even more of a consideration than the monthly cost of the contracted recovery site. Depending on where the recovery site is and how air travel works in that area, you may be looking at higher-than-usual expenses for the cost of tickets. But that is only part of the travel cost that has to be considered.

The cost in man-hours should be considered as well. A quick look on Priceline (**http://airlines.priceline.com/airlines/flights/flights-to.html**) might allow you to see the following information besides the price of the ticket. With this information you can infer more information that may impact the decision of the company as to which recovery site to take.

For example, if you are working for a company in Clarendon, Texas, the closest airport is in Amarillo. If the recovery site is in Boulder, Colorado, it could take you an hour to get to the airport, up to five hours, if luck is on your side, to get to Denver (the closest airport to Boulder), and then an hour or more by car to get to the hotel or the recovery site. You could drive nearly as quickly.

And it gets worse. If you work for a company in Lubbock, Texas, it could take you eight hours to fly to Denver, and many carriers route you through Dallas and Chicago. Add the drive time to Boulder, and the time it might take you to get to the airport in Lubbock, plus the wait time for the flight because you never know how close to the flight time the disaster will be declared, and you could be chewing up a significant number of man-hours, not to mention recovery hours, in the process.

These are all hours that you can't spend recovering your data or your systems. But they are hours that count against those hours in your SLAs.

FYI   *Air Travel*

Keep in mind that, in the event of a declared disaster, you won't be able to rely on getting the best prices from somewhere like Orbitz or Priceline. You will likely have to walk up to the ticket counter at the local airport and pay whatever the asking price is for the next flight out. And you may not be lucky enough for that flight to be leaving right when you want it to. You may find that you will have to wait extended periods of time for the flight that you need and pay a premium for that wait. All these costs are costs associated with the choice of recovery site.

Cost of Temporary Living   No employee, no matter how good-hearted, will foot the bill for the cost of temporary living expenses incurred while they are either at a recovery test drill or at an actual recovery. The company will have to compensate the employee for the temporary living costs. The more people involved, the more that expense can add up. This is yet another expense to be taken into account. The cost of living in Clarendon, Texas, is likely to be somewhat less than the cost of living in Boulder, Colorado, and the cost associated with living in Boulder during peak tourist season for extended, though temporary, periods of time can get to be excessive.

This is not usually a cost that is considered in association with the location of the disaster recovery site, but it ought to be taken into consideration.

Contract

Naturally, the contract should be considered when looking at the recovery site. Terms of the contract, what is included in each contract that the company is evaluating, the duration of the contract, and any additional costs for goods or services that may not be included in any given contract should be considered.

Designing Recovery Solutions

Without the ability to recover, there is no purpose for any backup other than to waste media. Going hand in hand with whatever backup solution is in place, or that you are putting into place, is the knowledge that at some point you will likely have to recover using these backups.

We have to establish a recovery site, select backup and recovery strategies, identify the tools necessary to meet our storage needs for the backups we have taken, and identify those places where creative solutions need to come into play.

Establishing a Disaster Recovery Site

One of the first decisions that has to be made in the disaster recovery planning process is how you intend to structure your backups and your planned recovery. Will there be automatic failover and no intervention will be necessary? Or will you have to retrieve tapes from offsite storage and have them transported to an alternative recovery site? Each alternative comes with its own advantages and disadvantages. Each also comes with trade-offs and costs. Some costs are direct, as in the physical outlay of capital, and some are indirect, as in the cost of bodies and time to recover the organization.

Choosing a Site: Hot, Warm, or Cold Standby   The choice of sites often comes down to a matter of money and practicality. Many companies would rather have a hot backup site, where they can fail their entire business over within a matter of minutes to hours. This kind of assurance, however, costs money—typically a lot of money. It means providing an entire office complex in another location (almost always another city, and usually another state). If the company is a manufacturing company, this could also mean the contracting of another facility or subcontracting work out in case the primary facility becomes unavailable.

This choice may be influenced by clients, stakeholders, and shareholders, but ultimately it is a matter of measuring the return on investment and determining how long your organization can withstand the risk of being without its ability to process work.

There are cases where a hot backup is necessary. Recall that we undertook a risk analysis in Chapter 3. We can begin to think in terms of identification of that risk as it pertains to the identification of recovery solutions. The acceptance, or the non-acceptance, of risk will drive many of the decisions that the organization makes surrounding the backup and recovery solution decisions. Recall that risk is the chance that an event will occur. This chance of an event occurring, coupled with the loss of revenue that will occur if that event occurs and the cost that is associated with it, are all factors that have to play into the organization's determination of whether the cost of the recovery solution is justified.

If you determine that there is little chance that a disaster or even an emergency event will occur, then you have minimized the risk from the beginning, and the choices that you make concerning recovery solutions is very much simplified. If, however, the organization determines that there is a significant enough risk surrounding the organization, there will be additional amounts of investment that the organization will have to be willing to make.

IN PRACTICE: Small Business

Risk, and how an organization chooses to deal with mitigating that risk, is relative. Big businesses tend to be able to throw more money at a solution than smaller businesses, but the size and complexity of solutions is relative. They may not be throwing any larger a percentage of their money at the solution than a small business or a home-based business might be in similar circumstances.

Small businesses are sometimes less adaptable to disaster than large companies. Someone who has turned a room in their house into a small-scale manufacturing line may not be any more or less able to withstand the occurrence of a disaster than Ford, Dodge, or Westinghouse. If all the capital and thought is tied up in creating the product, and little is tied up in learning what they would have to do if a disaster levels their house, they are in little better position than a large organization in a similar situation.

However, an accounting company that is based out of the home office of the accountant may be totally recoverable with minimal downtime if that company invests in the time and material necessary to make a periodic backup of the software and records on its system and stores those backups in a waterproof, fireproof file cabinet in a closet and makes two duplicate copies (DVDs are even getting cheaper today) and sends one to a relative in Pennsylvania and puts the other in a safety deposit box in a local bank.

Simply replacing damaged or destroyed hardware from a local commodity hardware store (electronics store, office supply store, or even from the mall) and recovering the backups would be all that it would take to recover the business in a storefront three miles from the primary location or in an apartment or hotel room nearby.

It is up to every individual organization to assess the risk and determine what it will mean to that organization and how best to recover should the worst happen.

Build vs. Rent or Share   The decision over whether to build a recovery site (whether dedicated to nothing but being a recovery site or as a line of business of its own) or to rent or share a recovery site with other companies is often a difficult one. The level of trust that has to be involved between two organizations in order to share a recovery site implies a special kind of relationship. Although this kind of relationship may exist fairly easily between two home-based businesses where there may already exist a trust relationship, the same level of trust may not exist between two larger organizations. Not only is there a level of trust that has to exist, but there has to be a small chance that both organizations will need to use the recovery site at the same time and that both are going to be able to uphold their end of the agreement over time. On the other hand, it is typically more affordable to establish a share relationship than to shoulder the entire cost of the recovery site. In the end, the decision to rent or share comes down to total cost.

Selecting Backup and Restoration Strategies

The choice of backup strategies in order to make the optimal use of both time for backup and time and effort for recovery is often a decision that will be based as much on guess work and art as it is on facts and figures. Many times the backup strategy that is chosen by a company is simply the favorite of one of the administrators or is just something that everyone seems comfortable with. These, however, are not valid and sound justifications for a backup strategy.

Full backups are complete backups of a system. They are a snapshot of how a system looked at a given point in time. Full backups (often referred to as cold backups) are invaluable to an organization for many reasons, and should always be a part of any backup and recovery solution. They may not, however, be the all-inclusive solution to a company's every need. In order to take a full backup, all the applications and databases on a system need to be shut down. This means that time needs to be taken to complete the shutdown and the restart after the backup is taken, and a backup taken of the full system. The disadvantages of full backups are that they take time and that you can only recover to that specific point in time, if that is the only backup on which the company is relying.

Incremental backups are those backups that gather together, in a perfect scenario, only those changes that have occurred since the last full or incremental backup. This kind of backup is not always possible without the assistance of third-party backup tools to assist with the backing up of the data and surrounding application. Incremental backups provide the fastest backup scenario, because you are only backing up the data that has changed in the period of time since the last incremental or full backup. What's more, because you are backing up the minimal amount of data that is practical, the storage space for these backups is the smallest. The trade-off here is that your recovery scenario can be longer because you have to incrementally restore each of the files from the original full backup to the point in time to where you need to recover. If you don't take full backups very often, this can be extensive.

Differential backups are those backups that contain all changes since the last full backup. The advantage of a differential backup is that you only have to restore the cold backup and one additional backup in order to restore the system to any given point in time. The disadvantage is that you have to back up and store the backups of redundant data. For example, if you take full backups every Saturday night, and differential backups on Sunday, Monday, Tuesday, Wednesday, Thursday, and Friday, by Friday you have duplicated the data that you backed up on Sunday five times.

Mirror backups are those backups that directly copy all selected files, directories, mount points, and file systems from one set of disks to another. A mirror backup is conceptually identical to a full backup except that the data in question cannot be compressed in any manner and cannot be password protected. Mirror backups are often made when using RAID by splitting the mirrored device and maintaining one of the mirrors (or backing up one of the mirrors) as the backup. The space required for a mirror backup is equal to that of the data that it is backing up, but typically (as long as the backup stays on disk) the recovery from failure is faster. This solution, however, is not typically practical in a disaster situation because a disk array is difficult to store and transport and a disaster at the primary site will likely wipe out the backup as well. Rather, a mirror backup is normally used as the source for an incremental, differential, or full backup so that the backups can be carried out without impact to the source system. The requirement for a duplicate set of hardware (or triplicate, depending on the RAID configuration and redundancy requirements of the organization) remains, but the recoverability of the system is greater when the mirror is used as a backup source rather than the backup itself.

Most organizations will come up with their own combination of these backup strategies. They may delineate their backup strategy based on the amount of activity on a system or on the features available to a given system by the underlying architecture. It may be easy to back up the entire system weekly with a full backup and then forget about most of the executable programs because they don't change much. The data in a transactional database (a database that has users inserting data into and altering data already resident in the database) will likely change minute to minute. That data will need to be backed up frequently, either incrementally or differentially (the choice of how has to be based on your organization's recovery requirements), in order to be sure that you can recover the data as quickly as possible to any given point in time. The data in a data warehouse, because it is far less volatile, may change only once or twice a week, depending on your load strategy, thus a single differential or incremental backup after those loads would be sufficient and similar to each other in recoverability and storage.

Hot backup is another alternative that is becoming more popular with larger organizations. With a hot backup, the entire decision (backup site location selection, backup and recovery strategy, vendor, etc.) is a package deal because the recovery location is in constant communication with the primary systems. This means that, in the event of an emergency or disaster, connectivity to the systems automatically fails over to the backup site and there is effectively no downtime noticed. This is an optimal solution for many organizations that have multiple data centers or multiple locations that can be used as data centers.

Although any backup solution has to effectively fit within the window available to you for the backup, the primary consideration in these different options needs to be the recovery needs of the organization. The most elegant backup strategy is worthless if you cannot effectively recover using the backup in a timely manner, and in a manner that meets all the needs of the organization. It is not practical to believe that, if it takes 10 hours to take a full backup of a system and each incremental backup takes 5 hours, and you need to restore a full backup and five incremental backups, that your recovery window will be any less than 35 hours, and this does not take into account the fact that tapes will likely have to be changed out at the end of each step or that restoration from tape usually takes longer than backing up to tapes. If you have a contractual agreement with your customers that your data and applications will be available for them within 72 hours, your recovery strategy, barring any difficulties along the line, takes at least half of that time. In a case like this, differential backups may be a solution to your problem, at least for some of your systems.

The combination of the consideration of backup strategies to fit within the confines of the organization's requirements and the ability of those backups to meet the requirements of the organization is considered to be matching the strategy to the operational constraints. In all aspects of backup and recovery, disaster recovery, or business continuity planning, it is critical to remember the operational constraints of the organization. If any part of the plan doesn't fit within those constraints it may be functional, but it will not likely meet the needs of the organization and will therefore not be a valid solution or consideration.

Although the backups we have talked about so far can provide a solution to the recoverability of the electronic files stored by a company, the DR team must be aware that not all the company's records are stored on computer systems. There will be a certain number of records that are stored on other media, such as paper or microfiche. Planning for the storage, backup, and recoverability of these records is as important as for the computerized records.

Backing up paper documents is as simple and as labor and space intensive as making copies and shipping those copies offsite to be stored in a climate- and access-controlled location. Alternatively, an organization can choose to digitize these paper documents, having those documents scanned and stored electronically on tape, disk, CD, or DVD. Similarly, with microfiche and other non-electronic documents, duplicate copies, in one form or another, should be created and stored in a secure location.

These non-electronic documents are often overlooked in the disaster recovery effort, and are often critical pieces of information that get the organization into trouble. Older data, data from before much of the information was stored digitally, is required by governmental regulations to be available for inspection for up to 20 years or more. If an organization finds itself in need of this information and finds that it is later unavailable, it can be catastrophic.

Storage area networks (SANs) and network-attached storage (NAS) have had an impact on the backup and recovery decisions that an organization makes. Because the amount of data that can be stored on a SAN or a NAS can be significantly greater than that stored simply on internal or regular RAID array, the time required to back up these devices can be significantly greater than on common storage devices. Further, because on any given network storage device an organization can store data from multiple heterogeneous operating systems, the backup and recovery solution needs to take these differences into account.

For more information, see the following article: **http://www.ameinfo.com/ 39672.html**.

Storage Backup and Recovery Tools

There are many backup and recovery tools on the market today. It is important to not tie yourself to a tool that is proprietary enough that you can't find a recovery site easily that will be able to handle your recovery needs or that you couldn't change recovery sites after a period of time if an earlier site no longer meets your needs.

Managing Stored Data and Applications   Different vendors bring a variety of products to market. A simple search for data backup solutions yields links to many products that could provide you with the solutions that you are looking for. There are many others, and a fairly exhaustive search should be carried out to determine the optimal fit not only for an organization's situation but also for the environment it has as its infrastructure. Many solutions are targeted to Windows and Unix, whereas other vendors target primarily IBM-based products.

The following is a list of storage solutions that are applicable for many businesses.

- Veritas (**www.veritas.com**) provides storage protection, automation, and performance solutions for a wide variety of operating systems and databases.

- EMC (**www.emc.com**) has a full line of data management and backup and recovery solutions.

- EMC Legato (**www.legato.com**) provides data protection and availability products for an assortment of operating systems and platforms.

- Network Appliance (**www.netapp.com**) is a high-performance file server, filer, and caching system for Windows and Unix systems that provides the ability to back up and recover data in an extremely rapid manner. It also provides access to analyst reports, customer stories, data sheets, technical reports, videos online, and a substantial glossary of terms.

- Storage Tek (**www.storagetek.com**) brings with it data protection, archiving, storage productivity, and industry solutions. It also has a substantial library of case studies and technical and white papers.

There are, of course, other alternatives, and there is always the home-grown method that relies on scripts and utilities that are resident in either the operating system or that can be built and stored in the organization's software and script library.

> ## FYI *Backing Up Scripts for Recovery*
>
> If you are maintaining your own backup and recovery scripts, you should take care to have an external source for those scripts—one that is not reliant on the recovery of the data to the server as a means to access the scripts. It would be very difficult to recover the scripts if the scripts are needed to recover the data. A minimal backup would include a script library that is maintained independently and retrievable with just the operating system utilities such as copy (regardless of the OS there is a copy command).

The Impact of Storage Area Networks (SANs) on Recovery It is often difficult to find an elegant and cost-effective method of disaster recovery solution for an environment that uses a SAN infrastructure. SANs are being used more and more as a solution to an organization's data storage challenges.

A SAN is a network of storage disks. A SAN typically connects multiple servers, usually with heterogeneous operating systems, to a centralized pool of storage. The idea is that rather than having to manage hundreds or thousands of servers, each with their own set of storage disks, by using SAN technology you can improve overall system administration. Organizations choose this type of architecture so that they can centrally manage the storage resources with a single backup and recovery solution, a single disk maintenance solution, and a single schedule over the entire organization. This architecture can create issues, however, when it comes time to perform disaster recovery because of the heterogeneity of the operating systems and the pooled storage model.

As a pooled storage solution, the SAN doesn't care what is put on it, what the format is, what the operating system is, or whether the data is ASCII or EBCDIC. But you will have to take care that your backup and recovery solutions take into account that there may be data included from multiple operating systems and for multiple purposes.

Further, because the storage solution is likely to be used by nearly every system in the organization, additional care needs to be taken when considering the recovery timeline, the order in which the data needs to be recovered, and the criticality of the data. It may be that none of your data will be available until all of your data has been recovered, and this may not be acceptable to the business as an entity.

Determining what a cost-effective DR solution is when you have standardized to any extent on a SAN storage solution is based on your organization's needs. Some solutions are based on host-based data replication over a network (LAN or WAN) to a remote and often dissimilar SAN technology. Alternatively, storage virtualization is seeing growing acceptance and can allow for the replication of the data across the SAN or to dissimilar storage arrays.

5

> ## FYI   *Storage Virtualization*
>
> Storage virtualization sounds like a complex concept, but it is simply the transparent amalgamation of multiple storage devices into what appears to the end user and the other hardware to be a single storage unit. A high-speed network is typically key to allowing for the elegant use by multiple heterogeneous operating systems and hardware solutions to access this virtual pool rapidly. Storage virtualization is typically handled by software masking the underlying hardware details.

Current Trends in Recovery   In recent years, more and more organizations have realized that any event that is disruptive of their business can be a crisis. Acknowledgment of the impact of the Sarbanes-Oxley Act, the Gramm-Leach-Bliley Act, and HIPAA (the Health Insurance Portability and Accountability Act) as realities of everyday life and of nearly every business's daily life has driven many of these realizations. These kinds of regulatory issues have been the impetus for many organizations to launch their own disaster recovery planning.

> ## FYI   *Governmental Regulations*
>
> The Gramm-Leach-Bliley Act, also known as the Financial Modernization Act of 1999, includes provisions to protect consumers' personal financial information that is held by financial institutions. (**www.ftc.gov/ privacy/privacyinitiatives/glbact.html**)
>
> The Sarbanes-Oxley Act was designed to radically change the way that publicly traded companies recorded and reported inancial information. (**www.ey.com/global/download.nsf/ Russia_E/EY_Sarbanes_9_12_02e/$file/EY_Sarbanes_ 9_12_02e.pdf**)
>
> HIPAA addresses health and insurance information privacy protection for individuals. (**www.hipaa.org/**)

More governmental regulations will likely come in the near future, and with these regulations will come evolving requirements for disaster recovery and implications for additional organizations.

Terrorism is becoming more widespread and is impacting more and more lives daily, but until recent events (9/11/2001 in the United States, London's transportation system bombings in 2005, and the continuing global strife over the recent years) it was not always looked on as an event that

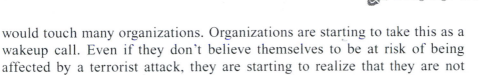

would touch many organizations. Organizations are starting to take this as a wakeup call. Even if they don't believe themselves to be at risk of being affected by a terrorist attack, they are starting to realize that they are not beyond the effects of disasters. They are also realizing that they are relying on organizations that might be affected by terrorist attacks (utility companies or transportation companies, for example) and are taking steps to mitigate these risks.

Data and information are becoming more of a critical concept for more organizations, and the demand for realistic 24/7 access to data is becoming the norm rather than the outlier in the statistical analysis of organizations. This demand for continuous access to data and information is impacting more disaster recovery plans, and service level agreements are equally impacted by the tightening timelines. This means that backing up data has to evolve to meet the need, as do recovery techniques and attempts to meet the tighter requirements.

Because email is becoming more critical as a means of business communication, and because it is becoming more relied upon as evidence in litigation, lost emails, or emails that are not retained in a sufficiently secure manner, can be a disaster recovery event. With more organizations based entirely on the Internet and with email being the primary means of communication with even a greater number organizations, the necessity of maintaining accessibility to the email system and to the historic information gathered from this email information is critical. This is true not only from a disaster recoverability perspective, but from the perspective of security as a whole. We not only have to be able to accurately recover and provide access to email information, but also be able to accurately report on and restrict users who have had access to that email and provide its relevant change history.

Restoring Communications and Recovering Users

Recovery of the business is nearly pointless unless you can restore communication with and recover all processes to the ultimate end users. Not only will this allow your business to continue its line of business and to hopefully grow and thrive, it will foster the goodwill that is necessary in doing business with both your customer and every stakeholder in the organization.

Determining Vital Users with BIA   Recall that you previously have done a business impact analysis (BIA). When it comes to determining which users to restore connectivity to and in what order, this will become, yet again, an invaluable tool. One of the areas of analysis for the BIA would have included those users, both known and implied, that would be impacted by an event. Assigning weights to these users allows you to determine in what order to recover not only the software and hardware resources, but in which order to restore connectivity and accessibility to given users or given user types. It is important to restore user access in a logical and correct order not only to critical systems and functionality but also to those areas that will be most directly impacted by service level agreements.

Rerouting Voice, Mail, and Goods Delivery　So you have relocated your systems and you have relocated many of your users and business units if necessary, and you need to get back to business as usual. But to really be back to normal, communication (other than strictly electronic digital communication) also needs to be re-established. Mail (payments and invoices, naturally, but other communication as well), voice communication, and delivery of goods to alternate locations need to be taken into account.

Voice communication is a vital link in nearly any organization's business. What's more, there is no acceptable alternative to voice communication in many situations. It is the manual alternative in most cases for any other alternatives, and it remains the communication solution of choice for most people. The ability to know from the tone of voice that both parties understand what you are discussing is important. The sound of another human voice on the other end of the line to provide information or to hear out a situation is often necessary to allow all parties to maintain a comfortable relationship.

There are different techniques that allow you to minimize the chances that voice communication will be affected, including redundancy and diversity of implementation. But these don't address what to do if there is a catastrophic disruption in service. In this case, you will need to work with the telephone company to determine the best way to handle the situation. Discuss location with them *before* there is a disaster situation. If you wait until there is a disaster, you may not be the only one making similar requests, and this could cause delays. An ongoing relationship with the telephone company or companies involved will prove useful when the disaster is declared.

Rerouting voice communication can be a challenge, depending on your location and your method of communication. The simplest solution is to standardize your organization on the technology of Voice Over IP (VOIP). VOIP is a method of taking audio and analog signals, converting them to digital signals, and transmitting them, at least part of the way, over the Internet. In this way voice communication can be routed to anywhere, the IP address implies routing. Redefinition of the IP address in a routing table can mean that the voice communication can be routed to an alternative location.

Mail is much easier to reroute. Simply submitting the proper forms will allow mail to find its proper locations, and this solution is customizable enough to route mail directly to where the receiving location needs to be, even when multiple locations are involved. Again, however, a working knowledge of where to get the proper forms, or maintaining a stock of the proper forms with the disaster recovery materials, can minimize downtime.

Rerouting deliveries of goods and services may not be as simple as rerouting mail delivery. Special arrangements will need to be made for delivery, either in postponing the delivery or in rerouting deliveries during the time that you are in a temporary location. This should include not only the time you are in the new location but also the period shortly after, to take into account orders that are in process and not yet delivered at any point in time.

There may be orders that are in process at the time of disaster and already out for delivery. These orders may need to be rerouted and there may be additional cost associated with either the return of the orders or with rerouting the deliveries to an alternate location. This will be a sunk cost that won't likely be recoverable, but most suppliers will work with you.

Eliminating Network Single Points of Failure This is by far the most important thing to take into consideration when looking at backup and recovery. For every single point of failure that you can eliminate, that is one place where your system may be robust enough to make disaster recovery, regardless of the level of loss, irrelevant.

A single point of failure is any point in your system where a failure will result in loss of the system, loss of the network, or loss of ability to access information. This single point can be hardware or software, and is often not even thought of as a point where something might fail. Some single points are difficult to eliminate. Even if they can't be eliminated completely, recognizing them as points where failure can occur and taking steps to monitor and maintain these points is a way to keep them healthy and to recognize that if any issues appear to be presenting themselves they can be taken care of as quickly as possible.

Elimination of these single points of failure doesn't come without cost. You will be duplicating hardware and, often, software systems. The cost-benefit trade-off in each case needs to be considered at each point that you uncover.

But wait. Not every single point of failure is directly connected to your computer. Often the single point of failure is a user who is overly tired, under trained or who thinks that he or she knows more than they actually do. Several years ago, the I LOVE YOU virus wreaked havoc on many organizations. An accounting user at one company knew just enough to understand the language in which the virus was written but didn't realize exactly what the ramifications might be if the virus was opened. He associated the virus with Adobe Acrobat, thankfully, and called the local help desk to help him to unassociate the virus with the software so he could find another way to open it and read the code.

Just as often, a user whose IT department is less diligent in keeping computers updated with the current security patches and virus definitions can be the cause of failure in a system or in an organization. Remember, a disaster is not necessarily the catastrophic loss that accompanies a hurricane or tornado, it can be simply the extended inability of an organization to continue with the work that needs to get done.

One way to eliminate this kind of single point of failure situation is open communication and training. Another is diligence in the maintenance of the systems connected to the system. Your system is only as robust as its least secure single point of failure, regardless of whether that point is hardware, software, or humanware.

This is just as important when recovering the organization as it is when examining the organization's home network. When you are looking at where to recover, examine where there might be single points of failure. When constructing the contracts, make sure that you read carefully and negotiate appropriately so that you eliminate as many points of failure as possible. Once you are at the disaster recovery site, there are few alternatives if there are further disasters.

Connecting End Users   One of the things that is often overlooked when considering disaster recovery is where your end users will be located, and what kind of connectivity they will be able to rely upon. Although you will likely have control over the definition of IP addresses assigned to the new hardware, you may have to take into account firewall ports and VPN or dial-in access to the network.

Further, you may need to find a location to house your users. Many organizations rely on temporary trailers or set up temporary office space in conference rooms in locations not affected by the event. It is important to think through where these users will need to be, and plan for the rapid implementation of establishing these people into their temporary office space.

Not only is it important to make sure that these end users can connect as rapidly as possible so that the company can return to business as usual as rapidly as possible, it will allow your users to regain a sense of control over their lives and over their surroundings. At a time when they are likely feeling that things are out of their control, the security that you provide to them will allow them to get back to normal as rapidly as possible.

Summary

You should now understand the critical steps in assessing a system to help you best address any vulnerability in the system. It is also imperative that the person conducting the security audit document the specific steps taken as well as any flaws found, and what corrective actions were taken.

Test Your Skills

MULTIPLE CHOICE QUESTIONS

1. One of the first considerations that comes into play in a disaster recovery plan is _____.
   A. data recovery
   B. data backup
   C. data recording
   D. business process

2. The quickest recovery methodology is _____, because your access times do not include the time that it takes to transfer data from another medium.
   A. tape backup
   B. floppy disk
   C. disk-to-disk
   D. portable drive

3. When determining a backup schedule, you need to take which of the following factors into account?
   A. Recovery point objective
   B. Recovery time objective
   C. Maximum allowable downtime
   D. All of the above

4. Which of the following types of failure often goes undetected for extended periods of time?
   A. Software
   B. Hardware
   C. Technical
   D. File recovery

5. Locations, other than your typical business site, where a duplicate of your data is stored and ready for access in a moment's notice are known as _____ sites.
   A. backup
   B. hot
   C. warm
   D. cold

6. A facility that is already stocked with all the hardware that it takes to create a reasonable facsimile of what you have in your primary data center is known as a _____ site.

    A. backup

    B. hot

    C. warm

    D. cold

7. The agreement of two or more companies to join together and act as partners in disaster recovery is known as a _____ agreement.

    A. reciprocal

    B. mutual

    C. coordinated

    D. group

8. Written agreements for the specific recovery alternatives should not include _____.

    A. contract duration

    B. termination conditions

    C. testing

    D. specific personnel names

9. Which of the following is most overlooked in a disaster recovery plan and in the selection of the disaster recovery site location?

    A. Location

    B. Office supplies

    C. Shelter

    D. Record storage

10. The overall cost of the site should include _____ cost.

    A. site and travel

    B. site and supply

    C. travel and supply

    D. None of the above

11. The choice of a backup site often comes down to a matter of _____.

    A. money and location

    B. money and practicality

    C. practicality and location

    D. location and site design

12. Complete backups of systems are known as _____ backups.

   A. mirror

   B. full

   C. disaster

   D. precautionary

13. Backups that directly copy all selected files, directories, mount points, and file systems from one set of disks to another are known as _____ backups.

   A. mirror

   B. full

   C. disaster

   D. precautionary

14. A network of storage disks is known as a(n) _____.

   A. ASCII array

   B. RAID file

   C. NET

   D. SAN

15. The act that includes provisions to protect consumers' personal financial information that is being held by financial institutions is the _____ Act.

   A. HIPAA

   B. Gramm-Leach-Bliley

   C. Sarbanes-Oxley

   D. Privacy Modernization

16. One thing that often gets overlooked when considering disaster recovery is _____.

   A. where your end users are going to be located

   B. what kind of connectivity the end users are going to rely upon in connecting

   C. finding a location to house your users

   D. All of the above

EXERCISES

Exercise 5.1: Pick Backup Software

1. Imagine a data center that has about 300 computers, roughly divided as 75% Windows, 20% UNIX variants, and 5% running other operating systems (Novell, etc.).

2. Thinking back to the backup considerations, make a list of possible backup software to use in your data center.

3. Prioritize your list of backup software, using restore performance and options as your primary consideration.

4. Assuming a different primary consideration, such as price or some other feature of your choice, decide if your priorities would be different.

Exercise 5.2: Pick Backup Media

1. Using the search engine of your choice, make a list of the various tape technologies available, and pick the best tape technology for the data center in Exercise 1.

2. Compare the tape drives available for the media you have chosen and pick a favorite drive.

3. Look at the tape robot systems available from the major vendors, and see if your media and drives will fit into that system.

Exercise 5.3: Offsite versus On Site

1. Your organization has approximately 10TB of data, and you need to decide if your organization should have on-site or offsite tape storage.

2. Your organization must be able to easily recover data no older than one month, as an operational requirement.

3. Your organization's further requirement is that recovery operations must resume at minimal levels for all systems within two weeks of a total catastrophe at the data center.

4. Decide how your organization should house its backups.

Exercise 5.4: Asset Classification

1. Imagine a small business with no more than 50 employees.

2. Develop a list of the hardware assets for the company you have imagined.

3. Develop a list of the other assets that the company has, from the information assets to the human resources.

Exercise 5.5: Picking an Alternative Site

1. Your company has decided to contract with an outsource center for a warm backup site.

2. Assume that your company needs 20 critical employees to oversee the technical recovery at the warm backup site should a disaster occur.

3. Develop a budget for a recovery using the warm backup site and the ongoing operational costs for the site. Does using a warm backup site make the recovery costs lower?

PROJECTS

5

Project 5.1: Develop a Complete Backup Solution

1. Assume you have a large data center consisting of over 300 systems with multiple operating systems.

2. The entire data center produces approximately 10TB of data today, grows approximately 1TB per year, and only changes about 10% per week.

3. Develop a complete backup system for the data center that allows the organization to quickly recover any system to data no older than one week with tapes in the facility.

Project 5.2: Bench Testing the Window

1. Consider a data center housing 150 computers with a normal performance distribution, that is, some systems run very slowly and a few others very quickly, but a graph of all the systems' performance is a smooth curve.

2. Using available performance data for common tape and optical storage technologies, attempt to determine how long the backup window needs to be to completely back up the entire data center.

3. Each system must be fully backed up each week, and you cannot need more than two sets of media to restore a system to within 1 day of a complete failure.

4. Divide the data for these systems in the following volumes: 5TB, 100TB, and 500TB.

Case **Study**

A large multinational company has three regional data centers to support the operations of the three major geographic regions where the company operates. A fourth data center serves as the central data warehouse for the company and resides in one of the three geographic regions, but government regulations prevent the two data centers from being located within 250 miles of each other. Consider the discussion of hot, warm, and cold sites in this chapter and write a brief position paper on how this company should approach the data recovery of their data centers with respect to an alternate site strategy. All four centers have equal importance in the processing of information for the company, and a disaster at any one of them impacts all four.

Chapter | **6**

Developing Plans, Procedures, and Relationships

Chapter Objectives

After reading this chapter and completing the exercises, you will be able to do the following:

- Determine what documents and contact information is necessary to support the disaster recovery effort.
- Choose the tools necessary to support the disaster recovery effort.
- Determine the best way to direct the disaster recovery team.
- Choose a backup strategy that will allow you to meet your recovery objectives.
- Describe how upstream vendors can affect your organization's ability to do work.
- Understand how your organization can affect downstream clients' ability to do their jobs.
- Describe how the organization's SLAs impacts not only itself, but also its downstream partners.
- Begin to pull together the recovery documentation.

Introduction

Now that we have assembled a lot of information, the time has come to start to pull it all together. This chapter will help you determine what the disaster recovery plan is all about—what goes into it and what shouldn't go into it. It will help you make decisions concerning what the plan is attempting to accomplish. What is produced from this exercise is a living document, but a document that is only as good as the effort that the disaster recovery team puts into it.

Who else is impacted? Special considerations need to be thought through when determining how and when to interact with those from whom you get your data and those who rely on getting their data from you. Hardware considerations, vendor-specific licensing issues for both software and hardware, and emergency support are all issues that need to be addressed in the plan.

You will need to determine the impact on your upstream vendors and downstream customers, regardless of who those vendors and customers are (internal or external to the organization). Your declaration of a disaster affects not only you but also these other parties.

What Documents Will You Need?

One of the first things that you need to determine is what documents you will need as support for the disaster recovery team. Although one of the most important documents is the recovery plan itself, other support documents will likely be as important, if not critical, to a successful recovery.

Installation instructions and media for all software that is resident on the systems should be included with the disaster recovery plan. You normally won't need to install the software during the disaster recovery, but there is always a chance that something in the backup may go wrong and one or more of the programs will need to be installed. Having the media and instructions as a part of the kit at the recovery site will expedite this.

License keys for all software on the systems should also be included. Again, although often not necessary, there are occasions (as when an organization is working with a mainframe and the operating system is tied by license to the hardware) when you will need access to that information. Software companies will be more helpful during a disaster recovery if you can assure them that you have legal access to that information.

Metadata associated with the data and systems is also important to include in the recovery plan. Although exhaustive metadata—the details on every piece of data that the organization has—is not necessary, the knowledge of every system, every interface, and every kind of software that the organization has should be contained in a document within the DR plan.

Having every interface documented, every user of the system identified, and all relevant data feeds documented may be even more important in an actual disaster situation, given that everyone on the team will be tired and stressed, and this is when mistakes are likely to be made. Mistakes are most likely to happen in the mundane details, such as the creation of users and groups, the granting of appropriate privileges to users and groups, and even the execution of the recovery scripts. Because of this, it is useful to add to the recovery documentation a set of scripts that can be used to perform these tasks. It is even desirable to have an electronic copy of the scripts available outside of the primary backups. What follows are scripts that can be used to create users on a UNIX/Linux server. Useradd will create the user, -c shows you the real name of the user created, -s shows you the shell that they will be using by default, and user1 through user6 is the UNIX logon user ID that each will use to log onto the system.

```
# useradd -m -c"Adam Weston" -s/opt/free/bin/ksh user1
# useradd -m -c"Amandya Jones" -s/opt/free/bin/ksh
  user2
# useradd -m -c"Larry Freeman" -s/opt/free/bin/ksh
  user3
# useradd -m -c"Lonny West" -s/opt/free/bin/ksh user4
# useradd -m -c"Angela Leigh Lynn" -s/opt/free/bin/ksh
  user5
# useradd -m -c"Leon Lawrence" -s/opt/free/bin/ksh
  user6
```

Once you have created the users, you can add the users to groups. First, edit the /etc/group file (or better yet, copy that file from an alternative backup into the target server). The etc/group is a flat text file that contains a list of the groups on the UNIX or Linux server, with each group on a separate line. Each line contains four colon-delimited fields that include the following information:

> **Group name:** The name of the group. This information is used by various utility programs to identify the group and its permissions.

> **Group password:** The optional group password allows users who are not part of the group to join the group by using the newgrp command and typing the password stored in this field. If a lowercase x is stored in this field, then shadow group passwords are being used.

> **Group ID (GID):** This is the numerical equivalent of the group name as it is understood by the system. It is used by the system and applications when determining access privileges.

> **Member list:** A comma-delimited list of users in the group.

Here is an example line from /etc/group:

```
General:x:101:user1,user2,user3
```

This line shows that the general group is using shadow passwords, has a GID of 101, and that the users we just created (user1, user2, and user3) are members of the group. Permissions in UNIX will follow the files, because resetting the permissions on thousands or millions of files is impractical.

Most backup utilities, and often storage solutions as well, come with their own recovery utilities. These utilities are optimized to recover files that have been backed up with the corresponding backup utilities. It is beneficial to keep a copy of the recovery commands associated with each kind of utility that you use in the recovery documentation. You might also keep a copy of a straight file transfer command that will allow you to transfer individual files or groups of files from the backup media to the recovery site in case it is needed.

```
Cp myfile1 /my/destination/myfile1
```

By simply adding these kinds of script to your recovery documentation, you can add to your ability to recover your systems regardless of what might befall the recovery team.

It is important that the system administrators be involved in this level of planning and documenting. You need to have experts in each different platform that you will be recovering. Ask them for their help and advice in pulling together all the scripts and step-by-step instructions that will be necessary.

Collecting Contact Information

Contact information on several different kinds of people needs to be included in the disaster recovery documentation. Although no one can be sure who will be accessible in the event of an emergency, knowing how to get in touch with relevant people as they are needed will be critical. The following people should be included in the list. Again, it is important to note that, regardless of the size of the organization, these are guidelines of what will be important. Also remember that the list is a living part of a living document, and should be updated as changes to systems and to the organization are made.

Computer Vendor

One of the most important lists of contact information that needs to be included in the disaster recovery plan is the information necessary to contact vendors for computer components, both hardware and software. Include not only information on contacting the vendor directly, but also customer service and help desk functions when provided. It is important for the organization to be able to quickly contact these vendors to report disaster conditions, particularly if custom hardware replacement may be needed or license agreements violated.

A situation where license compliance may be in question is when replacement hardware or hardware at recovery sites may have somewhat different configurations than that at the primary site. Some software companies' licensing practices are tied to hardware configuration. Most will be more than willing to work with the organization in a disaster situation and will provide comparable temporary licenses to see the organization through the rough patches, but they will be much more willing to help if they are contacted directly and early.

Suppliers

For organizations involved in retail resale of products, manufacturing raw material into final products, or assembling components into final products, maintaining an accurate contact list of suppliers will prove to be critical in the event of a declared disaster situation, particularly in a situation where the primary business location needs to be relocated for a period of time. Shipments will likely need to be cancelled, postponed, or redirected, and other considerations may need to be taken because of the situation at hand.

Although contacting these suppliers may not be necessary in all cases (for instance, for an author whose supply chain includes whatever office supply store is closest), because of the nature of disaster recovery planning, and planning for all levels of disaster, inclusion of this detail in a company's plan will help in the event that the information becomes necessary.

Emergency Services

One of the most important pieces of information for all organizations is the contact information and location of emergency services. This information should be maintained for not only the primary business location but also for the recovery location, so that those involved in the recovery can have the peace of mind of knowing where these services are located should they be needed.

The location of the two or three nearest fire departments, police stations, and hospitals should be included in the documentation. Also helpful is a map to each of these locations, preferably by more than one route from either the primary business location (for those associated with the primary business location) or the recovery location (for use when the business needs to have a recovery test or a true recovery).

Other useful emergency services to include are towing, dentists, opticians and glasses repair, automotive repair, and other handy but not quite emergency services for the recovery location. Most people overlook these more mundane services but, for those involved in the recovery location, the information will likely prove to be invaluable.

FYI *Supply Chain*

It is often presented that supply chains are a given in any business or organization, and they should be taken into account in nearly every business decision. Supply chains should not be taken lightly, but keep in mind that a supply chain may only be as big as the business or organization that is doing the planning and deciding.

>> CONTINUED

A business should be aware of the importance of being able to locate a source for the supplies necessary to function as a business, regardless of the size and complexity of the chain. The supply chain for a large organization can be broad and complex, but the less complex supply chain of a smaller organization, such as a home-based business, is just as critical, even if that chain simply includes access to a national chain of stores. Making note of where supplies are currently acquired can greatly help if a disaster occurs and the business is forced, for any reason, to relocate.

Customers

Vendors may be obvious inclusions in your disaster recovery plan, but customers are almost as important as vendors. Although it may never be necessary to notify any of the organization's customers, having the ability to contact those who may be impacted should be included in the plan. It is likely impossible to have contact information for all customers ready and printed, or on disk, in the disaster recovery kit, but it is advisable to have some sort of access to the information. This allows an organization to not only contact those customers who are going to be directly or indirectly impacted by a disaster situation, but to also ensure that anyone attempting to make contact with the organization has legitimate reason to make such contact. Remember, not all disasters are going to be natural disasters, and someone causing a DoS attack or other electronically generated interruption may want to gain information on the extent of the interruption.

Different organizations will preserve different levels of customers. Small companies (single proprietors) and organizations whose customers are either tangential, as in people involved in craft bazaars for their primary client base, or who have their customers' contact information easily accessible, as in an author with a list of publishers, will have a different take on the necessity of having ready access to all of their customer base, but ensuring that the critical customers can be contacted is important.

Key DR Personnel

The necessity of accessing those individuals who are critical to the disaster recovery effort is obvious, but it bears saying anyway. An organization should have contact information for the key personnel and also for their backups.

Contact information for the subject matter experts for the organization should also be included in the package. After the recovery effort is started, these auxiliary personnel can be called in to assist with the recovery effort, as testers and as people who can be called if issues are uncovered in the process.

Management for the Organization

Typically upper management doesn't encourage contact from every level of the organization. However, in a disaster situation they need to be kept abreast of all milestones, both met and unmet, and every situation that may make recovery in a timely manner less likely. In many situations, these people will be logged onto a conference call for much of the duration of the recovery effort, or will be the ones to initiate contact with the recovery team. However, their contact information should always be maintained and up to date with the disaster recovery documentation.

Evaluating Your Support Tools

Support is important for the ongoing, day-to-day operations of the organization; it is no less (and often much more) important in the event of an emergency situation. People are going to be feeling insecure during that period of time and will rely even more heavily on their support tools.

People

It is politically incorrect to refer to people as tools, but there are different categories of people who will help to support your organization in a declared disaster. It is not necessary to always have them on hand to support your efforts, but recognizing upon whom you may need to call and how they will be needed to help you in your recovery efforts is important.

Included in this category will likely be information on those people that we discussed earlier: the subject matter experts, the system administrators, and system owners of the systems being recovered. Help desk support needs to be ensured for users as they come back online. Help desk information for software and hardware that supports the organization's systems also needs to be available.

Supplies

Logically, most supplies can be acquired whenever the team arrives at the recovery site. However, there may be specialized supplies that an organization requires. If the organization uses supplies that are difficult to come by or that are specialized for the organization, it would be wise to hold back enough of these kinds of supplies to see the recovery team through a period of time until they can have the supply chain changed to allow them access to these supplies. If it is not possible to maintain a sufficient quantity of these types of supplies, a list of potential alternatives would be useful.

Proof That Your Vendors Are Planning

Completed questionnaires verifying that the vendors are planning for their own disaster recovery may also be included as a support tool or as supporting documentation. Although it is important that an organization be assured that they can recover from a disaster or that they can weather the disaster and come out on the other side maintaining the ability to be a profitable venture, an organization should also desire that their vendors be as prepared as they are. This is particularly important for vendors in the same location as the organization in question, although all vendors should be prepared. An organization is less likely to be able to recover successfully if they can't ensure that they are provided with the necessary supplies when their recovery is complete.

Remember, an organization's plan to maintain its profitability is only as good as its supply chain's ability to fulfill its needs. All the work that a disaster recovery team does is only as good as the organization's ability to do business. If the organization can't get the necessary parts, supplies, or raw materials, all of the disaster recovery efforts may not be enough to fully recover the business.

A sample questionnaire is included in the appendix to this book as well as in a download on the companion Web site. It can be customized to any organization regardless of size.

Emergency Operations Center

The emergency operations center is a central location where information on the current status of the organization during the emergency recovery is available. This information will be disseminated to the various stakeholders as they become concerned with the recovery progress. Whether it is to employees, governmental agencies, or vendors and clients, this central location will be the one-stop point of contact so that all information that is given out is the same regardless of to whom and when it is given. It is the coordinating point for the effective management of the recovery efforts. Through this center will pass requests for financial assistance, information on the current status of all systems, and information on locating assistance and relocation details for those who have to change their location in response to the disaster. All financial expenditures occurring during the recovery effort and surrounding the recovery activities should be reported to the operations center personnel, as they will be the final word on post-incident reimbursement for most expenses. Many day-to-day expenses will be approved without question. Some, however, will have to be approved beforehand. Those assigned to the center will be called upon to track and manage the assets, personnel, and tasks surrounding the recovery effort.

The emergency operations center will be the central location of information for all members of the recovery team, particularly those who are assisting the recovery effort remotely from the central recovery location. The rapid forwarding of information to geographically dispersed team members will prove critical in the effective and efficient recovery effort. The center's personnel will be the ultimate authority on the current state of the recovery effort, both public and private, and will be responsible for ensuring that the proper people receive the appropriate information.

The emergency operations center will also be the central location for processing offers of assistance and coordinating that assistance.

Creating Backups

It is important to note that if you do not have a backup of at least your data, you will have virtually no opportunity to recover. Think about it. How many times have you heard anyone ask (maybe when overhearing that someone lost a file that they had worked on for hours) "When was the last time you backed it up?" How often have you heard someone give the right answer (10 minutes ago, half an hour ago, or even yesterday, depending on the data)?

Backing up can take many forms. For small businesses or individuals a backup might mean nothing more extensive or expensive than copying data files and software that are important or that cause problems when not installed to a CD or DVD. Even for the smallest business, there is no longer any reason for backups not to be a routine event.

An organization needs to consider how much data it can easily recreate or how much it can live without when deciding when to do its backups. If students were to consider how much work they would like to have to recreate on a term paper, the answer would likely be "not much." An organization would likely have a similar response. However, there are some systems that can withstand a week between backups.

Full Backups

Full backups are complete backups of all the files and software on a system or on all the systems in an organization. Often these backups are facilitated with backup software. The software makes the backups simpler and easier to schedule. Using this software also means that the same software has to be available at a recovery facility, and can make recovery in the event of a declared disaster slightly more complicated than it might be otherwise.

Many organizations opt for full backups because historically they were the only type of backups that organizations have had to rely on. Often, organizations that rely on other types of backups to bring them up-to-date rely on full backups as the basis on which they build. Incremental backups can be added to full backups to bring an organization's data to a more current point in time.

Small businesses usually do full backups because that is the most practical approach for them to take. They usually have a minimal amount of data, comparatively, to worry about, and the time that it would take them to do a backup that compares the data already backed up to the data that needs to be backed up and write out the changes would take as long as , and maybe longer than, a full backup. The cost involved in full backups is well within the budget of any organization, and full backups are simple for anyone to do. Most ***commercial off-the-shelf (COTS)*** products that are readily available to anyone—home users and small businesses alike, are simple to use, and have robust features that will allow anyone to schedule off-hours backups and verify that the backups were successful. Often the most important feature of these products is the fact that anyone can use them and they come with simple, easy-to-use directions.

Incremental Backups

Incremental backups record the changes in the data and the system that have occurred since the last full or incremental backup. These backups are particularly good for organizations that have a significant amount of data, much of which remains unchanged but some of which changes frequently. Software may or may not change often, but because of the amount of data involved, and the fact that the majority of this data is unchanging, it is practical to maintain only the changes on backup media.

Let's look at an example.

A major retail chain maintains transactional data for all its stores in a transactional database and historical data in a data warehouse. It maintains shipping, inventory, and payroll information. Much of the information that it maintains will change rarely, if ever.

The chain carries, for the most part, the same items in inventory all the time. The amount of stock in inventory will change as will the cost and the price that the stores charge, but the vendor from whom it receives that inventory will likely not change often, nor will the description of the items.

The chain will likely maintain the same set of vendors for a long period of time. It may add more, and may drop some, but the majority will remain unchanged. Those that it keeps may have changes in address or other contact information, but for the most part, this data also is static.

The transactional data will change almost continuously, and the incremental backup of this system may approach a full backup, but even here there will be commonalities that will not need to be backed up. The same merchandise will be bought, because that is what the stores have in inventory. Many of the same customers will be involved in the transactions; the same payment methods will be involved.

Even the payroll system will remain mostly static for long periods of time. Seasonal workers will be hired and laid off at the end of the busy seasons. Some people will be temporary workers and not stay for an extended period of time, but for the most part, workers will be hired and will spend months or years working for the company. They may move and their addresses will change. They may receive a raise or a promotion and their pay rates will change. They will work different numbers of hours and their weekly paychecks will vary somewhat, but most of the information in that system will be static.

In the case of this organization, it may be beneficial to do incremental backups to capture just the data that has changed since the last backup. The amount of data that will need to be backed up will likely be less than that which will not need to be, and the time and storage trade-offs will be significant.

Backing Up the Mirror

As the size of the data needed to support many large companies grows, so does the time and resources that it takes those companies to back up and recover their data. Most large companies today require that their systems be available 99.999 percent of the time, virtually 24/7. This is less than 10 minutes a year that is set aside for maintenance, emergencies, and backups, which means that either companies have to get very creative with their time and resources, or they have to have systems that never break, are never backed up, or that never need any kind of maintenance. The latter is neither practical nor feasible. Therefore, they have to find every way possible to get creative.

One means that is often used to achieve very high availability of systems is know as ***split-mirror backups.*** With this kind of backup technology very large amounts of data can be backed up in a matter of seconds or just a few minutes, whereas it may have taken hours using a different backup method. Further, the time to recover from a backup of this type will be extremely short, comparatively, as well. It may sound too good to be true, but remember, with everything there is a trade-off. This kind of backup requires specialized hardware and software. It requires that all the data that will be backed up reside on a disk subsystem, typically a NAS or a SAN that is mirrored. Mirroring is the process of writing files (typically database files, but any files can be stored on these systems) to two different disks simultaneously. The primary disk set holds the primary copy of the data, whereas its mirror holds an exact replica of the data.

There are, of course, other disk solutions that can help with high availability for your organization. Servers can be mirrored for ease and transparency of failover. This can be put into place as one part of a disaster recovery solution but can also double as a high-availability solution for minimizing the downtime for systems, which can allow an organization to meet more of its user needs while still being able to maintain its systems' health.

Server clusters have long been a solution for high availability as well. In a server cluster, one or more servers in the cluster can fail, resulting in the failure of the applications relying on the availability of the system. Although there are software versions of this concept that either leverage the hardware version of clustering or not, hardware clustering has been proven to be a high-availability solution to the increasing demands of a global society and it can be a linchpin of a disaster recovery (or rather a disaster avoidance) solution.

Naturally, introducing these elements to your organization will likely mean that changes need to occur in your backup and recovery strategies and in the contracts that may already be in place for your recovery location.

Under normal operation, writes occur to all the disk groups simultaneously. This can be seen in Figure 6.1. The writes to both the primary disks and the mirror disk sets are temporarily suspended (this means that the data being entered into the systems needs to be cached in memory for a period of time) while the mirror is broken. Figure 6.2 shows what occurs when the mirror is broken and backups are taking place. Once the split occurs, the writes can continue on the primary disk set while the backup is occurring from the mirror set. Once the backup is complete, the writes are once again suspended while the mirrors re-marry and the writes can continue. This is seen in Figure 6.3. Because the mirror was split for a period of time, resynchronization needs to occur between the primary disk set and the mirror disk set before they can be considered to be an exact copy again.

Breaking the mirror (splitting the image of your data into two pieces, one that is being updated and one that is caught in time) is a manual operation that can be scripted to occur on a set schedule. It should be done when the system is at its least busy so that the resynchronization process can occur as rapidly as possible.

Because the companies that typically use this kind of backup strategy are global in nature and have the need for assured high availability, and because during the time that the mirror is broken (if there are two disk groups involved)

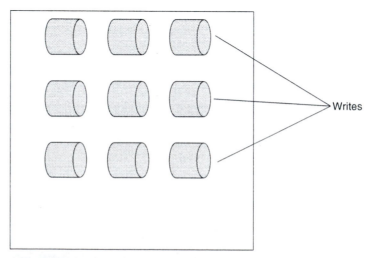

FIGURE 6.1 Normal operations.

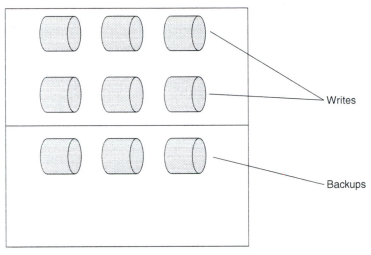

FIGURE 6.2 Backup operations.

there is the possibility of hardware failure causing an outage, it is important to note that most companies that follow this path will not have a mirror of two sets of disk groups, but will have three sets.

Many SAN vendors and NAS vendors, Hewlett-Packard for example, have products that can perform a zero downtime backup (ZDB) for use on their storage solutions. It is a great advance for organizations that can take advantage of this technology and backup solution as it ensures absolute maximum uptime for all systems impacted by the network attached storage, while providing a facility to ensure a successful backup of the system to use should it become necessary to recover to an alternative location.

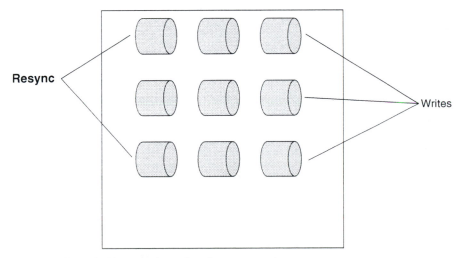

FIGURE 6.3 Resynchronization operations.

These assurances don't come without a cost, however. The price for the solution is not inexpensive, as you can imagine. You are not only buying the software, you are also buying the peace of mind that your applications can be available as close to 99.999 percent of the time as is possible while still dealing with hardware, software, human, and natural inconsistencies. That assurance does not come cheaply.

Organizations need to understand that those options are available should they choose to take advantage of them and be able to afford the technology.

Creating the Recovery Plan

The time has come to discuss the meat of the chapter, the creation of the recovery plan. It is important to remember that the recovery plan is a living document. Changes will be made to the document periodically.

There should be an owner of the document, someone who is ultimately responsible for the maintenance of the document, who oversees the changes and change control. Although this person should not be ultimately responsible for every update to the document that needs to be made, and indeed should not make most changes, he or she will be responsible for accumulating the changes that are made and making sure that they jell into a unified document.

This means that an added measure of responsibility falls upon this person. He or she not only shoulders the added duties of the owner, but has to be able to assure the organization that the document will be available, in its most current condition, to the recovery team in the event of a disaster recovery test or declared disaster. These documents and their associated appendices can often get very large, and care needs to be taken to make sure that all of the pieces of the document are kept in sync.

Capturing the Planning Output in the DR Plan

It is important that all discussions and interviews be captured so that they can be incorporated into what will evolve into the disaster recovery plan. This can be accomplished by using a tape recorder or videotaping interviews and meetings, or by designating someone with very accurate shorthand and note-taking skills as team secretary. It is important, however, that nothing be left simply to memory. No one's memory is accurate enough to remember all the comments and nuances of those conversations. It is important that nothing, even an offhand comment that is assumed to be unimportant, be lost. It is hard to tell at this point what will prove important later, and they can always be culled if they prove not to be important.

Creating Recovery Team Charters   One of the first, and arguably one of the most important, things to add to the planning document is the team charter.

The charter spells out the particular duties, responsibilities, and resources available to each member of the team as well as the team as a whole in the event of a disaster. This document will give the planning team a feeling of cohesiveness and add a level of stability to the recovery team in the event that a disaster is declared. At a time that will be decidedly unstable for everyone involved, this can prove to be critical to the mental wellbeing of the team.

The team charter includes the following sections:

Opportunity/Problem Statement: With the increase in computer purchases and growth within the information technology area, there is a growing need for the disaster recovery team and their ability to look at various recovery techniques and approaches. These tools help the organization to monitor and control its destiny in recovering in the event of a disaster or an emergency. They will help to control recovery network equipment and other physical resources, administer users and key logical and physical resources, and optimize the performance, reliability, and availability of the organization's systems in the event of a disaster. Disaster management standards and guidelines give the disaster recovery team a framework for identification of the best ways to meet the organization's needs.

Mission Statement: The disaster recovery team is charged by the management of the organization to serve in an advisory capacity to senior staff and assist with the recovery of the systems of the organization in the eventuality of the organization facing a disaster or an emergency situation. The primary focus of the disaster recovery planning team is developing, implementing, and ensuring the recommendations and maximum efforts of the resources and for the strategic direction of the organization.

Description: The description section will include a description of not only the recovery team but of the situation that is going to be occurring in the near future surrounding the disaster and the team. This will have to, by design, be somewhat vague. Specific team members will not be able to be named. It may list a position level or a description of the people who will need to be in place. Also, every disaster is somewhat different, and the specific details will need to be included as an aside in the documentation that is created during the disaster recovery.

Background: The background section will give the business case surrounding the team: why it and the documentation were created, the problem that it is intended to help, and some information about the business. This part of the document can be used as a backup document for clients who ask about your disaster recovery planning efforts. It may be that the background includes the fact that no comprehensive disaster recovery plan exists and this project will include the creation of that plan, the surrounding documentation, and tests so that the organization can successfully recover in the event of a disaster. If this is the situation at the onset of the planning process, this is a perfectly acceptable background statement. However, recall that this is a living document and many people who end up on the disaster recovery planning team will not be involved in the initial team that created the foundations. This background will become as much a living testimonial to the progress as the rest of the document.

Scope: The disaster recovery planning project needs to be just as aware of scope creep as any other project. Concrete and measurable goals (as measurable as possible) need to be included in the recovery document.

Timeframe for Project Completion: There needs to be put in writing a time limit to the initial planning phase of the disaster planning process. It is not something that can be accomplished in a day, but neither should it be something that is allowed to continue without any measurable deadlines and milestones. In this section, outline the timelines for the team meetings (be they once a week or once a month), the date of the launch of the project (regardless of whether it is the initial planning of the document or the continuing planning and revision process for the document), and concrete dates for when different parts of the planning and documentation process need to occur. Early identification of the milestones required for the team will provide a basis for this. Recall, inventory of the assets needs to be accomplished; the inventory of the processes, functions, and planning steps needs to be broken down into discrete units. Each of these milestones should have a concrete and realistic date assigned to it.

Team Participants: A list of team participants should accompany this charter. At this point it is not only acceptable but helpful to assign specific people to positions in the charter. Although the charter may need to be amended as people and positions change, it is important that the participants' section provide people the opportunity to take ownership of their position and shoulder their own responsibilities. It is important to include everyone in this section. Leaving people out will leave those left out with the feeling that their input is not of value to the team and will eliminate much of the team spirit that needs to accompany the project. The section can be broken down into the following subsections:

- *Sponsor:* sponsor's name

- *Process owner:* owner's name

- *Team leader:* team leader's name

- *Facilitator:* facilitator's name if there is one, or name of the secretary or person holding other position that is relevant

- *Team members:* list all team members with their respective positions in the organization and their area of expertise. If they are titled members of the organization, it is appropriate to accompany the name with the position.

List of Resources: The list of resources includes auxiliary teams that may be called upon for their input into the process, whether internal or external to the organization. If a small company is asking for the advice of the local fire department, police department, or other governmental organization, this is where to list this information. If local or university library systems will be used in the gathering of data, whether it be for the information needed to determine the hazards and risks for a given organization in a given location or as a means to determine where further information can be gathered, those resources should be listed. Further, it is important that any resources that have been used in the preparation of the documentation be listed in as complete a means as possible. People involved in the recovery during a disaster situation may need to refer back to the information gathered, and easing their search needs to be uppermost in the minds of the people involved in the planning process.

Potential Stakeholders: This list includes all potentially affected parties, both internal and external to the organization. A complete list allows an organization to facilitate better communication during the planning process and in the event that a disaster occurs. This does not mean that every customer or every client of a large organization needs to be included; it does mean that "customers" should be included, and potentially the location of where a full list of these stakeholders can be found. It may be that the list will be included in the data to be recovered, and that is to be expected, but a designation as to in which system the information can be found needs to be included. For governmental agencies included in the list of stakeholders, include a URL reference to where actual names and contact information for individuals can be found and the location of any relevant documentation and forms that may be needed. Include not only those for the home location of the organization, but for any location that might be relevant to the recovery location.

Team Contract: The team contract is simply a statement that everyone on the team has read the charter and understands the responsibilities associated with being a member of the team. It can simply be a clear and concise statement that, "We have read the preceding document, understand our roles, and agree with the sponsor or process owner as to the problem that we are attempting to address. If at any time it becomes apparent that the charter needs to be modified we will consult the team and the sponsor and come to an agreement as to those modifications." This needs to be followed by a section where the team members can sign the document.

Recovery Scenarios   In the case of the recovery document, recovery scenarios are not the instructions on how to recover but the different kinds of ways that the organization may be called upon to recover. Not every emergency will result in a declared disaster. And not every declared disaster will result in the same kind of recovery. Recall our discussion from Chapter 3 on disasters and emergencies and how these might impact a company.

A rampant virus loose in the email system might cause that system to be completely unavailable, or might cause an overload on the network such that immediate action is needed to stop the storm. This will not result in a declared disaster and a trip to an offsite recovery location, but it will mean that certain parts of the disaster recovery document will be called into play. Because the organization has taken the time to document all the systems on which it relies and assigned each of these systems relative importance and determined the measures necessary to recover any and all of these systems, it will mean that a portion of the disaster recovery documents will be used, even if that use is implicit rather than explicit.

Corrupt data in a file or a database might call for another kind of recovery scenario. Again, this is not likely one in which the company has to failover to a recovery site, but one that will have different ramifications and impacts than the email example. In this example, clients may have to be notified, customers alerted, or orders in process may have to be delayed or cancelled due to the corruption.

Loss of a server, set of servers, or storage subsystem may call for immediate assistance from the hardware provider, and, based on that provider's timelines, may also call for the temporary relocation of a portion of the company's systems to a recovery site. Natural or manmade disasters of catastrophic scope will likely call for the relocation of the organization for a period of time to the recovery site.

Brainstorming sessions should surround this portion of the document as different players will have a better understanding of the ramifications for different kinds of emergencies and the potential timelines, resource requirements, and auxiliary resources necessary for many of the potential scenarios.

No matter how many scenarios and situations are included in this section, it is likely that one or more will be missed. This is to be expected and is one of the reasons that this document needs to be viewed as a living document. The inclusion of as many as can be foreseen, however, will assist the organization over time to be as prepared as possible.

Directories and Inventories   As this is the single point of information for the disaster recovery effort, in both the planning effort and the recovery effort in a drill or declared disaster, it should have as complete a reference section as possible. Include a directory of all the people involved in the planning as resources for the recovery team. Also include names and numbers for organizational management of the emergency response teams in both the primary business location and in the disaster recovery location. A complete directory of all software and hardware vendors that have support contracts with the company, their contact information, and all license information should also accompany this part of the document.

FYI   *It Isn't All About the Business*

It is important that the disaster recovery team look at more than just the organization. There needs to be some outside information built into the plan to make life easier for those who are on the recovery team, and even for those on the planning team.

For those on the recovery team, add a directory of services local to the recovery site. Have the team members do their homework and find things like local restaurants, both ones that deliver and ones that are nearby but offsite, both sit down and fast food. If possible, include business cards and menus from local restaurants as an appendix to the disaster recovery document. Include a variety of dining choices. Include locations where members can rent videos, borrow reading material or music, attend movies, and engage in other recreational activities. Due to the nature of a disaster situation, it is easy for team members to burn out quickly. Anticipation of much-needed downtime recreation is critical and will make the recovery effort much less difficult.

Don't take the planning team for granted, either. Often the meetings that the team attends stretch for long periods of time and may last well into the evening on occasion. Include in the planning documents the name and numbers of restaurants that deliver or that are local to the planning sessions. A well-deserved break will go far to make sure that the morale of those involved remains high.

Taking human factors into consideration make not only the planning sessions but also the recovery and even the drills go much smoother.

Inventories of hardware and software products, systems affected or potentially affected by any disaster, and interfaces between systems (both within and external to the organization) should be included in the inventories section.

No organization stands alone. Just as no man is an island, neither is any company an island. There are relationships with vendors, partners, and clients or customers. These people are all affected by an organization's decision to declare a disaster. The following sections look at these relationships and how to manage them so that they are not damaged or destroyed by a disaster declaration.

Upstream Relationships

Relationships, from an organizational perspective, can be upstream or downstream. Upstream relationships are those that an organization has with its vendors and suppliers.

Vendor Emergencies

As you have probably already gleaned by now, emergencies happen to everyone. You can't automatically assume that your company will be the only one affected by any given disaster situation or that other companies will be any better (or even as well) prepared should a disaster occur.

People from whom you acquire supplies may be in a similar situation as you in the event of an emergency. They may be undergoing their own disaster recovery attempts at the same time you are. Or if they are not as prepared, they may be scrambling to figure out what they need to do in order to try to get back to a functioning company while you are trying to make demands on them for supplies that they may not be able to either locate or supply to you when you need them.

Also, unless the vendor supplies specialty items that may be needed only by your organization or other companies involved in similar businesses, then other businesses affected by the disaster or by similar emergency situations may be attempting to order supplies to help ease their own emergency situations. This can cause the supplier to run low on inventory as it will likely not stock in warehouses to be able to supply all the needs required in emergency situations.

To further complicate the situation, it is important to take into consideration not only your company's suppliers but to extend the scope of consideration to include their suppliers and even their suppliers' suppliers when considering what may need to be done in the event of a disaster. The organization need not be overly concerned with the plans that all the other companies in the chain may have made or not made, but should consider the ramifications of what may happen in a widespread emergency situation.

You may have to make preliminary contingency plans for securing alternative sources of supplies, particularly for those that will be critical for the organization to continue doing business and that may not be commodity in nature. Office supplies can be acquired anywhere. If needed, discount department stores can become a supplier of those kinds of supplies. However, if the supplies in question are something less easily acquired, or that require a longer lead time, it is important to know the alternative sources for obtaining them.

IN PRACTICE: The Steel Industry

Steel companies that rely on traditional blast furnaces to create the molten iron necessary in the steel-making process rely on sources of raw materials. One of these raw materials is a taconite pellet, or rather a large quantity of these pellets. These high-iron-content pellets are the key raw material necessary to make high-quality steel. This is

important in turn because steel manufacturers are the suppliers of steel for the auto industry and appliance manufacturing industry.

For the steel company, the company producing the taconite pellets is a direct supplier. However, in order to get the pellets from where they are produced to the steel plant, they have to be transported. This means either shipping by train or by train and boat.

The biggest taconite producers in the United States are located in northern Minnesota. The boats travel on the Great Lakes and the trains travel by rail. Consider what would happen if a major emergency were to occur with the rail system in northern Minnesota for an extended period of time. Most steel companies don't operate on the just-in-time system of having their raw materials arrive at just the point in time when they are needed, but maintain a working stockpile of resources sufficient to carry them through some period of time should the supply line be interrupted.

What would happen to the taconite industry if the shipping provider were unable to ship product? It would either have to scale back manufacturing significantly or find a way to stockpile product for an extended period of time.

What would happen to the steel industry? It would have to scale back because even if the taconite manufacturers were able to produce the material, they would be unable to get it to the customer. Alternatively, they would have to locate and secure an interim supply of taconite to see them through the necessary period of time. This alternative source likely didn't anticipate the additional need and would have to ramp up production in order to provide the necessary material. This would likely cause a premium to be placed on the material ordered to cover the additional operating cost of the producer.

What would happen to the auto industry and the appliance manufacturing industry that was relying on the steel mill to supply it steel? They would have to scale back their operations or acquire alternative sources of their raw materials.

So you see, any emergency or disaster can have far-reaching consequences and can cause a ripple effect through not only the industries or customers that it touches directly but in the customers of the customers of the customers.

It soon becomes apparent that disaster recovery planning isn't only concerned with the disasters that might befall the organization, but with anything that might happen to impact the organization aversely, whether directly or indirectly.

Vendor Handoffs

It is increasingly the case that vendors and client companies are more than just buyers and sellers. Depending on the organization and the business models involved, many organizations are developing what can be viewed as partnerships with their neighbors in the supply chain rather than simple vendor-customer relationships.

This can mean a lot of different things. It often means that information changes hands at a much broader and more continuous level than in less open models. Many organizations find that their business processing relies upon the availability of the data feeds and information handoffs from these vendors to be able to adequately process their own internal information and vice versa.

Anticipated needs might be handed off to a vendor from a company and in turn available inventory levels might be sent back. This can allow for more appropriate planning on the part of both companies. If a company's information processing relies on the availability of this information, it may be that a company not affected by a disaster may be indirectly affected due to its inability to process internal information as a result of the business partner's inability to provide that information.

Further, the apparently unaffected company may find that it cannot send files to an affected company because of a disaster situation and the files that would, ordinarily, have changed hands either stack up on the unaffected company's servers or are overwritten and the information is lost. In either of these situations, contingency plans are needed concerning what to do with the files and how to make sure that all the information finds its way to where it should be whenever the connections are restored.

Hardware Support

What happens if your vendor supplies you hardware? In the event of a disaster in your company, will it be able to sufficiently supply enough of your hardware needs in this fast-moving and ramped-up situation?

If the workstations for a large number of end users need to be replaced, they will be needed in very little time and with very little notice. If specialized configurations are necessary, it may be that the vendor will not be able to deliver in a timely enough manner or with the exact specifications necessary. You may need to obtain similar hardware from an alternative vendor.

Alternatively, consider a situation where you have a standing order for a number of hardware components with your vendor and an emergency occurs at the vendor site resulting in its inability to fulfill the requirements of the order. Will you be able to acquire similar hardware from another vendor to complete the order and will that acquisition be in a timely enough manner to not cause deleterious effects to your organization?

Special Considerations Some hardware requires lead time because it is specialized to either the requirements of the customer (your company, for example)

or because it is ordered infrequently enough that there is a chance that the configuration in question will become outdated before the preconfigured system is sold. If this is the case and a disaster befalls the client company, it may not be in a position to take delivery of the hardware either when scheduled or in the foreseeable future. Alternatively, if the hardware vendor finds itself in a disaster situation, it may not be able to fulfill specialized orders in a timely manner.

Another special situation arises when your systems are hosted on someone else's hardware or your hardware is housed in someone else's data center. In such cases, little of the actual maintenance and administration are at your disposal. This can be a benefit if you are short of trained staff or budget to obtain one. This can be a drawback if you are concerned about disaster recovery. Nearly all the precautions and planning are outside the control of the organization. Although this may make the company's planning tasks more streamlined, it also means that there are few actual precautions that you can take independent of the facility to ensure that your data is secure and available.

Another way that an organization can be impacted by having all or a portion of its systems hosted and outsourced occurs when Web services are hosted external to the organization. In these cases, even denial of service attacks are outside the control of the organization's system administrators. It also means, again, that much of the control of the organization's disaster recovery planning is in the hands of other people.

When a portion of the disaster recovery responsibility will be in the hands of other people, it is important that the organization take precautions to make sure that legally binding agreements exist with all involved parties to cover the contingencies that may arise. These agreements should include documentation similar to that which the organization itself would accumulate in the disaster recovery planning process and should cover the additional security measures that will be enacted should any kind of emergency situation arise to ensure that the organization's data will not be compromised or that any other organization be allowed to come into contact with the organization's data.

FYI *Floor Space for Rent*

There are data centers that simply provide floor space, utilities, and connectivity for your hardware. Although these centers are more the exception than the rule, they are a handy way for a company to either provide itself with disaster recovery failover capability or with additional (or even primary) data center real estate. This is particularly useful for clients that are currently space constrained or when the per-square-foot cost for building in their own locations are cost prohibitive.

> ▶▶ CONTINUED
>
> Although there are times when someone has to physically access the data center, which may come at an added cost either in terms of additional fees or in terms of time necessary to make such arrangements, there are situations where this kind of service can be very profitable for both parties.

Software Support

The other kind of special vendors that you should pay particular attention to in your planning efforts is software vendors. In your planning documents you should already have a list of all the software assets of the organization, along with the hardware, information, and human assets. Software vendors, or rather their support departments, will be some of your most important assets when the time comes to recover systems. It is important that you understand that if you run into difficulty in your recovery efforts, help desk personnel will become your most relied-upon allies. They will help you through the difficulties that you doubtless will encounter in your endeavors.

Licensing   It is important that you maintain not only the name and contact information of your vendors but licensing information as well. It is often the case that software is licensed for a particular hardware configuration. When that software needs to be installed on a disaster recovery hardware configuration, the recovery will not work without a temporary license for that software on that hardware configuration. Hardware and software vendors are more than willing to assist you in your recovery planning and testing efforts and in your actual recoveries as long as they know that the company has a legitimate license to begin with.

Other software vendors base their support efforts on the level of licensing for your organization in their agreement. Support help desks often are more than willing to assist your efforts, but are occasionally limited in the efforts they can put forth on your behalf based on the level of support your organization has purchased.

Considerations   Another consideration to take into account is the fact that most software vendors support only those releases of their software that are currently active. They maintain on their sites the actively supported versions of their software, and this is the primary set of software that they will help you with. Some will be able to help you with recovery efforts if your organization has access to the software media necessary to do the installation, but if the release you are dealing with is old enough it may not be possible to locate people within the software vendor's organization with sufficient experience with the releases that your organization is dealing with.

6

Downstream Relationships

Not only do you need to make plans for your upstream partners, your vendors, you also need to take into account your downstream relationships, your customers. They are relying on your organization to be there, to be able to operate effectively and efficiently, and to fulfill the requirements of any and all agreements and contracts into which they have entered.

Service Level Agreements with Customers

Recall that service level agreements (SLAs) are legally binding agreements that spell out the available uptime for an organization's systems or the anticipated response time required of an organization should an outage occur.

These agreements are even more important if your organization is the vendor involved in a partnership with the client and file transfers are taking place. If your organization is required to exchange data with its clients or if it is in the position of providing outsourcing or hosting services, it behooves the organization to make sure that all SLAs are in place and that it is capable and prepared for the eventualities of either not being able to deliver on the services contracted upon or the client organization not being able to accept the services when they are delivered.

Directing the Disaster Recovering Team

It will fall to one individual in the disaster recovery drills and in the disaster recovery effort to lead and direct the activities surrounding the exercise.

This person will have to maintain leadership and a strong sense of organization throughout the event. It is important that at no time will the team in a drill be allowed to consider that what they are doing is anything other than the real thing. Drills need to be approached in the same manner as an actual disaster.

It is important to note that many organizations do not announce that a drill will be occurring. There is an announcement (perhaps a phone call in the middle of the night to all relevant individuals or a surprise announcement during working hours) that there is currently a disaster situation and the disaster recovery team should report to the recovery site prepared to recover the organization. This allows those organizations to not only test the mechanics of recovering the organization, but to "stress test," if you will, the process and the participants. It is better to pretend that there is a disaster and uncover potentially fatal (for the organization) flaws in the plan than to uncover those flaws when an actual disaster occurs and there is no margin for error.

Defining Roles and Responsibilities One of the most important things that the disaster recovery team leader needs to do, regardless of the situation, is to define and assign roles and responsibilities as the players arrive at the recovery site. Although these roles may change over the duration of the recovery, it is important that a cohesive team with clearly defined roles is in effect. Allowing individuals to own their positions and responsibilities allows them to perform to the best of their ability and to realize the importance that they play in the overall plan. If, however, the person to whom a role is assigned is unable to fulfill that role, the recovery team leader needs to not hesitate to reassign the role to make sure that the recovery effort goes as planned.

One of the most important roles assigned to a person is to be on site at all times and take notes on the timing, issues, and unexpected occurrences that accompany the disaster recovery. These notes will be invaluable in subsequent planning sessions as a means to work out the issues and the inefficiencies that pop up in the exercise.

This is not to say that everyone involved doesn't need to make their own notes; it is critical to future drills and recoveries that as many notes be taken as possible, without assigning blame and without feeling like those notes will be used against anyone after the recovery. These notes need to be as objective and nonjudgmental as possible. The purpose is not to assign blame but to find where improvements in the process can occur in the future. There should, however, be one single person responsible for maintaining a central copy of everyone's notes so that nothing is lost or forgotten.

Team Actions Following a Disaster or After a Drill

Once a drill or a disaster recovery is completed, the end is still not in sight. Remember, this is a living document, one that will grow over time as the organization grows, that will need to be revisited with every purchase and every change in the way that the organization does business, and that will allow for the additions and changes that are necessary to achieve an efficient recovery.

Debriefing   One of the first things to be done after the recovery, whether it is a true disaster or a drill, is to have everyone that was involved sit down and debrief. This should occur after everyone has had a chance to relax and sleep after the recovery, but it should follow closely on the heels of the recovery effort so people have minimal chance to forget what occurred.

This is often a time when a relaxed road trip will prove useful. With the team members in a central, nonthreatening location where they can talk in a relaxed atmosphere, many things will come out that may not have in a more formal setting. Again, careful notes or audio recording of the proceeding are needed so that nothing is forgotten or missed.

What comes out of this debriefing should be all the wins that the team saw in the process (those places where things went particularly well, or where there were efficiencies gained because of a way that something was handled) and where the team saw losses (those places where things didn't go as planned, or where it was impossible to recover a system at all because of something that may have been out of anyone's control). It is important that both wins and losses are uncovered because there are lessons to be learned from each, and those lessons can be applied to different systems or different places in the process the next time there is a drill or a recovery.

Future Planning   Again, it is important that the organization and all involved view this process as never ending. The document is meant to change over time and evolve as the business evolves. There should never be any doubt that there will continue to be a disaster recovery planning team, although members of the team may need to change over time as the needs of the business and needs of the team change.

This planning will start with the debriefing and lessons learned at the recovery and will continue until the next drill or recovery. There may be a flurry of meetings immediately following the recovery effort, and then the meetings may wane for several months to give everyone time to fully recover from the effort, but they will need to continue. It is critical to the business that they do so.

Summary

You should now be able to identify the documents necessary to support any recovery effort, and maintain the contact information for people inside and outside your organization that you'll need to disseminate information to during a recovery effort. No organization stands alone. Regardless of the type of business you're in, there are vendors upstream who provide you with supplies, raw material, services or information and clients downstream demanding the same from your organization. It is important that these people be kept in mind when creating, testing, and executing your disaster recovery plan. This chapter points out locations where it is necessary to take special precautions and involve these partners to make these relationships disaster-proof.

Test Your Skills

MULTIPLE CHOICE QUESTIONS

1. One of the first things that you need to determine is what _____ you will need as support for the disaster recovery team.

    A. data

    B. software

    C. hardware

    D. documents

2. What should be included with the disaster recovery plan?

    A. installation instructions for any software that is resident on any of the systems

    B. installation media for any software that is resident on any of the systems

    C. license keys for all software on the systems

    D. all of the above

3. One of the most important lists of contact information that needs to be included in the disaster recovery plan is the information necessary to contact _____.

    A. software developers

    B. hardware maintenance

    C. vendors for computer components

    D. support staff

4. Which of the following people should have contact information included in the disaster recovery plan?

    A. subject matter experts

    B. system administrators

    C. system owners of the systems that are being recovered

    D. all of the above

5. A central location where information on the current status of the organization during the emergency recovery is available is known as the _____.

   A. emergency operations center

   B. emergency operations area

   C. emergency operations network

   D. emergency operations core

6. A complete backup of all the files and software on a system or on all the systems in an organization is known as a(n) _____.

   A. incremental backup

   B. hot backup

   C. full backup

   D. cold backup

7. One means that is often used to achieve very high availability of systems is know as _____ backups.

   A. mirror

   B. split-mirror

   C. disaster

   D. precautionary

8. What will spell out the particular duties, responsibilities, and resources available to each member of the team as well as the team as a whole in the event of a disaster?

   A. plan charter

   B. team charter

   C. group charter

   D. backup charter

9. Recovery scenarios are _____.

   A. instructions on how to recover

   B. the different kinds of ways that the organization may be called upon to recover

   C. ways to practice recovery

   D. none of the above

10. Relationships that an organization has with its vendors and suppliers are known as _____ relationships.

    A. material

    B. supply line

    C. downstream

    D. upstream

11. If the supplies you need are something less easily acquired, or that require a longer lead time, it might be important to know about _____.

    A. manufacturing methods

    B. alternate objects

    C. alternative sources

    D. all of the above

12. Some hardware requires _____ because it is specialized to the requirements of the customer.

    A. preparation staging

    B. lead time

    C. development time

    D. staging time

13. When you have your systems hosted on someone else's hardware or you have your hardware housed in someone else's data center _____.

    A. you do not have to worry about disaster recovery

    B. little of the disaster recovery planning is your responsibility

    C. little of the actual maintenance and administration are at your disposal

    D. you should have access to all maintenance and administration

14. It is important that you maintain not only the name and contact information for the software vendors but _____ as well.

    A. software keys

    B. software files

    C. data key files

    D. licensing information

15. It is important to upgrade software so that you stay with supportable versions because _____.

    A. your organization might require time-critical support

    B. it might not be practical to find individuals with appropriate expertise in an older, unsupported release

    C. software companies are usually willing to support releases one behind the currently supported versions, but not much past that

    D. all of the above

16. Not only do you need to make plans for your upstream partners, your vendors, you also need to take into account your downstream relationships, your _____.

    A. vendors

    B. customers

    C. suppliers

    D. service partners

17. Legally binding agreements that spell out the available uptime for an organization's systems or the anticipated response time required of an organization should an outage occur are known as _____.

    A. service level agreements

    B. service level licenses

    C. software level agreements

    D. working level agreements

18. One of the first things to be done after the recovery, whether it is a true disaster or a drill, is to have everyone that was involved sit down and _____.

    A. debrief

    B. relax

    C. explain the plan

    D. all of the above

EXERCISES

Exercise 6.1: Accounting Recovery

1. Imagine working for a small accounting firm in your area. You are in charge of developing its recovery plan. All records for the firm are kept on the computers in the office.

2. There are five computers that contain accounting records in the office, and all are critical to the operation of the firm. Assume that the firm uses a standard Windows application for its accounting practices.

3. Develop a written procedure to recover a computer in the firm if the hard drive in the computer fails. The only application on the computer is the accounting application, and a backup of the data is taken each night to a local tape drive that all of the computers share over a small network.

Exercise 6.2: Complex Application Recovery

1. You have been tasked to write the recovery procedure for a complex Web-based application at your small brokerage house.

2. The firm uses outsourced resources to maintain the level of uptime required by both its users and federal regulations.

3. Assume that the outsourcing firm only provides the "hands" to maintain the applications. Develop the procedure to recover the customer trading portal. The recovery procedure serves two purposes, a recovery procedure in case of complete disaster at the outsourcing company and an installation guide for the outsourcing company to set up the application for the first time.

Exercise 6.3: Mirrors, Mirrors Everywhere

1. Disk mirroring technology is fairly straightforward, but each vendor has its own unique twist.

2. Using the Dell, EMC, and StorageTek Web sites, describe the hardware technologies offered by these companies for mirrors used on individual servers, not those for use by multiple computers.

3. Create a chart to describe the differentiating factors of each solution. It is important to note if any vendor offers a complete solution, that is, whether the solution relies on preexisting server hardware to complete the solution.

Exercise 6.4: Electronic Mail Is Critical

1. You work for an IT organization that maintains the Microsoft Exchange 2003 environment for 10,000 users. Your organization considers the electronic mail to be a mission-critical application.

2. Users must have access to their mail at any time. Using the resources at the Microsoft Web site, develop the list of tools you would need to maintain the 24-hour access that users need.

Exercise 6.5: Backup Plan

1. You have 300 users with their files on a single file server, and you need to back up that data so that a user never loses a file.

2. Develop the backup plan to ensure that your users never lose a file more than an hour old.

3. Develop the recovery procedure to recover a file if a user should happen to accidentally delete a file.

Exercise 6.6: Mainframe Failure

1. You have a central data center with a large enterprise-class mainframe that handles all the processing for your organization.

2. While working on the air conditioning of the building a contractor accidentally hit the cooling line to the mainframe, allowing the mainframe to overheat and require serious repair.

3. What agreements should the center have in place to make this emergency not cause a long-term outage for the company?

Exercise 6.7: Software Support

1. Your company has a large software investment with a single software vendor that supplies most of the components for your administrative system.

2. Are there special considerations you should have with this vendor to ensure a smooth recovery in case of a disaster in your company?

Exercise 6.8: Service Level Agreements

1. Almost all agreements with vendors involve a service level agreement, which defines the level of performance that each company will expect from each other.

2. You are evaluating the agreements that your company has with your software vendors.

3. Describe how you will measure the performance of an agreement with a software vendor and what considerations you should include in the agreement.

PROJECTS

Project 6.1: Advanced Recovery

1. Your company has a high-use Web application that allows your users to order your products and track their orders.

2. The Web-based application uses a back-end database server to hold all data. The database is backed up each day and the transaction logs are written to tape every hour.

3. Assume a total disaster where you must recover the application from scratch. The disaster destroyed the servers, but remarkably did not damage any of the tapes that were still in the tape backup system.

4. Develop a general plan to recover the application as quickly as possible, which will require bringing back both the front- and back-end servers.

Project 6.2: Emergency Operations

1. A major hurricane has struck the area where your company has its central data center. There are offsite backups and hardware at three other centers around the country.

2. Assume that the area is suffering greatly from the hurricane's impact, and your company cannot continue operations until the central data center's operations resume.

3. Briefly describe the activities that need to occur to set up the emergency operation center for your company, and where your company should locate the center.

Project 6.3: Complex Vendor Emergency

1. Your company has relationships with several upstream vendors. Many of these vendors are local to your operation from a supply perspective.

2. Your company can do without components from any single vendor for up to one week but no longer, or production of your primary product will cease.

3. The executive management has asked that the company consider developing a strategy for surviving a longer outage with up to three suppliers. Develop a plan or strategy that would allow the company to survive for up to two weeks without supplies from three of the primary vendors.

▶▶ Case **Study**

You are helping to prepare the recovery plan for a medium-sized business in the manufacturing industry that has one physical location. All operations occur at this location. Construct a recovery charter for this company.

Chapter | 7

Developing Procedures for Special Circumstances

Chapter Objectives

After reading this chapter and completing the exercises, you will be able to do the following:

- Identify emergency situations that may occur during a recovery.
- Determine what can be done if an emergency occurs during an emergency situation.
- Assess the risks associated with disaster recovery.
- Identify gaps in emergency recovery situations and plan accordingly.

Introduction

The best-laid plans often go awry. What will happen when all the hard work you have done suddenly hits a snag and you have to deal with emergencies during the emergencies? We have seen that it is important to have a plan for just about any contingency that might arise in an organization. If the primary plan cannot be followed, having a backup plan will assist with alleviating the stress that will occur. This will also provide you and your organization with a fall back point to assist those performing the recovery and provide stability for them when they will likely need it most.

The disaster recovery effort, whether a planned practice or an actual emergency situation, is stressful enough. Change is difficult for many people, and the added change of changing the changes may be too much for them in such a short time. Knowing that there is a plan for this kind of situation will ease the peace of mind of not only those involved, but also those stakeholders who are relying on the recovery to occur seamlessly.

Emergencies During the Emergency

Planning for emergencies is something that a well-prepared organization does. But what happens when—even if you have a disaster recovery plan, have tested it, and are comfortable with the plan and its execution—the unimaginable occurs: you have to declare a disaster and go through the recovery plan for real? Do you think that is the worst that could happen? It isn't.

Imagine that you have declared your disaster and are proceeding with the recovery. Something happens during the recovery that constitutes an emergency or yet another disaster. What can happen now?

Does your organization's preparedness plan encompass the potential eventuality of having to face an emergency at the disaster recovery site? Have you prepared for such an eventuality? Have the necessary steps been taken to ensure that you could pick up and move to yet another site in order to recover your organization? What will this do to the SLAs that your organization has in place? Does your recovery site have plans in place for these kinds of eventualities?

FYI · *Wording SLAs*

It is possible to word SLAs in such a way as to make sure that the organization is covered in the eventuality that an emergency within an emergency should present itself. It is in an organization's best interest to make sure that the SLAs that are in place are written such that, should an emergency occur during the recovery effort, the clock is reset to that time and the SLAs are not violated.

Concrete, realistic, and measurable commitments are important for a successful SLA. If your SLA includes a clause identifying the potential for an intra-emergency emergency, specify that your organization will have the additional days necessary to relocate and re-recover the data. If you have agreed upon 72 hours for recovery, word your additional emergency clause to specify that, in the event that a disaster that is declared within a disaster, an additional 72 hours will be allotted for the recovery from the second disaster and that this 72 hours will commence at the declaration of the disaster and will supersede the time allotted for the declaration of the original disaster.

Not limiting the extra disasters to a second one will also cover any eventuality that may occur that causes the organization to declare disaster after disaster. Although this is definitely a worst case scenario, it should not be discounted.

Support Contracts

Chapter 2 looked at the necessity for support contracts for your organization as well as for a disaster situation. But what about support contracts as they might apply should a second emergency or disaster occur while the organization is in the process of recovery from the initial disaster? Does the organization have the contracts in line to be able to cover itself should this kind of situation arise? Arrangements with many software vendors can put the organization on better footing should the need arise to make this kind of adjustment in recovery.

Further, it is important that the organization have support contracts with the recovery location should it become necessary to relocate the disaster recovery effort to another location. Although it may seem overly cautious to talk to the recovery site company about the eventuality of the recovery site either not being available when needed by the organization or needing to relocate to an alternative site in the midst of an ongoing recovery, it is in the best interests of both the organization and the recovery site to have all of the relevant information on the table up front.

Because of the nature of its business, the recovery company should already have in place arrangements for this kind of eventuality. If it does not it should raise questions about the suitability of the recovery site for the choice of recovery location. Because the organization doing the planning should have any emergency eventuality uppermost in its mind when determining what contracts to sign and what recommendations to make, the question of what would happen should an emergency befall the recovery site should be among the questions asked. However, often these questions are not asked, and the contracts that should be in place are not.

FYI   *Home-Based Businesses*

Although this section appears to be directed primarily at organizations of significant size, it is just as important for small organizations, including home-based businesses, to be aware of the need for plans for what might happen should additional emergency situations occur.

Many of the needs of this type of organization are commodity in nature, and they can be acquired in almost any location with very little notice. However, many cottage industries rely on either customized software or software that is not always freely accessible in all locations. Special arrangements may need to be made with software, hardware, or machine vendors to speed shipment of specialized tools to alternative locations. If those alternative locations should have to change, it is important that the shipments be re-routable with little burden on either the manufacturer (reseller) or the buyer.

Disaster Recovery Contracts

As we have already discussed to a small degree, it is important for all concerned to have disaster recovery contracts and contracts concerning what to do in the eventuality of an emergency occurring in the midst of an emergency. But what happens once you have your contracts? Organizations typically keep these documents in safe locations, locked up where they will not be affected by emergency situations or where they can be easily accessed in the event that they need to be referenced or renegotiated. These precautions are all well and good, but how accessible will these documents be in the midst of an emergency? If they are needed for reference at any point, are they in a location or format that is easily accessible to the recovery team? If it becomes necessary to move the recovery location, can the necessary documents be easily and readily accessed?

It is important that all relevant documents, or more appropriately either electronic or photocopies of these documents, be kept with every set of backups that the organization maintains for the eventuality of a disaster recovery.

IN PRACTICE: BS Sunlight Application Service Provider

BS Sunlight is an application service provider to many organizations. It has in place a disaster recovery plan and tests it every year to some degree. It has a backup strategy that is commensurate with its recovery plan, which covers all SLAs.

The backup strategy dictates that a full set of backup tapes be maintained in waterproof cases and stored offsite in a secure location, and that these backups can be obtained only by a certain set of management members and only under certain circumstances.

The waterproof cases contain a full set of all manuals on CDs and DVDs for all of the systems that will be necessary to recover. The recovery documents—in hard copy, on CD and DVD, and embedded within the backups of the servers—are included, as are copies of all contracts that may become necessary, complete with full contact information for all vendors and all support information in both hard copy and scanned or stored on CD and DVD format.

Because BS Sunlight has determined that it wants to be able to recover the business regardless of the severity of the emergency situation and regardless of the situation in which it finds itself, it has made the business decision to take these steps so that it can recover the business regardless of what may befall either the primary site or one of the backup sites with which it has contracted.

Preparations

When an organization prepares for the eventuality of an emergency in its primary location, it takes certain steps in order to become prepared. Backups are put in place and are taken routinely. Security measures are put in place and followed. But when individuals are thrust into unfamiliar surroundings or are working under conditions of additional stress, shortcuts are often taken, either deliberately or inadvertently, that could cause the organization to be at risk.

Under these circumstances, backup are often not undertaken at as regular an interval as they were in the primary location. There are even organizations who have made the decision to outsource their IT services to better fit with their business plan yet who assign their backup tape rotation to one or more employees whose main job (due primarily or in part to the outsourcing) is not IT related. The employees are supposed to care for the tapes and make sure that they stay safe and that the logical rotation is maintained. Because the employees do not understand the ramifications of what is being asked, backup jobs may be missed, tape rotation may not occur in a timely manner, tapes may not be maintained as diligently as necessary, or rotation may not occur in the correct order and the necessary backup may be overwritten before it should have been. It is often necessary to make sure that the persons assigned to the backups are either IT trained or have sufficient understanding of the steps necessary and the criticality of the job before they are assigned to perform the tasks. Even well-written documentation, if there is not underlying understanding at some level, may not be enough.

7

Identifying the Gaps in Your Recovery Plans

In any organization's attempts—particularly early attempts—at disaster recovery planning and testing, gaps in what people think will happen and what actually happens appear. One prime example occurred in the wake of the September 11th terrorist attacks. Many organizations realized that their disaster recovery plans were lacking and decided that they needed to do something about it. The gaps that many organizations found were made apparent because of their inability to recover in a timely manner from the disaster.

When gaps were discovered the companies worked hard to overcome them, and nearly 2 years later, when the August 2003 blackout hit the East Coast of the United States, many organizations had installed electrical generators that would provide their computer systems with power. This allowed them to continue to do business on a limited scale. Even companies not directly affected by the terrorist attacks worked on making their DR plans more robust and were better prepared for the blackouts that crippled much of the Northeast for more than a day.

Many of the gaps that organizations strove to fill in this example were not gaps that were found in the process of testing efforts or even in the midst of their own disaster recovery. They were, however, still gaps in planning.

In the cycle of planning, backing up, testing recovery, and restarting the cycle, organizations typically find their own gaps, such as places where backups have been insufficient, where systems were missed entirely in the inventory phases, and where the knowledge and ability of those involved in the exercise is found to need augmenting. These are discussed next.

Backups

Backups are one of the first areas where gaps are identified. Either the backup is not broad enough to capture enough of the system to be able to recover in a disaster situation, or the backup media and methods are not entirely compatible with the hardware and topology of the recovery location.

IN PRACTICE: BS Sunlight's Backup Strategy

BS Sunlight put its disaster recovery plans in place. Backups were taken on a regular basis and testing was planned for the summer months.

The disaster recovery team made the journey to the recovery site and started the recovery drill as if it were a disaster. The recovery media made it to the recovery site successfully and on time. Most of the systems were up and running with sufficient time to make sure that the SLAs would not have been missed had this been an actual disaster recovery situation.

However, on one set of systems, it was discovered that the hardware that the recovery center had substituted in place of the hardware that the organization was using (the recovery center substituted newer models for older, which was within the bounds of the contract) was not completely compatible with the backup media or the backup method chosen by the organization. This meant that several key systems in the organization were unable to be recovered during the testing. Both the methods and media used for the backups and the contracts with the recovery location company were examined in an effort to make sure that this gap did not continue and was accounted for in subsequent tests.

Testing

Gaps are often discovered in testing efforts. These typically are not found during the testing session in which the gaps occur. They often are discovered in subsequent testing when tests fail, or in actual disaster situations when systems that are turned over to the end user do not perform adequately.

These gaps normally can be uncovered if the test is run as if it were an actual disaster situation. In this case, the actual systems at the primary location are left intact and running, but the recovery effort progresses as if it were a disaster. Often, those involved in the recovery effort are not entirely sure if it is a test or a recovery.

When the recovery is complete, the entire system is switched from the primary location to the backup location and business continues for a period of time on the recovered system as if it were the primary location. In this way, more of the system can be tested and more gaps in testing are likely to be discovered.

Systems

It may seem counterintuitive that an organization can overlook critical systems in its planning and recovery efforts. However, it is not uncommon for an organization to find that, either in the midst of a test or, worse, in the midst of a recovery, one or more functional areas of the organization have overlooked a PC or server sitting under someone's desk that is business critical to some process.

Typically these oversights are honest mistakes. A department will have acquired a system that runs only on a platform that the organization does not have the expertise to maintain. They don't think about the system unless there is a problem with it, and then only to the extent necessary to keep the system functioning.

Backups are often not done on a regular basis. If they are done, they may not be tested fully. Further, accurate records on license and support details may not be readily available.

Because functional people often consider that they only work on "the accounting system" or the "HR system" they don't (and maybe shouldn't have to) delineate the difference between using the primarily supported systems and the ones that are supported outside official administration circles.

Hopefully these missing pieces are found in the testing phase of the disaster recovery planning. If they are not uncovered until a true disaster recovery there may be little recourse for the organization other than to attempt to, as rapidly as possible, recreate the system to whatever extent possible and attempt to recover the functionality, possibly with limited or no access to data that might be associated with the system. At best, the organization may see the recovery take longer than expected. At worst, it may see an extended impact on the ability to do business for a longer period of time than should be possible otherwise.

If the missing system is identified in the testing situation, extensive notes should be made on what the gap is and what systems are affected by the missing system and its functionality. When the trial recovery is over, special effort should be made to make sure that the system in question complies with the organizational standards on backups and recoverability. At the very least, the contact information and the knowledge of the system should make it into the recovery documentation.

People

Some of the biggest gaps found in disaster recovery planning concern the people involved. People gaps are discovered in not only the area of people involved in the disaster recovery (or the recovery test) but in the areas of planning and end-user testing.

If the wrong people are involved in the planning effort, other gaps can be discovered because of the missing knowledge of systems that need to be included or in the ways that backups need to be accomplished to meet the need of recovery. If all levels of management are not included, or all stakeholders in the planning process are not taken into account, the potential of not meeting SLAs might prove to be costly to the organization.

People gaps that occur in the disaster recovery testing effort, particularly in early testing efforts, can be equally as costly. Although eventually the organization will want to have as many people as possible involved so that they can be considered trained in the recovery process, in early testing attempts it is important that knowledgeable people be involved because these tests will provide the foundation for all future testing and for the ultimate test, an actual recovery.

In later testing efforts, it is often beneficial to have inexperienced individuals placed into roles that they may not be well suited for. This will show where there are inconsistencies in the plan or in the documentation. Once the plan is established and the tests have been successful for a period of time, it is important to foolproof the tests so that anyone that needs to be drafted to fill positions can follow the documentation successfully. This can give the organization the assurance that anyone can be called upon in a disaster to fill the position and provide the needed support.

Disaster recovery professionals often suggest that you write your disaster recovery instructions so that anyone (even employees with no ties to the IT department or even the day-to-day workings of the company) could use them to recover the system. If this is the case, you can rest assured that your documentation is sufficiently thorough to provide the necessary coverage. It is not a comforting thought that most organizations are not sufficiently well prepared enough to make this claim.

You may have all the right people involved in the planning and recovery efforts, but if you don't have the right people involved in testing that the recovery is successful and accurate, then all of the effort that has been put into the planning, the backups, and the recovery will be for naught.

Again, finding out that you don't have the right people in place isn't the worst thing that can happen, particularly if you find out before a disaster has been declared. First, you have gained the insight of the people that you do

have, right or wrong, and no insight will have gone to waste. Further, you can augment the team, wherever the inconsistencies are, with more appropriate people. It would not be the recommended way to staff the planning or the recovery testing team, but experience is gained from the existence of the inconsistencies.

Identifying Disaster Recovery Risks

There are always risks associated with doing business, even in a perfect world. There are additional risks associated with being in a disaster recovery situation.

Location

One of the risks associated with a disaster recovery situation involves the fact that everyone is in an unfamiliar location. Although this is not typically considered a risk in itself, it contributes to risk because of the heightened stress associated even with a testing situation. It can have one of two effects. Often those involved will become overly cautious in their actions and not perform as rapidly or as efficiently as necessary. This can be even more of an issue if everyone is aware that the drill that they are involved in is not an actual disaster situation but a testing situation. Conversely, the individuals can become less cautious than they may be in other situations, more aggressive, and pay less attention to detail than might be prudent. In this case, mistakes can be made. These can be costly if the drill is not a testing situation; they could mean the difference between the company meeting its SLAs and having to pay fines for not meeting them.

If the individuals involved in the recovery are aware that it is a test and not a true disaster, the exercise may be viewed as a paid working holiday, and receive less seriousness than should be accorded. When this is the situation often less is accomplished than should be. This is one reason that some organizations, when planning tests, don't include everyone in the planning, but spring the trip on them under the guise of an actual disaster. This means that fewer people will have the tendency to look on the situation as relaxed free time and will more likely strive to meet the deliverable timelines.

Situation

Because the recovery team is in an unfamiliar location and working in an unfamiliar environment, they are likely to be less mindful of security precautions if they are different than those at the primary work location. Security measures often are more stringent at a recovery site, and people accustomed to more lax security measures may inadvertently counter the security measures that are in place.

Further, old work habits and working hours may remain. Disaster situations, regardless of whether tests or declared disasters, call for extraordinary practices—longer than usual work hours, altered work schedules, and working under conditions other than what everyone is used to. Unaccustomed managers will deliver instructions and directions and unusual work environments will make many of those involved uncomfortable.

Systems

There are additional risks in that recovery will be performed on different systems than everyone is used to dealing with. This may not seem like an apparent risk—after all, a system is a system. It is little more than a bunch of commodity pieces put together to form more commodity pieces on which the recovery team will recover the organization's software and systems. However, every system has its own idiosyncrasies and its own security precautions in place to keep intruders out.

It is common to assume that because there are contracts in place, the recovery will go smoothly because the hardware is compatible. Hardware is often considered to be interchangeable because it is a commodity item. This is not necessarily the case, however. There are occasions when, even though contracts are in place and hardware has been provided as compatible, it is difficult, if not impossible, to recover.

IN PRACTICE: BS Sunlight

The systems administrator and database administrator for BS Sunlight run a regularly scheduled recovery test, which proceeds in the usual manner. However, for this recovery testing, the hardware (which the contract states must be compatible with what the organization has) was changed because the hardware that BS Sunlight used for tape backups was outdated and newer hardware, capable of reading the same kinds of tapes, was substituted.

No one, even after being alerted to the substitution, anticipated that it would be an issue. However, when the recovery started, it quickly became apparent that the new tape drives were in fact not able to read the tapes brought for the recovery. Despite the best efforts of the organization's contracts with the recovery site and the software support contracts with all of the software vendors, it was impossible to recover the operating system to such a state that it was able to be used, let alone any of the databases that

▶▶ CONTINUED ON NEXT PAGE

resided on that system. The gap was not in the people or in having the necessary contracts in place. The gap was that the recovery site did not have a proven method for assuring that the contracted hardware was provided and in place when needed, and that any contracted organization could successfully recover its systems should the need arise.

Summary

Emergencies can happen at any time, even when you're already in the midst of one. This chapter demonstrates the importance of preparing your organization for an emergency situation, or even a disaster situation, in the midst of an existing emergency. These emergencies may be similar to the existing emergency, or they can arise because insufficient or misdirected testing or other preparedness issues. This chapter should help you identify potential issues and protect yourself from further harm.

7

Test Your Skills

MULTIPLE CHOICE QUESTIONS

1. Having a(n) _____ plan for the eventuality that the primary plan cannot be followed will assist in alleviating the stress that occurs during a disaster.

   A. fallback

   B. operational

   C. backup

   D. functional

2. Knowing that there is a secondary plan when the primary plan cannot be followed will ease the minds of _____ who are relying on the recovery to occur seamlessly.

   A. stakeholders

   B. employees

   C. company officials

   D. all of the above

3. It is in an organization's best interest to make sure that the _____ that are in place are written such that, should an emergency occur during the recovery effort, the clock is reset to that time.

    A. plans

    B. contingency plans

    C. SLAs

    D. emergency notes

4. The question of what would happen should an emergency befall the _____ should be among the questions asked when determining what contracts to sign.

    A. recovery site

    B. recovery team

    C. primary site

    D. backup team

5. If alternative locations should have to change, it is important that shipments be _____ with little burden on either the manufacturer (reseller) or the buyer.

    A. canceled

    B. reroutable

    C. reordered

    D. none of the above

6. When individuals are thrust into unfamiliar surroundings or are working under conditions of additional stress, _____ are often taken that could cause the organization to be at risk.

    A. contingencies

    B. thoughtless actions

    C. shortcuts

    D. security risks

7. Typically, in the cycle of planning, backing up, testing recovery, and restarting the cycle, organizations find _____ in planning.

    A. gaps

    B. inconsistencies

    C. problems

    D. organizational discrepancies

8. One of the first areas in which people identify gaps is in _____.

    A. planning

    B. virtual security

    C. physical security

    D. backups

9. Gaps are often discovered in _____ efforts.

    A. planning

    B. security

    C. testing

    D. none of the above

10. It is not uncommon for an organization to find that one or more
    functional areas of the organization have overlooked a PC or
    server sitting under someone's desk that is _____ to some
    process.

    A. business critical

    B. security dependent

    C. organizationally imperative

    D. mission dependent

11. It often occurs that some of the biggest gaps found in disaster recovery
    planning is in the area of the _____ involved.

    A. systems

    B. security

    C. vendors

    D. people

12. If the _____ are involved in the planning effort, gaps can be
    discovered because of the missing knowledge of systems that need to
    be included or in the ways that backups need to be accomplished to
    meet the need of recovery.

    A. wrong people

    B. wrong vendors

    C. stakeholders

    D. wrong system administrators

7

13. One of the risks associated with a disaster recovery situation involves the fact that everyone is in an unfamiliar _____.

    A. situation

    B. area

    C. location

    D. arena

14. Because the recovery team is in an unfamiliar location, they are likely to be less mindful of _____ if they are different than those at the primary work location.

    A. system usage logs

    B. security precautions

    C. logon procedures

    D. system adaptations

15. Hardware is often considered to be interchangeable because it is a(n) _____ item.

    A. common

    B. inexpensive

    C. interchangeable

    D. commodity

EXERCISES

Exercise 7.1: Testing

1. You have been asked to test the disaster recovery plan for a small business in your area. The company has a backup plan that is well documented.

2. Describe the steps you would use to test the plan to ensure that the backup plan would function in case of an actual emergency.

Exercise 7.2: Risks

1. All disaster recoveries are at risk during a recovery. Many agencies have specific minimum requirements for recovery plans.

2. Research the minimum requirements for state agencies in your home state as well as the minimum requirements for federal agencies. Write a summary of these requirements.

Exercise 7.3: Filling the Human Gap

1. You work for a medium-sized manufacturing company that has a well-developed disaster recovery plan. The plan is well tested and the testing has revealed a serious personnel gap.

2. During a recovery, key personnel in the manufacturing process are unionized (the collective bargaining agreement specifies that only union workers may complete these tasks), and the collective bargaining agreement does not specify either payment for union employees or the use of alternative personnel during emergencies.

3. Provide a well-reasoned argument that would allow your company to use nonunion workers or allow the company to correct the personnel gap during an emergency.

Exercise 7.4: Conduct a Poll

1. Locate five similar companies in your area and ask those that have tested recovery plans if there are gaps in their plan.

2. Of those companies that respond that they do have gaps, document how they plan to address those gaps in their recovery plans.

PROJECTS

Project 7.1: Overcoming Flaws

1. There are risks to any company's recovery location. Identify a company in your area and ask about its recovery location.

2. List the risks associated with the company's choice of recovery location and possible mitigation strategies.

Case Study

A new application service provider has asked for help in developing a recovery plan. Develop a set of guidelines that can help the company develop a comprehensive recovery plan, including emergencies during a recovery.

Chapter | 8

Testing the Disaster Recovery Plan

Chapter Objectives

After reading this chapter and completing the exercises, you will be able to do the following:

- Explain the necessity of practicing the DR plan.
- Describe the different kinds of tests that can be performed.
- Determine the impact of testing activities.
- Understand the need for change control.
- Describe methods of change control.

Introduction

Now you have a plan, but a plan is only as good as its ability to work. It isn't a recovery if you cannot recover. This chapter will walk you through the test and help you to learn from the testing situation so that in the event of an actual emergency you know where to turn for information.

Rehearsing the DR Plan

Everyone has to rehearse. Athletes practice (alone and as a team), actors and actresses practice their lines (both at formal practices and alone), and musicians rehearse (alone with their music and as a group). The disaster recovery team needs to be no less diligent. There are times and places where people can practice different recovery scenarios alone (in a test environment, for example) to make sure that scripts and techniques are working as anticipated. However, to work effectively as a team recovery drills need to occur and notes need to be taken so everyone can learn from what has been done.

It is vital to the organization and the success of the disaster recovery plan that the plan be thoroughly tested on an annual basis. It is often not practical to test it more frequently. A well tuned and repeatable test plan needs to be written that documents what is to be included in the testing, the anticipated time lines and outcomes, and the criteria for a successful test or the criteria for failing a portion of the test. The test will provide the organization with the assurance that all necessary steps are included in the disaster recovery plan, and that the organization is in good standing and will be able to recover sufficiently rapidly so as to continue to do business in a profitable manner.

Although this is the primary reason to test the recovery plan, there are also other reasons for testing, which are discussed next.

Reasons for Testing the Disaster Recovery Plan

By testing the recovery plan you can determine the feasibility and compatibility of backup facilities and procedures. You may find places where data is not being backed up as anticipated or where you have forgotten that a set of files cannot be backed up while open, yet the backup procedure does not account for this inconsistency.

By testing the plan, you can identify areas that need modification. You may anticipate that one part can be done at the same time as another, but in testing you discover that one relies on the other being done first. You may find that the time to recover a component is shorter than anticipated, resulting in wasted downtime. You may find that you have not allocated enough time and there is no way to have it done in time for the next steps to occur.

Testing is an optimal way of providing training to the team's managers and members, and even potential team members, on how to recover the organization from a disaster. It is also good training for administrators on how to recover their systems in the event of loss of service that is not deemed to be a disaster, but that impacts the system or the organization aversely. Through testing, it is possible to provide (to business partners, stakeholders, and shareholders) proof that the organization can recover from a disaster in a timely manner and that the bottom line will be minimally impacted.

Testing can also be a means of providing motivation for maintaining and updating the recovery plan, to keep it a living document. Without the impetus of testing the recoverability of the organization based on the outcome of tests based on the plan, it is easy for an organization and a team to become complacent. Without the shot of adrenaline that accompanies the testing, without the change of pace that accompanies doing something radically different from the day-to-day business of keeping the business running, it is easy for the team to lose momentum and interest in the process.

If testing is so critical to a recovery plan, why doesn't everyone do it? Organizations that don't do testing state that they don't because it is a drain on time and resources (human as well as monetary). Rarely do they think through what might happen with an untested and untried recovery plan.

Considering the Impact of Testing on the Organization's Activities

One of the considerations in disaster recovery testing is the impact that the exercise will have on the organization. Business as usual will have to continue for the majority of the organization. The systems that are being recovered on alternate hardware have to continue to work as normal on the hardware that they are running on for the production systems.

This may sound obvious, but it is important that those involved remember this. The testers will have left positions where they have full-time jobs. The duties associated with keeping the primary business running will have to be picked up by other members of the organization. Work can't stop just because the team members are doing something else. Often the recovery team does the testing over a weekend, when most of the organization is not likely to be working. This minimizes the impact of the missing people to the organization. It makes for a long week for those on the team, however.

Network addresses and IP address also have to be addressed as potential places where the organization could be impacted. The systems that are being recovered will have, at least initially, the same IP addresses as their production counterparts. This means that the same network that is used for production cannot be used for these recoveries at the same time. It also means that the recovery team has limited access to the outside world.

IN PRACTICE: Database Recovery Gone Bad

GBS Company was practicing its recovery on a set of servers in the basement of one of its IT employees. It was decided that a few run-throughs would allow it to find the bugs in the plan before spending the money needed to move the trial to another cold site location. The company recovered most of the servers and services without a hitch. However, when it brought up the database it drove its work-flow processing, hundreds of purchase orders (orders that had

▶▶ CONTINUED ON NEXT PAGE

already been processed, many of which had already been filled) went out to vendors via email.

GBS had not disabled outgoing email from the servers because it had hoped to test all of its systems. Because these new servers had the same IP addresses as their production counterparts, the emails were sent from an appropriately named server. All purchase orders had to be tracked down and vendors contacted to prevent duplicate orders from being processed.

Had the IP addresses been changed, the data in the database that routed the purchase order requests to the mail server would have failed (GBS set up its servers to allow only outgoing mail sent from inside the firewall to be routed through the mail servers, so any attempt that the workflow mailer might have made to send the purchase orders would have been fruitless).

In the end, part of the disaster recovery testing resulted in a small disaster of its own making.

It is important to remember that because the recovery is taking place at an alternative site, a cost is associated with the recovery testing, as well as a recovery proper. There will likely be a travel cost associated with getting the team there, housing cost, meals cost, car rental cost, and other associated costs. This can detract, in the eyes of the organization, from the desirability of testing overall. It is important to understand that the cost, however, is minimal when compared to the potential savings that can result from actually having exercised the recovery plan and knowing that the plan will work.

Developing Testing Criteria and Procedures

As with any kind of test, the disaster recovery test needs to have a set of criteria set so that everyone knows whether the plan and the team have passed. Care should be taken when determining what needs to occur for it to pass and how many errors the test can have, and in what places, before it fails.

The criteria for what constitutes a disaster need to be established at the organizational level. At what point is it necessary to announce to the world that a recovery situation is imminent and at what point is it still an internal recovery? There are often events in an organization (database crashes, network issues, even data corruption issues) that can be handled internally without anyone having to be alerted.

The criteria for what passing means and the limits within which the test needs to be passed must be determined in advance. There will likely be deviations, particularly in early attempts. These deviations may be in response time or in network settings or connectivity. Many will be easily fixed within the time allotted for the recovery test; some will not. Accurate notes should be taken concerning what issues presented themselves and what was done to fix them.

It is possible, in parallel, to create the procedures that need to be followed in order to not only arrive safely at the recovery site, but also those leading up to the beginning of the recovery test and in the test proper. These procedures often include flight information from the nearest airport or to the airport closest to the recovery site (for those sites that are far enough away to require that kind of information). Although flight information may change from one recovery test or recovery to the next, it will give everyone an idea of what schedules will be like and can be kept easily updated during the periods between tests. Because the type and severity of a potential disaster is hard to predict, it is often wise to include more than one airport in the procedures because the closest airport may be affected by the same emergency as the organization. Further, several copies of maps from the organization to the recovery site can be included in the documentation to assist those who will not be flying or in the event that flight is not an option.

The procedure document needs to include information on determining what constitutes a disaster that can be recovered at the organization site and what constitutes one that needs to be declared and recovered offsite. (See Appendix A.) The procedure for declaring a disaster and contact information for everyone internal and external to the organization needs to be included in those procedures, or referenced as an external document if it is located elsewhere in the disaster recovery plan.

IN PRACTICE: Geekbooks Inc

Joy, sole proprietor and writer for Geekbooks Inc, located in Taylor, Texas, has created her company testing criteria and processes. She determined that if she could acquire a replacement PC or laptop comparable to the one that she uses and recover her system to a productive state within a day of an emergency, then she would not have to relocate herself and her business and would not have to declare her situation a disaster.

She determined that if she had to relocate herself for the purpose of recovery, she would relocate her family and her business to eastern Ohio, which is far enough away for the disaster to likely not be affected, has easy access, and where she still has family. She located several hotels in the area that would be adequate to house her recovery and several hardware and software vendors in the area that

▶▶ CONTINUED ON NEXT PAGE

would likely be able to fill the needs of her business. Further, because she was storing an auxiliary backup of her data with family in the area, she would have ready access to those backups.

She determined what milestones her organization would have to pass in order to be recoverable, and what level of data inaccuracy and incompleteness she was willing to accept in order to claim to be recovered.

She added this document to her soft copy documentation, sent a copy of the document offsite to the local bank where she stores one set of her backups, and sent another copy to her family with whom she stores her auxiliary documentation and backups. In this way, she can access the documentation wherever she needs to recover her systems and she doesn't have to worry about what she needs to have readily packed should she need to relocate.

These procedures are typically a higher level plan than the nuts and bolts of performing the recovery and testing it afterwards, but it is important that nothing be left out or taken for granted at this point.

After testing and recovery procedures and criteria have been completed, an initial test of the plan should be performed. This can be done by conducting a structured walk-through test, which will provide you with additional information on any further steps that may need to be included in the planning documents, changes in procedures that are not effective, and other appropriate adjustments to the plan. The plan should be adjusted to correct any problems that are identified by the initial test and any subsequent tests.

Using a Step-By-Step Process to Test the Plan

The testing of the plan should be broken into sections. The least intrusive sections of the plan can be tested during normal business hours as a means to minimize disruptions to the overall operations of the organization. Other portions of the early testing could be scheduled during maintenance windows when access to the system is greatly minimized or not allowed.

A step-by-step process should be created and followed for everything that is to be tested, along with expected results of the tests that are performed during the recovery test. This is just as important in the smaller tests as it is in an over-all system recovery test. It is often the case that not every system will be tested by every recovery test. This can be attributed to resource limitations (typically time or human) or to fear of attempting to accomplish too much in too short a time period.

By creating a step-by-step process, you create a test that is infinitely repeatable by not only those intimately familiar with the systems, but by anyone who has to step into the position. If the steps are detailed enough, even someone marginally familiar with the process and the systems can step in and perform the process adequately.

There are several types of tests that the organization can perform. The following is a sample of the way that tests can be broken down.

Checklist Tests   A checklist test will likely be the initial test that the organization will perform. This test consists of a series of checklists associated with the different systems that make up the overall disaster recovery effort of the organization. It will also be the basis of the step-by-step instructions for the final overall recovery. Walk through this set of checklists, thinking carefully about the ramifications of each step, and what issues may present themselves with each. A sample of this checklist can be found in Appendix B.

This will be a nonintrusive set of tests and should be walked through several times, preferably by several different people who have an understanding of the system involved with each. Each additional set of eyes that looks at each checklist will likely see different places where there may be issues or where things are missing.

These checklists should be added to the other documents in the disaster recovery plan along with any notes that have been added and associated changes for the next version of the document.

Because these tests can be done at any time, they should be done frequently and by as many people as is practical. That way there is general familiarity with the process, so when the time comes to go through more tests or through the recovery proper they can step in and perform the recovery. This is good for the organization, as well. It is important from a business continuity perspective to make sure that more than one person can recover any given system. There is no way to ensure that a single identified individual will be in a position to recover the organization should a disaster occur, nor to prevent that person from leaving the organization.

Only in a very small organization (sole proprietorship with probably less than five employees) can one person recover an organization. One person can, typically, recover a system (or maybe even several systems), but it takes a team of people (often then entire organization) to fully recover an organization. That is often the distinction between disaster recovery (which we have also learned takes a team) and business continuity planning (where the team is even larger).

Simulation Tests   Simulation tests pretend to be actual recovery scenarios but they do not impact the systems that are running in production. This can be a logical next step to the checklist tests and could be performed at the primary organization location, as it is nonintrusive.

Many vendors are including this in their software offerings, either free of charge or as an additional fee service. By running a utility it is possible to check an individual product for recoverability. Although this will help in some cases, each vendor's utility is likely specially written to ensure the recoverability of just that vendor's product. It will not likely assist in the testing of the recoverability of any other product.

Appendix A has a sample list of procedures and audit reports that an organization might make use of for this type of testing.

FYI *XOsoft*

Software products that are specially written to test recovery plans can often help with simulation testing. Software from vendors such as XOsoft **(http://www.xosoft.com)** can be used to simulate what a recovery might mean to the organization. This software product can run on a backup of your data, recover to an alternative set of hardware, and determine whether the system will be successfully recovered. These tests can be run on demand or on a predetermined schedule. This can remove at least one set of the barriers to testing from the organizational equation (time and human resources).

If you would like to try WANSyncHA (XOsoft's business continuity offering) you can download it from their site and take a look at what it might offer to an organization.

This step is often skipped. Without being able to run tests on the recovered systems, it is difficult to justify what amounts to little more than exercising the checklists to a somewhat greater degree. As with the planning, testing plans and testing needs to be flexible and customized to the situation and the organization. What is most important is to test to the greatest extent possible.

Parallel Tests Parallel tests often follow checklist testing. In parallel testing a system is recovered on parallel hardware to the production version. Although this infers that there will be parallel hardware available, hardware is often leased for a short period of time for testing.

The production systems need not be brought down for the end users to test the recovered system. The testing of the recovery and the recovered system also can be done when there is free time. This means that the recovery and subsequent testing can stretch out over an extended period of time. This tests the recoverability, but if no time limit is set on the testing or the recovery, it will not prove whether the recovery can happen in sufficient time to meet the set service level agreements (SLAs).

Often when disaster recovery tests are conducted offsite, they are conducted as parallel tests. The recovery is conducted in isolation while the production systems are fully functional and being accessed by the end users. A minimal number of users are requested to access the recovered system and perform tests against the recovered systems.

Although this does not limit the impact to the organization of resources or time, it minimizes the impact to the production system as the two systems are allowed to run in parallel. This can be very important to customer-facing sites that allow access to the public, such as in e-business organizations (such as Amazon.com, eBay, Travelocity, and others). In cases of these customer-facing sites, minimizing the impact to the public and making the recovery testing totally transparent to the ultimate end user is often as important—or more important—than minimizing impact to the resources or time of the organization. In these cases, profit will likely take a front seat to the cost associated with recovering in parallel.

Full Interruption Tests   Full interruption tests are the ultimate disaster recovery test. A full interruption test takes, as input, all information gathered in any and all of the previous testing scenarios and (as completely as is possible) exercises the plan so that the organization can be assured that it can rapidly and fully recover. The reason that an organization, after successfully completing a full interruption test, can be assured that they can recover is because the testing is creating a situation where the organization is facing a mock disaster and the recovery is being done as if it were for real. At the point when the recovery is complete, the organization fails over to the recovered system as if it were business as usual.

This is also the kind of recovery test that is done when an organization has set up a hot recovery site, or a site that is updated in real time. In situations like this, failing over to the backup site is as simple as toggling settings off on one system and on for the other—recovery is complete and testing can begin. This kind of recovery testing can be done with little or no notice and can be relied upon to be sure that there can be a full recovery in the case of a disaster.

It is important to remember, however, that there is a trade-off in the assurance that the disaster recovery can occur seamlessly and nearly effortlessly. There needs to be duplicated hardware and software, and there is often an extra software licensing cost associated with this kind of high availability. Most of the time only international organizations have sufficient resources or justification for this kind of availability.

Developing Test Scenarios and Using Test Results Effectively

Although simply testing what people can remember may be adequate, leaving everything to memory gives you nothing to measure against and always leaves

the possibility that something will be missed. Often what is missed is something that occurs only on special occasions (such as quarter end, end of fiscal year in accounting, or during a special sale cycle for marketing and sales). Creating written testing scenarios helps to work through these situations and helps the functional areas to remember those special processing situations that may otherwise be missed in haste or in the interest of getting as much done as efficiently and as effectively as possible.

Writing testing scenarios not only helps the functional units to determine whether all the scenarios are covered, it also provides the organization with a document that will provide a place to tally the results of the testing in an organized manner. This not only ensures that everything is tested, it ensures that all of the tests are either marked as a success or a failure. This documentation is a valued addition to the recovery document. It will point out what changes need to be made to the recovery plan and potentially to the security measures and backup measures in the organization.

Each functional area requires a unique set of test scenarios, written by subject matter experts who know best what they do day to day, month to month, and at the end of the quarter and end of the fiscal year. It will likely be these people who have to execute the test plans. If the scenarios are created step-by-step and each step is checked off as it is executed along with an analysis of the results, it will benefit in the long run when the recovery is completely successful in the event that the plan needs to be fully executed in an emergency situation.

It isn't likely that the functional units will be thrilled with the prospect of creating the scenarios, due to the extra effort needed to write them and provide the organization with anticipated result sets. But cooperation can be gained if they are approached with the attitude that this will help not only the disaster recovery team and the organization as a whole, but will help them in the long run by making sure that they have the data and access that they need to do their job better in the event that an emergency is declared.

Examine the sample set of test scenarios in Appendix B to assist in determining what should be examined for this part of the testing and planning.

Maintaining the DR Plan

Once the organization has the results from one of the tests, it is important that that the findings be analyzed and that the overall determination be added to the disaster recovery plan if they are found to be lacking.

It is important for the organization to remain cognizant of the fact that the recovery plan is a living document. It needs to be updated whenever there is any addition to the hardware or software or whenever one of the existing components is removed.

It is even more critical that the plan be updated whenever there is a successful recovery test or when places are found to be lacking in the existing document. It is a good practice to examine and review the documentation at least annually, or semiannually if possible, to make sure that the documentation still follows the business processes and still matches the hardware and software involved in these processes.

Applying Change Control: Why and How

Wikipedia (wikipedia.org) describes *change control* as a formal process used to ensure a product, service, or process is only modified in line with the identified necessary change. It applies to disaster recovery in that the recovery plan needs to be changed only in ways that apply to what is necessary to ensure that the recovery will be successful and that changes that occur in the organization also occur as is related to the disaster recovery plan. Change for change's sake is not what needs to happen, but accurate changes reflecting changes in needs or changes in assets and processes need to be made.

Change control typically implies that there is a document or a section of a document through which changes to the document can be tracked and signed off on. Change control can occur to the document for the following reasons:

- Requirement changes

- Problems arising in current process

- Request for enhancements

- Requests for new additions to the process

It applies to the baseline work and all associated works that are created by the members of the team as well as to all associated documents including:

- Software that has been added into production

- Requirements specifications

- Procedures and processes

- Assets

- User and technical documentation

- Licenses and contact information

Typically, there are times when pieces of the recovery plan are exempt from the change control process. Ordinarily exempt from the process are parts of the project that are currently under development, interim and temporary work, and completed tests as they are added to the recovery plan or notes for any part of the work that is intended for individual use only.

Changes usually have to pass through the change control board or committee. In the case of the disaster recovery planning change control, this will be

Revision History

Name	Date	Reason For Changes	Version
		initial draft	1.0 draft 1

Approval History

Name	Date	Position

FIGURE 8.1 Change control.

a subset of the disaster recovery planning team that is responsible for the change control approvals. An example of a simple change control that can be associated with a document is shown in Figure 8.1.

Ensuring Normal Developments Are Accounted for in the DR Plan

Because no organization is completely static; because software development occurs internally; and because new files, systems, databases and software are added to existing systems; it is important that all of the normal developments are accounted for in the recovery plan.

Generally people do not think of updating the disaster recovery plan each time there are additions or changes to systems. This is when discipline is necessary, particularly in smaller organizations where many of the decisions on changes are made by either the only person, or one of the only people, in the company.

In larger organizations, change control is often built into the movement of software additions and changes through the system. If this is the case, it is easy to tie changes in the disaster recovery plans to changes as they migrate through the system.

However it is handled, making sure that all appropriate changes make it into the disaster recovery plan when they occur, over time, and with as little effort as is necessary to get them done is in the best interest of not only the disaster recovery team but the organization as a whole. If changes are made as they occur, it will take less time to address the inputs and outputs to the new or altered system because they will be well documented and many people will have a basic understanding of the overall system. There will be documentation concerning the system and the changes, and these can easily be incorporated into the recovery plan. With the increasing time that passes after the new system is added to the organization, more details will be forgotten, more research will have to be done, and more research (and therefore time) will have to be dedicated to adding the new or revised system to the plan.

Scheduling Regular Reviews

Even the most diligent organization will have things that slip through without making it into the recovery plan. Some of the changes aren't well documented to begin with. Organizations are often lax with even their production systems' change control. Small organizations often forget that when they invest in new software or hardware it needs to be added to the plan so that the plan stays current. It is also often the case that organizations may remove systems and hardware from production without those changes having to go through any change control process.

Optimally, the disaster recovery team should have meetings scheduled every month, regardless of what is or isn't taking place in the organization. This will keep them thinking more as a team and will keep the need for recovery planning fresh in everyone's mind. It allows minimal time to pass between sessions—minimal time in which changes can occur that affect the organization and potentially the recovery plan.

This, however, is not always realistic. Small companies may not be able to spare the team at the same time every month. Home offices often don't think to schedule time to sit down with the plan and review what has happened since the last review. Worse, often the smallest businesses don't think to review the plan until something happens that prompts the thought of disaster. This can be as simple as a Windows protection fault, or the realization that the files that they thought they had backed up as works in progress are really not the versions they thought they were and they lose at least several hours of time in rework. Although this isn't necessarily a disaster, it is often enough of a wake-up call to prompt a review of the plan and the backups to make sure that what should be being done really is being done.

Whatever frequency is determined to be appropriate, it is vital to the recovery document and to the organization that ongoing reviews of the recovery plan and associated organizational systems take place with the disaster recovery team, and with any additional functional areas as can be convinced to attend. This will allow all concerned to stay abreast of what is occurring in the recovery document and in future planning sessions.

Managing and Documenting the Recovery

Whether the recovery in question is a recovery test or a declared disaster, it is critical that management be involved at every step of the recovery and that the recovery and all milestones be documented along with the successes, failures, and any issues that may occur at every step of the recovery.

The disaster recovery plan and recovery testing may be one of the most critical projects (or series of projects) that the organization can undertake. Although the overall planning process is in itself a project, it is important to remember that the testing (or recovery) is a self-contained unit of processing and can therefore be viewed as a project standing on its own.

Creating a project plan, determining identifiable and measurable milestones, and associating discrete costs with many of the milestones will benefit the overall organization in a reporting and planning standpoint. The organization will be able to look back at the historical projects and determine if they are getting more successful over time, and if they are getting more cost effective over time relative to the economy.

By creating a formalized project plan, it will be easier to manage the project during the recovery and to report on it later. Because the plan will be in writing and will be repeatable, it will be easy to take that same plan, or one very similar to it, and use it in the event that the recovery has to occur for real.

Identifying Stakeholders

As with any project plan, it is important to keep in mind all of the stakeholders of the project, both local and extended. These people, to some extent, need to be kept informed about the progress that is being made towards recovery.

To this end, it is wise to at least do mock updates to the stakeholders as the recovery test occurs. Internal stakeholders should be contacted routinely as milestones are met or missed and a pretend attempt be made to keep external stakeholders informed. This should be faked in an attempt to make sure that none of the external stakeholders are unduly alarmed at receiving an update. As many external stakeholders as possible should be aware of the testing to let them know that if they do receive an update they shouldn't worry about the organization.

Copies of correspondences should be kept, either electronically or in hard copy, in connection with the recovery plan so they can be referred to later.

Defining Clear Goals at the Start

The goal for either a recovery or a recovery test is success, and measurable goals and milestones will help to keep the project on track. Realistic time limits should be assigned to each step of the plan. This means that everyone assigned to those tasks should be held responsible for whether the milestones are met or missed, and during a debriefing after the recovery they should be held responsible for helping to determine what went wrong and what could be done better. This is not to say that blame should be assigned to anyone either during or following the recovery; however, by having everyone take ownership in the recovery, the plan, and the ultimate results there is a better chance of success and that the testing will be taken seriously.

Reporting

After the recovery, and after a debriefing following the recovery, it is important that formal reporting, complete with findings, both positive and negative, be given to the organization. These reports will become a part of the recovery document and will become the basis for future planning sessions and changes in the backup and recovery strategy and for the recovery plan proper.

Of particular importance in disaster recovery testing is performing a postmortem of the success and failure of the disaster recovery test. This postmortem should include all incidents in the process as they were discovered, and whether recovery was possible. A complete list of best practices and lessons learned should be kept with the disaster recovery document so the next recovery will be able to make use of the lessons learned from all past recovery efforts.

Summary

Testing the plan is as important to a successful recovery as the planning itself. Successful teams work together, drill together, and prepare for the ultimate recovery.

Management should be involved at every step of the testing and should oversee the process in a manner similar to that of any major project in the organization. They will be looked to as leaders and role models in the process and will have their example followed by most of those involved. For the same reason, it is important that the most appropriate people be chosen for the testing.

All of the relevant people in the company, management as well as other stakeholders, should be kept abreast of the progress during and after the testing and results should be presented, without assigning blame, to upper management.

Test Your Skills

MULTIPLE CHOICE QUESTIONS

1. There are times and places where people can practice different recovery _____.

   A. materials

   B. plans

   C. situations

   D. scenarios

2. It is vital to the organization and the success of the recovery plan that the plan be thoroughly tested, at least on a(n) _____ basis.

   A. annual

   B. biannual

   C. monthly

   D. bimonthly

3. By testing the recovery plan you can determine the _____ and _____ of backup facilities and procedures.

   A. feasibility, comparability

   B. capability, compatibility

   C. feasibility, compatibility

   D. feasibility, capability

4. Most organizations that don't do testing don't do so because it is a drain on _____ and _____.

   A. time, talent

   B. time, resources

   C. talent, resources

   D. time, money

5. One of the considerations that have to go along with disaster recovery testing is the impact that the exercise will have on the _____.

   A. suppliers

   B. vendors

   C. organization

   D. customers

6. Often the recovery team does the testing _____.

   A. over a weekend

   B. mid-week

   C. early Monday morning

   D. after close of business

7. As with any kind of test, the disaster recovery test needs to have a set of _____ so everyone knows whether the plan and the team have passed.

   A. standards

   B. minimums

   C. tests

   D. criteria

8

8. The criteria need to be established at the organizational level for what constitutes a(n) _____.

   A. emergency

   B. disaster

   C. trigger

   D. none of the above

9. Initially, the testing of the plan should be broken into _____.

   A. phases

   B. sections

   C. areas

   D. arenas

10. The checklists should be added to the other documents in the _____ along with any notes that have been added and associated changes for the next version of the document.

    A. disaster recovery plan

    B. planning notebook

    C. disaster notebook

    D. emergency recovery plan

11. _____ pretend to be actual recovery scenarios but they don't impact the systems that are running in production.

    A. Disaster tests

    B. Disaster drills

    C. Simulation drills

    D. Simulation tests

12. Parallel tests are often the tests that follow _____ testing.

    A. disaster

    B. simulation

    C. checklist

    D. operational

13. The ultimate type of disaster recovery testing is a _____ test.

    A. full interruption

    B. partial interruption

    C. full disruption

    D. partial disruption

14. Each _____ needs to create its own test scenarios.

    A. functional unit

    B. functional area

    C. user division

    D. none of the above

15. Change control can occur to the document for _____.

    A. requirement changes

    B. request for enhancements

    C. requests for new additions to the process

    D. all of the above

16. Optimally, the disaster recovery team should have meetings scheduled every _____, regardless of what is or isn't taking place in the organization.

    A. month

    B. 3 months

    C. 6 months

    D. year

17. Measurable _____ and _____ will help to keep the disaster recovery project on track.

    A. goals, team leaders

    B. teams, goals

    C. goals, milestones

    D. teams, milestones

8

EXERCISES

Exercise 8.1: Unit Testing

1. A large institution has deployed nearly identical network hardware across all wiring closets at a given location.

2. As part of their ongoing disaster testing plan, it has been decided that the networking group will select a closet at random each month and test the recovery of that closet.

3. If necessary, consult a networking expert, and develop a generic testing strategy that the networking group can use to perform these tests.

Exercise 8.2: Project Strategies

1. As part of the disaster recovery planning at a medium-sized business, you have been asked to develop a project plan to test the backups of production systems.

2. Develop an outline of the project plan for the testing.

Exercise 8.3: Change Control

1. Disaster recovery planning requires change management of the plan, as do the items involved in the recovery, since technological environments change over time.

2. In a well-supported essay, describe how you should attempt to incorporate the changes that occur to a large enterprise network over time in disaster recovery planning.

Exercise 8.4: Testing Methods

1. Sometimes it is not feasible to conduct a complete real-world test of a recovery.

2. Describe a recovery that would not be feasible to test with a real-world simulation.

PROJECTS

Project 8.1: Survey

1. Using a list of companies in your area, ask five of them about the testing of data backups or some other recovery area that needs testing.

2. Develop a comparison of how these companies approach the recovery testing and make a recommendation on how each company might improve its testing process.

▶ Case **Study**

Familiarize yourself with some of the technology used by an online technology vendor, such as Dell. Write a thorough discussion of how the vendor should approach testing the recovery of some aspect of their technology with respect to the online ordering process.

Chapter | 9

Continued Assessment of Needs, Threats, and Solutions

Chapter Objectives

After reading this chapter and completing the exercises, you will be able to do the following:

- Determine the lessons that were learned during the test disaster recovery.
- Decide how to overcome the threats that were uncovered.
- Use SWOT (strengths, weaknesses, opportunities, threats) analysis as an additional method of determining threats.
- Plan for eliminating threats going forward.

Introduction

The test is done; now it is time to determine what was learned in the test, and what can be taken from the experience and used so that the same issues (and there will be issues) aren't repeated the next time.

What to Do After the Disaster Recovery Test

After the test, it is important not only to step back and regroup, but also to meet as a team and discuss the lessons learned. This is not the time to assess or assign blame. This is the time to simply determine what was learned and what can be done better going forward. It is important that the team meet, before a long enough period of downtime that the they begin to forget, at least once (typically more than once) to discuss what was done well, what was done poorly, and what was learned.

Extensive notes should be taken during these meetings so everyone's perception of the lessons learned is captured. In the aftermath of the recovery or the recovery test, some thoughts may not seem important or relevant, but after a period of time they may appear to be more relevant.

What Was Learned?

The recovery test is over. The team has learned that either the organization can or cannot recover, and that is all that was learned, right?

Not exactly. There are many things that may have been learned. For example, the organization may be conducting backups at the wrong time. Missing critical information in a given time period may be captured if the time is changed by even a small fraction.

Perhaps the organization cannot recover because the tapes being used are incompatible with the hardware on which it is trying to recover. This can mean simply changing the kinds of tapes used, or changing the kind of hardware used for recovery. This depends largely on the recovery site and the recovery solution that may be under contract.

Perhaps there were missed applications, files, or databases that should have been backed up in order to fully recover the organization's systems. These missed applications are often the ones that are sitting on someone's PC that they never think of even being there until they need it; they are the only ones who use it, and they are the only ones who will notice that it is missing. This information needs to be captured so changes in strategy can be made.

There are often applications that people forget that they rely upon for their day-to-day jobs. For example, a reporting database, written in Access and residing on a user's computer but shared among all of the people in the department, might not make the list of critical applications. This application would likely be homegrown and might make use of information gathered from multiple databases and massaged into a format that is easier for the end users to work with. Without this application, it would take several times longer for the users to perform their daily reporting and decision-making duties. The users likely would take this application for granted (after all, it was likely not purchased but built internally by a member of the group rather than a member of the IT development staff), the computer on which it resides may not make it into the backup schedule, and the information contained could be lost.

Depending on your backup strategy and how much information and backup software you keep with each copy of your recovery backups, you may find that, when you attempt to recover, you are unable to because you have not taken into account that the software may not be loaded on the computer on which you recover. Or you may find that the version of the software that you have available is not the version that is required to read the files that you have restored. You may have upgraded your installation, but not the backup files of the software to reflect this upgrade.

Any number of things can be uncovered or unrecoverable during either the recovery testing or the recovery proper. It is just as important, however, to determine things that may have gone particularly well. If you have gone through the recovery process a number of times, you may have a general feel for how long each piece of the recovery process will take to accomplish. Perhaps someone in the organization came up with a new way to do the backups so that the recovery could be accomplished in half the time. The time savings shortened the timelines on the critical path and all the systems dependent on the shortened recovery were likewise finished early. This was brought out as a lesson leaned from the recovery at the next postmortem debriefing.

Although it is important not to assign blame for things that went badly, it is often beneficial to morale to give kudos for things that went particularly well. It is often to the team's benefit to praise even minor achievements. Although it is important to not appear to be insincere, it is also important to provide positive reinforcement.

IN PRACTICE: Lessons Learned

Radical Risk Management, a Miami, Florida company, had been holding recovery tests every January in Denver, Colorado for several years. The recovery team flew in to the recovery area, as was their standard practice. They requested that the company that stored their tapes send them to the recovery area so they were there when the team arrived, as was their standard practice.

The team arrived on time, but the tapes were running a bit behind schedule. When the tapes finally arrived, there was ice inside the tapes and water inside the tape case. Apparently there were problems during shipping (presumably only during shipping) and the tapes appeared to be unusable.

The team, in the spirit of disaster recovery, made the decision to attempt to recover anyway and see what they could salvage and what they could learn. After filing a claim with the tape storage company, they spent the entire first day of their recovery effort trying to dry out the tapes and restore them to a condition where they could be read from and written to.

Although they were unable—due in part to lack of time and in part to the degraded condition of the tapes—to completely recover, they were able to take back a new set of lessons learned on new and innovative ways to dry out wet tapes, which they shared not only with their organization, but also with their trading partners too.

9

During these sessions, it is important to remember to stay on task as much as possible. It is also important that the meetings not become a place to judge either processes or people but to find facts. If the meetings become a place where blame is assigned, people will become defensive and little will be learned. Remember, the team is just that—a team.

What Will Be Done Differently

Once the fact-finding meetings are complete, and this has to be decided by each individual organization, it is time to make decisions on what the organization, and the team, will do differently during the next recovery (whether it is a test or an actual recovery).

There are many places where things are likely to change, depending on what was uncovered in the meetings. There may simply need to be alterations made in the documentation, or there may need to be changes made in the overall process. Some will be small and simple to implement; others will be broader in scope and scale and will take cross-functional effort.

These meetings on changes to make should occur as soon after the recovery as possible. This is for two reasons: first, to make sure that you don't lose the momentum gained at the recovery and immediately following; and second, to allow as much time for the implementation of the changes as possible before the next recovery effort.

Changes should include any measures that can be added to make security tighter at the next event. These incremental security changes will be simpler to implement than if several iterations pass with no changes and then it becomes apparent that the changes are necessary. Because disasters deal almost entirely with security or lack of adequate security, it is important that security stay uppermost in everyone's mind.

The recovery planning process often seems to become rote and the real purpose lost in the process. People forget that the purpose is to recover the organization and get lost in the details of getting through the meetings and the recoveries. It likely will not be possible to get the people really excited about the prospect, but keeping a level of awareness and excitement is something that needs to be a goal of the team.

It is important that every item that ends up in the "what we learned" category be at least examined in the "what we will do differently" meetings. Even if all that the group does is state the situation and open it for discussion, at least the issue will have been aired and addressed as relevant or irrelevant and can then be put to rest. Not only does this allow all issues that arise to be addressed, it also allows the people involved to feel validated and their opinion valued. Remember, morale is as important in the recovery team as it is anywhere else.

Threat Determination in System

Based on the outcome of testing and the follow-up debriefing meetings, it is possible to determine what the uncovered risks are for the system. These threats include spoofing, tampering, repudiation, information disclosure, and denial of service, and level of privilege. It is important to note that in a static environment, for a given system design, the threats to that design don't really change. However, as the system evolves or as the systems surrounding it and feeding it evolve, so do the threats to the system. Organizations are, if nothing, continuously changing. This is becoming more and more the case. Look at *Who Moved My Cheese* and *Managing Chaos and Complexity,* two books about managing people and organizations in their times of change.

Ironically, once they have a disaster recovery plan, and even more so after they have started to test the plan, many organizations simply ignore that there may be emerging threats to their organization. They may feel that they have done due diligence and that is all they need to do. If they are lucky, they are right. It is more likely that something that they didn't notice sneaking up on them will cause issues later, or there will be an issue with the recovery site that they never considered. After all, it is a recovery site; they are supposed to have plugged all the holes, right? Maybe. Maybe not. Why take the chance?

Think about it. A new system may be created that feeds its information into a system that you are already backing up as a part of the recovery effort. The new system may or may not be included in the backups, but the connectivity between the new source system and the old target system may not be accounted for, and the dependencies between the two systems may not have made it into your documentation. This might mean that your recovery efforts are misplaced and that you are now recovering systems in the wrong order.

Or there may be holes in the security system that have been plugged in the primary location but that have not been plugged in the recovery site location. These security issues may include the screening of people who have the privilege to access the systems at the recovery site. You may find that information ends up being misappropriated by people that you are trusting at the recovery site or that people on the outside have gained access to your information in ways that you had not anticipated, but trusted the recovery site to have taken into consideration.

Threat Classification

In classifying the threats to each system and to each component of a system (including the human components), you can look at each kind of threat and determine what kinds of attacks associated with the threat could be launched at each component.

Each kind of threat attack can be further broken down as to whether they are mitigated threats or unmitigated threats. After recovery testing, the team should go back through the systems and look at the threats and determine which are mitigated (ones that have been taken into account in the recovery plan or removed from the equation) and which are unmitigated (those which still allow for vulnerabilities). Many unmitigated risks may go undiscovered until the tests have been conducted.

It is often beneficial to have someone on the team designated to attempt to find the holes in the system while the recovery is taking place. This is, in theory, the closest you are going to get to a replica of your production system, and allowing access to the system by someone who is determined to find the places where it may be broken is often a benefit. It may even be to an organization's benefit to schedule at least one test cycle that is dedicated to finding all the places where the system can be broken.

By throwing as many people at the problem as possible, it is possible to find many previously undetected holes. An organization may even consider hiring a consultant with experience in locating weaknesses in a system to point them out. Examples of some potential holes follow.

Spoofing Spoofing refers to one person or entity electronically masquerading as another by falsifying data, redirecting URLs, or redirecting messages to an alternative site. This masquerading can lead to an illegitimately gained competitive advantage by scavenging information from the business or to illegal activities by stealing information or money.

Spoofing can be the end result of many different kinds of attacks. Any attack that gains someone information can result in that information being used to spoof others into revealing even more information to the hacker or to trusting that person with business to which they should not be a party.

Spoofing can include phishing or Web page spoofing. In phishing, an organization's Web page or Web page design is copied (granted, easy enough to copy directly from the Internet, but why bother if you have access to the information directly from backup tapes, from recovery site servers, or from downed servers in a primary location left unguarded in an emergency situation), and unsuspecting victims provide personal information or make purchases of things that are not legitimate. This attack is often directed at banks and financial institutions (or rather, at the customers of these companies) and is often performed with the aid of URL spoofing, which exploits Web browser bugs in order to display incorrect URLs in the browser's location bar; or with DNS cache poisoning as a means to direct the legitimate user away from the initial target to the fake one. Once the user enters his or her password, the attack-code reports a password error, redirects the user back to the legitimate site, and poof—the user ID and password are grabbed. The easiest way to get the user to believe that the site is legitimate is to use the legitimate site (or a copy of it) as the bait.

Another form of spoofing is pharming. Pharming occurs when the spoofer sets up a redirection of a domain name from its intended IP address destination to an alternative destination in order to gain access to sensitive information (credit card numbers, account numbers, passwords, and PINs). The spoofer sets up a Web site that is almost identical to the original (PayPal is one common example) and gets people to log into the incorrect site, thereby farming—or pharming—the information that they want from the people who have been redirected. Often the redirect is accomplished by means of spam being sent to let people know that their account may have been compromised and that they will need to log in again to verify their account information. Another method of pharming can be set up to prevent the user's computer from contacting the legitimate DNS, by installing a virus on the victim's computer, by compromising the user's firewall or router, or by changing the user's hosts file so that domain names will map to an incorrect IP address. All these places can be easily obtained using information that you may have left behind during a recovery, during a test, on a set of backup tapes, or even on the server, left unguarded during a declared disaster.

Although spoofing isn't something that is necessarily more prevalent in a recovery situation, and keeping in mind that spoofing typically requires a close approximation of the "target's" Web site, the easy availability of the Web site from a recovery server may be a hole that no on considered.

Tampering   The tests may uncover places where tampering may occur, either at the primary business location or at the recovery site. It is important to make note of the differences between the primary business location and the recovery site when making the distinction in tampering, and special attention needs to be paid to the places where tampering can occur at the recovery site. Although you will not likely have control over, or even access to, all the places at the recovery location where tampering may occur, anywhere you find that might fall into the category of a tampering-prone location should be investigated and noted.

There may be times or places in the recovery location where people outside of the control of the recovering organization have access to system data. They may have custody of the recovery media (allowing them to make a copy) and they may have access to the data at a low level where they could scavenge or make alterations to the data while it is within their control. It is important to research where nonorganizational people might have access to either the recovery media or the servers on which the data is being recovered and place that information in the recovery document. Although changing the data during a test would not result in much of an effect on an organization, similar alteration during an actual declared disaster could potentially affect the entire organization and its relationship with its competition and upstream and downstream partners. These situations should be noted as potential risks of the recovery site and careful note should be made during testing and actual recoveries.

Are there sufficient firewalls and DMZs in place at the recovery site? Are your cryptography keys working as anticipated? Is the security to the network and physical security to the servers and the sever room allocated to your recovery sufficient?

If you are working on this as a small business/sole proprietorship (home based or otherwise), make sure that your LAN and/or wireless settings are adequate for the location. If necessary, get another computer (PDA or laptop) to check and make sure that the network is secure. Make note of any inconsistencies that you uncover and determine what, if anything, should be done in order to fill in the gaps.

Post recovery, these locations and situations should be investigated further and plans made to mitigate the chance that tampering can occur.

Repudiation   To explain repudiation, it is important to first look at nonrepudiation. In authentication terms, nonrepudiation means that a user or a server cannot later (after they have performed an action) deny that they performed the action in question.

This speaks to the ability of an organization to ensure the security and recoverability of their cryptographic keys. Compromised keys (did you remember to scrub the servers at the recovery site and remove all traces of the organization's data and systems from the servers?) can be used by someone with less-than-honorable intentions for fraud.

FYI   *Cryptographic Keys*

A cryptographic key is the piece of information that one computer uses to control its mathematical computation of the encryption algorithm to ensure that all secure messages are sent in encrypted format, (typically) with a digital signature that ensures the message originated with the sender and gets to the receiver in the same format as it was sent. This is critical to allowing a business to do business in many cases, because digital signatures are what allow a business transaction to occur digitally and remain a legally binding transaction.

Encryption with one private key requires decryption with its corresponding public key. Encryption with another key, or decryption with a different key, will result in either message text encrypted with an entirely different cryptographic key or the inability to decrypt the cipher when it is read.

Keeping your private key safe and secret is often one of the most difficult, yet most practical, issues with cryptography. Anyone who obtains the key can recover a message or set of messages, decrypt messages that are intercepted, or spoof other people by using your keys to get people to trust them rather than your business.

This information and process is key for the purpose of nonrepudiation for an organization. An organization, as well as a person, needs to be uniquely identifiable and needs to take every measure necessary to ensure that identity theft has not or cannot occur.

Denial of Service   Recall that denial of service attacks are a type of attack waged on a network in an attempt to flood the network, thereby bringing the network to its knees. Some exploit TCP/IP limitations, whereas others simply bombard a server in an attempt to render it unusable for a period of time.

Although an organization may have measures in place to limit its exposure to a DoS attack, these measures may not be entirely captured in a recovery plan and may not limit the exposure that the organization may face at the recovery site. Although uncovering this may be difficult, it is worth the effort to attempt to discover whether the measures that your organization has taken to limit DoS attacks and their effects will carry through to the recovery site. This will give you the added assurance that, should recovery to this site be necessary, your organization's existing efforts will be enough to make sure that you will be able to recover the measures to prevent these attacks as well. The results of these kinds of tests or hack attempts should be included in your recovery documents.

Threat Tree   After you have identified the points where the system or systems might be vulnerable and you have determined that you may be open to a threat at one or more of those points, consider the following types of questions:

- What security mechanism do we already have in place to protect this resource?

- What security mechanism can we put into place to protect the resource?

- Are there any associated interfaces or transactions that have to be taken into account when looking at the system or the threat?

One tool that is useful in setting up the test for threats (or in analyzing them after they have been discovered) is a threat (or attack) tree. A threat tree allows you to determine the level of risk associated with each threat of attack and determine if you, as a team or as an organization as a whole, have successfully mitigated that risk.

A threat tree is a diagram, bearing an uncanny likeness to a flowchart, showing a hierarchy of threats or vulnerabilities. It shows, graphically, what might be going on in the mind of someone mounting an attack. The ultimate goal of the attack or threat is at the top of the inverted tree. Each level shows the step-by-step process that might be required to carry out the attack. Figure 9.1 is a simple threat tree for someone who might be considering stealing a bicycle.

9

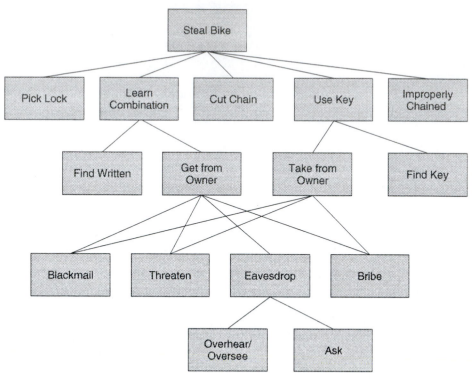

FIGURE 9.1. Threat tree for stealing a bicycle.

Outline   An alternative for the graphic flow diagram for an attack tree might be to take the same kind of approach, but rather than using a flow chart outline the same details. The bicycle theft example in an outline might be as follows:

1. Steal bicycle
   A. Pick the lock
   B. Learn the combination
      1. Find it written down somewhere
      2. Get it from owner
         a. by blackmail
         b. by bullying or threatening
         c. by eavesdropping on owner telling someone
            1. overhear or oversee
            2. just ask
         d. bribe the owner to tell
   C. Cut the chain (probable)

D. Use a key

    1. Take it from the owner

        a. by blackmail

        b. by bullying or threatening

        c. by bribery

    2. Find the key

E. Find the bike improperly chained

Notice that the flow chart entails less typing.

SWOT (Strengths, Weaknesses, Opportunities, Threats)

Another useful tool for disclosing not only where there are threats to the organization and the recovery process but also the strengths and weaknesses in the plan, as well as opportunities for improvement is SWOT analysis.

Typically organizations conduct SWOT analyses to determine where they stand with relation to their competitors or to the market as a whole. Marketing classes typically focus on SWOT analyses as a unit and time is spent looking at the different strengths, weaknesses, opportunities, and threats to the organization from competition. But if we look at anyone or anything attempting to break through our security measures, either deliberately or accidentally, we can apply the same kind of thought process to determining if our recovery plan and our testing scenario is sufficient.

FYI *Traditional SWOT Analysis*

Traditional SWOT analyses are tools used by organizations to audit the organization's environment. Typically, they are the first tools used by marketers to target key issues. SWOT stands for strengths, weaknesses, opportunities, and threats. Strengths and weaknesses are traditionally internal factors, and opportunities and threats are external factors.

Figure 9.2 is the graphic that typically accompanies a SWOT analysis. The further away from the center line a situation is, the further away it is from the opposite idea. The further away from a weakness a strength is, the stronger it is. The further away from an opportunity a threat is, the bigger the threat. Sometimes it is helpful to plot the location on the squares where you think each "thing" is. This will help you to see where they lie in relationship to each other and visualize how to mitigate them into the center.

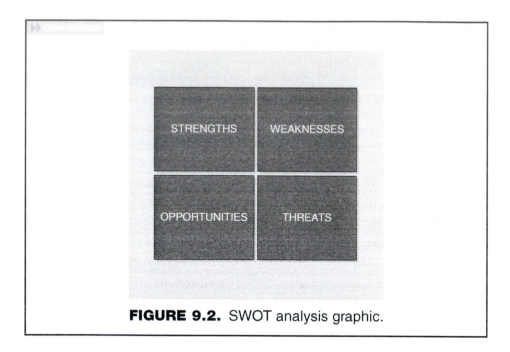

FIGURE 9.2. SWOT analysis graphic.

Strengths   The S in SWOT stands for strengths. What things were done particularly well in recovery planning and recovery testing? What steps were taken to mitigate the risk to the organization from a disaster that addressed a particularly sensitive area of potential disaster? These should be addressed in this part of the analysis.

Typically, strengths point out places where an organization might have core competencies or a competitive edge over the competition. Looking at it this way, what are the core competencies of your organization's plan? What special precautions or special techniques did your team employ to make sure that you were able to recover a particularly difficult system, or what technique did you use in a challenging situation in the recovery process that allowed you to overcome the situation?

Weaknesses   Where there are strengths, there are also weaknesses. What did your organization do that didn't work as well as it should have? What was missed as a potential risk? Were any of the systems unable to be recovered in the appropriate time?

If you undo all the thought processes that you employ to determine the strengths, you can better think through what the weaknesses might be. It is important that thinking through the weaknesses is done in neither a judgmental nor an accusatory manner, but only as a tool to find those situations that need to be addressed so that in the future you can either overcome the situation or put processes in place so that the weaknesses are less weak, less obvious, or eliminated and even made into strengths.

A weakness might be found to be a recovery process that is entirely too slow. Thinking through it, new ways of backing up might be used to better facilitate recovery. If you take the people involved in the process out of the equation and limit your analysis to simply the facts of the situation, it is easier to look at objectively and to turn it around.

Opportunities   Often, in the process of planning, recovering, and repeating the cycle, people will have what might be termed as "Aha!" moments—times when something that no one ever thought of, at least as it relates to the given situation—can be used to make better use of resources, speed the recovery, or allow the group to leverage the economies of scale or scope.

Someone might have read something in a magazine on the plane on the way to the recovery site, or on the way back from the recovery site, they think is something the organization might be able to leverage to their recovery advantage. Perhaps there is an emerging technology that the organization might be able to make use of, or perhaps the process might work better in a different order.

These thoughts should be jotted down—on a piece of note paper, in the margin of the recovery plan, on the back of a napkin—and brought into the notes that accompany the recovery plan in the post-recovery meetings. Although some of the opportunities may not end up in the planning and recovery scenario, if they are never considered they certainly won't be. Making note of an idea that might make the recovery quicker, more efficient, or less prone to human error might allow similar thought processes to occur later when the analysis phase of the post-recovery debriefing occurs. Many times people have wonderful ideas in the heat of the moment, in the midst of a trial (like the recovery testing), that they will have forgotten when the stress is less or when they are in a different situation. These might be tragically lost opportunities to make the recovery process better if they are not noted somewhere permanently.

Opportunities are often realized simply because someone has had the temerity to think outside the box. This should not only be tolerated but also encouraged. It is one reason why many people from different parts of the organization should be brought into the process as often as possible. Although younger members of the organization are often overlooked in the planning process because they don't have as much experience with the particular systems in question, they can often be a wonderful source of new ideas and innovative thinking.

Threat   Finally, we look at the threats—threats that have been considered or threats that have come to light because of the recovery testing and planning. Some threats may not become apparent until the recovery testing exercise begins and people start to think through what it is going to take, from a practical perspective, to recover the organization.

Threats might be situations that endanger the organization's security or cause hardware or software failure, which become apparent only when the recovery testing is in process. It might be an inadequacy in the recovery plan that is discovered only in the process of recovering. It may even be a deficiency in the backup strategy that ends up becoming an issue when the recovery is in process.

Solution Determination

Once you have discovered your latest list of threats, either as an ongoing security practice at your organization or as a result of your latest recovery test, you have to decide what you are going to do about them. Ideally, every threat should be addressed immediately, as it is a gap, a place where your organization may find that it is in danger of a future disaster, or at the very least an emergency situation. However, realistically, many of these uncovered threats will find themselves relegated to the back burner in the organization or discounted as being trivial or infrequent enough that they are simply not going to be dealt with.

Threats, like risks, can be weighted and categorized. Cost-benefit analysis can be done on allowing the risks to remain or on pursuing a solution to them. Many threats, particularly the ones uncovered during actual recovery attempts, will likely have to be dealt with. It may mean simply changing your backup strategy or including things in the backups that weren't there before. It may mean that additional testing will need to be done during the testing phase of the recovery.

Damage

What is the potential damage to your system from the threat? Will there be data loss in the system? Will there be compromised data in transmission? Will there be breached information? Is there potential for hardware damage or media failure?

Reproducible

Is the threat reproducible in the primary location? What is the chance that the threat will succeed in the primary location? What is the chance that the threat will succeed at the recovery location? (What is the difference in these two chances?) What are the chances that someone will stumble upon the threat or gap?

Exploitable

How much effort will have to be exercised to find the threat? How much benefit will there be if it is found and exploited? Don't think that businesses are the only ones concerned with cost-benefit analysis. Anyone trying to intercept data or wreak havoc with your systems and their data will try only as hard as it is worth trying for the benefit that they are liable to realize from the success.

Users/Systems Affected

How many people or systems can be affected by the threat if it comes to fruition? If the threat is that someone could use your Internet connection on your wireless network, but there is no data that they can access and there is no harm they can cause other than making use of the connections, the users affected may be minimal. However, what can someone do with a pirated Internet connection? Can they use your connection to bounce to another connection, and thereby point the finger at your connection when they wreak havoc on another system? Be realistic, but understand that what you view as minimal impact to your organization might be far more extensive than anticipated.

Discoverable

How difficult would it be for the threat to be discovered by someone who really wants to find it? Backdoors in some operating systems are well known by some people, and they are more than capable of testing systems to see if the backdoor is open. This means that the threat is very discoverable. However, an internal system that is used by one or two people, not connected to the network, and has one or two default passwords in some of its systems might be nearly impossible for anyone to detect and therefore is not very discoverable.

9

Summary

This chapter demonstrates how continued diligence is necessary in making sure that an organization's changing needs are taken into account and how planning needs to change along with them. We have found where we might be able to leverage processes that we have in one area to make another more efficient, and we have determined that thinking outside the box is just as important in a disaster recovery perspective as in any other. We have seen how to plan and execute a disaster recovery, whether as a drill or in actual fact. We can now go into an organization and become a productive member of the planning and recovery team.

Through practice (either in an organization or in our daily lives as users of systems and data), we can enable ourselves to think more critically and more productively over time so that we can make sure that (from term papers to the systems of Fortune 500 organizations) we can recover quickly and efficiently.

Test Your Skills

MULTIPLE CHOICE QUESTIONS

1. Once the testing is done, it is time to determine what was _____ in the test and what can be taken from the experience.

   A. learned

   B. found lacking

   C. successful

   D. done

2. The team needs to meet _____ to discuss what it was done well, what was done poorly, and what was learned.

   A. only once

   B. at least once

   C. twice

   D. continually

3. Extensive notes should be taken during post-test meetings so that everyone's _____ the lessons learned can be captured.

   A. experiences with

   B. concerns about

   C. perception of

   D. opinions about

4. One of the things that might be learned from testing is that _____.

   A. backups are being conducted at the wrong time

   B. critical information in a given time period could be captured if the time is changed by even a small fraction

   C. the organization cannot recover because the tapes being used are incompatible with the hardware on which it is trying to recover

   D. all of the above

5. Although it is important to not assign blame for things that went badly, it is often beneficial to morale to give _____ for things that went particularly well.

   A. critiques

   B. kudos

   C. punishments

   D. rewards

6. If the post-test meeting becomes a place where blame is assigned, people will become _____ and little will be learned.

    A. defensive

    B. concerned

    C. introverted

    D. none of the above

7. Changes should include any measures that can be added to make _____ tighter at the next event.

    A. processes

    B. record keeping

    C. security

    D. recording

8. The recovery planning process often seems to become _____ and the real purpose gets lost in the process.

    A. relaxed

    B. consistent

    C. systematic

    D. rote

9. Based on the outcome of testing and of the follow-up debriefing meetings, it is possible to determine what the _____ risks are for the system.

    A. problematic

    B. updated

    C. uncovered

    D. highest

10. _____refers to one person or entity electronically masquerading as another by falsifying data, redirecting URLs, or redirecting messages to an alternative site.

    A. Spoofing

    B. Cracking

    C. Duping

    D. Twinning

11. The tests may uncover places where _____ may occur, either at the primary business location or at the recovery site.

    A. hacking

    B. spoofing

    C. cracking

    D. tampering

12. A(n) _____ key is the piece of information that one computer uses to control its mathematical computation of the encryption algorithm to ensure that all secure messages are sent in encrypted format.

    A. cryptographic

    B. stenographic

    C. encryption

    D. data

13. A type of attack waged on a network in an attempt to flood the network, thereby bringing the network to its knees, is known as a(n) _____ attack.

    A. spoofing

    B. denial of service

    C. encryption

    D. spoof flooding

14. One tool that is useful in setting up the test for threats is a(n) _____ tree.

    A. emergency

    B. hacking

    C. threat

    D. assessment

15. Typically, organizations perform _____ analyses to determine where they stand with relation to their competitors or to the market as a whole.

    A. UNIT

    B. TOWS

    C. SWAT

    D. SWOT

16. _____ are often realized simply because someone thinks outside the box.

    A. Threats

    B. Opportunities

    C. Attacks

    D. none of the above

17. _____ can be done on allowing the risks to remain or on pursuing a solution to them.

    A. Return on investment

    B. Costing plan

    C. Problem planning

    D. Cost-benefit analysis

EXERCISES

Exercise 9.1: Denial of Service Tools

1. Using the Internet, look for denial of service tools.

2. Write a brief summary of the tools you found and some techniques to mitigate the threat of these tools.

Exercise 9.2: The Function of Denial of Service

1. Denial of service attacks are usually seen as a pointed attack, and not part of a larger attack on a system.

2. Describe a scenario in which a denial of service attack can play a role in a larger attack.

Exercise 9.3: Threat Tree

1. All systems are vulnerable to attack, even those that hold the most sensitive information.

2. Pretend you were going to attack the student information system with the intention of registering for a widely popular class.

3. Develop a threat tree for this attack.

Exercise 9.4: Recovery Security

1. Your company has a thorough security plan for the primary and recovery systems used to ensure that even during a recovery the information is protected.

2. Comprehensive plans are only one part of securing your recovery. Assuming that your company will use contract employees for part of the recovery, describe in a short paper how your company can mitigate the threat from using contract employees.

PROJECTS

Project 9.1 Blended Threats

1. Single vulnerabilities in a system are now commonplace, and every second Tuesday of each month sees the announcement of a new set of these single vulnerabilities.

2. Using a security Web site (McAfee, TrendMicro, or Symantec), write a list of five possible blended threats and the risks they pose to an organization, especially during a recovery.

Project 9.2 Pharming

1. Pharming is a threat to the reputations and business of many companies on the Internet today.

2. Pharming relies on successful spoofing, and a recovery can significantly increase the risk of an organization's vulnerability to such an attack.

3. Write a brief description of a pharming attack and describe ways in which a company can monitor for such an attack and mitigate against the attack in the event of a recovery.

▶▶ Case Study

Your company has recently conducted an extensive recovery test of its IT systems. Outline a sample SWOT that might be developed after a complete recovery test. The major areas to consider for the SWOT are operational recovery, system integration, and time to recover.

Sample Disaster Recovery Plan

This appendix contains a sample disaster recovery plan. It is by no means the only example that can be used, and it can be extended to encompass any organization's size and complexity.

Business Recovery Plan
April Wells
Emergency Operations Center (EOC)

Change Control

Change	Date	Made By	Approved By	Version Number

Current Changes

Initial Draft

Quick Reference Guide

I. Activation of EOC

The Emergency Operations Center (EOC) is activated by order of the crisis management team. The crisis management team consists of the company owner and the vice president.

II. Activation Levels/Staffing

Level 1

The incident impacts—or is likely to impact—a number of critical functions and possible use of recovery teams. Recovery can likely be accomplished in the primary work location. If this is the case, the recovery location will be the office of the primary residence or other convenient location.

Staff: Self, close staff
Auxiliary staff will stay on standby alert.

Level 2

The incident impacts—or is likely to impact—a moderate number of critical functions and a limited use of recovery teams. Recovery may or may not occur at the primary location or one of the alternative locations.

Staff: self, close staff, auxiliary staff

Level 3

The incident impacts—or is likely to impact—a large number of critical functions, and all recovery teams are activated. Recovery will primarily take place off site a one of the alternative locations.

Staff: EOC Manager
EOC staff members.
Users: Entire Crisis Management Team
All Recovery Team Leaders
All Recovery Team Scribes (In EOC work areas)

The primary recovery area is located at 1234 Anystreet, Mytown, Texas. If the area of the emergency includes the primary location, the secondary recovery is located at South Broad Street, Hibbing, Minnesota. If the primary and secondary locations are affected, the recovery location will be Waterberry Drive, Apollo, PA.

The primary staff member will report as quickly as possible to the recovery location. Upon arrival, any auxiliary staff will be called. The initial communications effort will likely require more than one staff member. When any or all of the staff required show up at the recovery location, he or she will call or page the primary staff member. These members will exchange information on status of recovery and the process necessary for shift change and handoff.

III. EOC Functions

A. Provide a Central Point of Contact

The primary recovery staff will act as a clearinghouse for all emergency responses and as a source of all recovery information for anyone with any interest. All inbound telephone numbers will be given to all recovery team members who will call relevant authorities to report injuries, to update interested parties concerning the progress of the recovery, or to find necessary resources, etc.

Everything that happens during the Response/Recovery Operations will be recorded and reported to any interested parties.

B. Initial Notification

The primary recovery staff will be responsible for notifying any necessary auxiliary team members and engaging any auxiliary team members should they become necessary.

Initial notification and all subsequent notifications will be logged on the Notification Checklist along with the appropriate contact, status code, and the time the calls were made in the Status and Time Called column. Times will be in the local time zone, regardless of where the recovery is taking place.

Multiple entries may need to be made for every contact attempt because not all attempts will be initially successful.

Contact Name	Contact Title	Status	Time Called	Call Returned

C. Record Inbound/Outbound Calls

All calls, inbound or outbound, will be logged on the telephone log sheets. Whoever takes or makes the call should enter his or her initials at the end of the log entry.

Contact Name	Contact Number or E-mail Address	Message	Time Called	Call Returned	Initials

D. Gather Critical Information

Reports will be posted on bulletin boards as a means of keeping track of the recovery effort. All key information will be written on these boards as well. This will be the central official means to keep the information tracking system up-to-date.

E. Requests for Resources

Record the resource requests (made and filled) as they come in. These requests can be for information resources, hardware resources or information, software resources or information, further office supplies, or human resources.

These requests will be filled as rapidly as possible, and the resource request fulfillment information will be posted on the appropriate Resolve or Unresolved Issues status boards. Unresolved issues will be moved to the Resolved Issues board whenever they are resolved.

F. Inform Key Personnel of Status

Communications personnel will monitor for changes in current situation and report on the changes in status and post the gathered information on the Response/Recovery Situation board.

All relevant personnel will be informed of critical information as soon as it is received or discovered. The recovery team may require auxiliary staff to assist with contacting specific people directly and with providing relevant people with critical information whenever necessary.

G. Contact Managers for Information

The primary recovery personnel may require more extensive information from specific individuals. The recovery personnel should do whatever is necessary to locate the individuals from whom the information can be acquired and obtain the information necessary to accomplish the recovery effort.

Make note of all requests and all responses in the telephone/e-mail log and transfer this contact information to the recovery document post-recovery. This will allow us to enrich our information on where further information can be obtained.

H. Recovery Operations Log

The Recovery Operations Log becomes our working record of the activities conducted by the recovery team. All activities (positive and negative) should be added to this log. This log will ultimately become a permanent part of the recovery documentation, and the lessons learned will be recorded and the recovery documentation will be altered to account for all lessons learned.

Contact Lists

I. Crisis Management Team Members

The following team members will be concerned at all levels of the recovery effort.

II. EOC Staff

The following staff members should be contacted in the event that an emergency be declared.

EOC Manager Name: April Wells Office Phone: 123-456-7890 Address: 1234 mystreet Anytown TX USA Home Phone: 234-567-1890 Other Phone:	Name: Office Phone: Address: Home Phone: Other Phone: Pager:
Pager: Staff Members Name: Office Phone: Address: Home Phone: Other Phone: Pager:	Name: Office Phone: Address: Home Phone: Other Phone: Pager:

Emergency Contacts

Name: Hospital Office Phone: 789-123-0987 Address: Home Phone: Other Phone: Pager:	Name: Fire/Police/Ambulance Office Phone: 911 Address: Home Phone: Other Phone: Pager:
Name: Office Phone: Address: Home Phone: Other Phone: Pager:	Name: Office Phone: Address: Home Phone: Other Phone: Pager:

Computer Contacts

Name: Dell Support Office Phone: Address:	Name: Sony Support Office Phone: Address:
Name: Microsoft Office Phone: Address:	Name: Oracle Office Phone: Address:
Name: Camtesia Office Phone: Address:	Name: Peach Tree Office Phone: Address:

Vendor Contacts

Name: Agent Office Phone: Address:	Name: O'Reilly Office Phone: Address:
Name: Prentice Hall Office Phone: Address:	Name: Wiley Office Phone: Address:
Name: Oracle Press Office Phone: Address:	Name: Que Office Phone: Address:
Name: 7 Hills Office Phone: Address:	Name: VTC Office Phone: Address:
Name: Past Agent Office Phone: Address:	Name: Internet Provider Office Phone: Address:

EOC Organization

The primary recovery staff is established in the following functional areas:

- Communications area
- Meeting area
- Media briefing area
- Workspace for individual team representatives

I. The Communications Area

The communications area needs to include a phone bank or at least access to two dedicated phone lines. It should include a television to monitor local and national news, and there should be access to print or electronic news. The preferable source of communication, as soon as it is possible, would be electronic as it is simpler and more central.

This area is to be set up in such a way as to prevent the sound from computers, televisions, and monitor devices to interfere with telephone communications. The room should be, if possible, separated from other functional areas so you can prevent others (family, visitors, or assistants) from congregating in the area and to keep those congregating in the communications area from interfering with the goings-on in the recovery area.

This room, if relocating in Apollo, Pennsylvania, is to be the back bedroom in the house on Waterberry Drive. If relocating in Hibbing, Minnesota, the room will be the office in the house on South Broad Street. Both are equipped with high-speed wireless Internet access. Both have a primary phone line, and both have two entrances, one to the inside of the house and one to the outside.

II. The Meeting Room

The meeting area should be large enough to comfortably seat not only the primary members of the recovery team, but also as many relevant visitors as are likely to attend any meeting in person. That number may include the crisis management team—if one exists, the recovery team leaders, and representatives from outside agencies. This area should be equipped with a white board or large paper on which we can track statuses as well as presentation pads and notepaper.

III. Recovery Team Workspace

The recovery workspace should be readily available at all times for the team and any auxiliary people that need to have access. It should include voice and data access as well as surge protected power or a generator. Extended battery support for the laptop would be critical.

EOC Supplies and Equipment

I. Communications

Telephone with hands-free capability

Fax access

Dedicated telephone line

Broadband connectivity

Cellular telephones with charger; can double as high-end walkie-talkie

Radio

Television, AM/FM radio, access to real-time weather updates

II. Office Supplies

Post-it notes

Lined legal pads

Pencils/pens

Markers and erasers for white boards

Tape

Tape-recorder and cassettes with spare batteries

Flashlights and spare batteries

Printer/copier paper

File folders, paper clips, rubber bands, ruler, scissors, staplers, etc.

III. Office Equipment

PCs or laptop

Printer/copier/scanner/fax machine and ink

Three-hole punch

Tape recorder

IV. Documents

Business continuity plans

Other recovery SOPs

Payroll and benefits SOPs

Bank and charging account information

Building blueprints (all buildings)

Area map showing all alternate facilities

Local street guide/map

Local telephone directories

Branch office contact lists

Procedures for installing BCP software

Procedures for installing and configuring all additional software, including passwords

Detailed Information

I. Activation of Recovery Team

When

The recovery team will be activated by order of April Wells, Larry Wells, or other appointed member. Activation notification will be made through phone or e-mail or other official so designated.

Where

The primary backup site is located at Round Rock, Texas. If the area of the emergency includes the primary business location, the secondary recovery is located at Hibbing, Minnesota. If the primary and secondary locations are affected the tertiary location in Apollo, Pennsylvania, will be activated.

Who

The primary staff personnel who are "on call" will report immediately to the recovery location. Upon arrival at the recovery location, he/she will call in the other support staff. The initial communications effort will often require more than one staff member at the recovery location.

The primary recovery staff will manage the recovery location. The day-to-day support functions will be handled primarily by the primary recovery staff with additional support, as required, from auxiliary recovery staff.

What

When the duty primary recovery staff arrives at the recovery location, he/she will call or page all of the auxiliary personnel and all concerned contacts that the recovery location is operational. The activating official may be calling other personnel and telephone may be busy.

Recovery Functions Details

I. Provide a Central Point of Contact

The recovery support staff will act as a clearinghouse for all recovery information and will provide all critical services during these times. The primary inbound phone number will be 888-999-0101, and the primary e-mail channel will be *myemail@myorg.com*. This information will be given to all team members, internal and external, primary as well as auxiliary. Reports all injuries, updates to the progress in appropriate areas, and location of support information and resources to this communication channel.

Everything that happens during the Response/Recovery Operations will eventually be recorded at the EOC.

Other EOC functions include:

- Initial notification

- Record inbound/outbound calls

- Gather critical information

- Receive requests for resources

- Inform key managers of status

- Contact managers for information

- Receive media questions (direct to public information officer)

II. Initial Notification

After the activating official notifies the EOC duty staff, April or Larry will begin the process of notifying key managers of the situation. When the duty EOC staff activates the EOC, the EOC staff assumes the responsibility of notifying the remaining key managers.

The activating official (regardless of whether it is April or Larry) will provide the EOC staff with the information to give to key managers and will also tell the EOC staff who to contact and when. The EOC staff will write down the information on whom and how to contact word-for-word and will remember to always read this message as it pertains to the recovery effort. They will then report back to the activating officer to ensure that the information was conveyed correctly and on any information conveyed back to the organization.

If either April or Larry or the EOC staff gets an answering machine when conveying messages, they should be sure to give a brief message explaining the situation, the current status, and ask them to call the EOC for further information.

The phone designated for incoming calls should not be used, if possible, for outgoing calls. Outgoing calls should be made on the cellular lines. The activating official will report to the EOC as soon as possible after activation and remain in periodic contact while in route to the recovery location. Upon arrival at the recovery location, the activating official will assume responsibility for the onsite recovery functions. The senior member of management will log and initial all subsequent notifications. Appropriate contact status and call time will be logged.

III. Record All Inbound and Outbound Calls

All calls will be logged on the telephone log sheets. The following information is required to be logged on all inbound and outbound calls:

- Date and time of call

- Name of person calling or being called

- What the call was about
- The relevant information on the call details

- For inbound calls, also include the action taken by the recovery member in relation to the call. Some examples include:
  - "Passed along information to (Name)"
  - "Answered caller's question concerning _____"
  - "Put information on status board"

- The initials of the person handling the call must be at the end of the log entry.

Telephone logs will be kept so confusion can be kept to a minimum in an emergency or disaster situation. Much of the information that is passed on by telephone is critical not only to the current recovery, but may be relevant to ongoing business and future recovery planning as well. This critical information could be lost unless all relevant information that occurs in telephone calls and e-mails are recorded accurately in a logbook.

After the emergency, the organization will study the conversation details and the resulting actions taken by all participants. This will be used to identify what we did right and what we did wrong, where we can leverage efficiencies in other areas, and what needs to be improved. Due to the nature of the emergency recovery situation, most of the actions taken during the emergency recovery will be by phone. It is difficult to study conversations or responses without an accurate record of all telephonic actions.

IV. Gather Critical Information

Accurate and timely information on the emergency situation that caused the recovery, information on the recovery, and information on the recovery location is essential for effective emergency response and disaster recovery. Relevant information to gather data on includes:

- Unresolved issues
- Additional resources
- How the recovery is progressing
- Who is working on what, and where they are

Daily written reports will provide most of this information. Other information will be provided through telephone conversations. A system will be established to help track this information, and periodic reports will be posted on bulletin boards.

Other key information that needs to be written on presentation boards or easel pads includes unresolved issues:

- Personnel
- Health and safety
- Recovery teams
- Business units
- Computer operations
- Production operations
- Communications
- Equipment
- Purchasing
  - Facilities' work orders
  - Invoices and receipts
- Disaster situation causing the recovery or that occur during the recovery (e.g., cresting of rivers, road closings, local utility damage, additional snowfall)

V. Requests for Resources

Recovery and disaster recovery requires many types of resources both from an initial staffing perspective and those that need to be accounted for later. These may include:

- People
- Security guards
- Cleaning staff
- Drivers
- Temporary employees
- Supporting vendors
- Supplies
- Computer printer paper, ribbons, etc.
- Food and water
- Medical supplies
- Additional or replacement production equipment
- Additional or replacement computer equipment

- Special recovery equipment
- Furniture

Staff needs to record the resource requests as well as the resources as they come in. This information will be used in future planning. That information needs to be posted on the appropriate Unresolved Issues status boards. Critical requests will be filled first; others as time and resources permit.

VI. Inform Key Managers of Status

Situations can change quickly during an emergency, during a recovery, or during disaster recovery operations. Whoever is in a decision-making position requires the latest, most up-to-date information so they can make the best decisions possible for the organization. The managers assigned to carry out the recovery tasks need to know as soon as possible of changes in those tasks or changes affecting those tasks. The staff will monitor the changes in the situation as they occur and post information on the Response/Recovery Situation board. This information will be disseminated as soon as it is discovered as relevant.

VII. Contact Managers for Information

The crisis management team may require additional information from specific individuals. The staff should locate the individuals necessary and obtain the needed information, write down the request and the response in the telephone logs, and post or update the information on the appropriate status boards.

VIII. Media Questions

Newspapers, radio, and television reporters may require information about the company and the current emergency situation. All team members are required to pass along those requests to management.

IX. EOC Operations Log

The EOC Operations Log is an official record of all activities conducted by the EOC. The managers will ensure that the following information is recorded:

- The time and date that operations begin and end.
  - Who is working in the EOC, shift changes, etc.
  - All relevant milestones and timing
- Any of the following:
  - Telephone logs
  - Briefings and reports
  - TV and radio press conferences
  - TV and radio announcements

- Copies of proclamations
- Pertinent newspaper stories
- Division daily reports
- Recovery meeting minutes
- Verbal and published directives

X. Recovery Preparedness

Team plans are intended to be living documents. They should reflect the most up-to-date and relevant information available. Recovery coordinators and team leaders are responsible for reviewing and updating their plans on at least a semi-annual basis. Team leaders or alternate team leader and other individuals who have copies of the team plan will be sent updates each time the plan is changed.

Cover sheets for plan updates will be attached to the end of this section.

A. Semiannual Plan Review

(Updates due January 1 and July 1)

Team leader and alternate team leader. This section identifies the persons assigned in the leadership positions. It should be reviewed by the team leader to identify changes in assigned personnel.

B. Training and Exercises

Updated plans are not enough to ensure organizational continuation if the people assigned to recovery teams don't know what is expected of them. Team members should receive relevant training on not only recovery concepts in general and their team's functions in particular, but also on all software that will be necessary to be recovered in the recovery situation. Tests will be conducted of the recovery plan to help identify needed improvements in strategies and plans. Exercises will give team members valuable experience in dealing with the challenges inherent in recovery operations.

C. Activity Schedule

Plan Reviews

Enter the dates when plan reviews were conducted.

Plan Holders

Due Jan 1 Done January 15
Due Jul 1
Team Leader (April Wells)
Alt. Team Leader (Larry Wells)
(Name)
(Name)
(Name)
(Name)

Training/Exercises

Enter the dates and number of participants for each activity. Each exercise type should be conducted at least once per year.

Activity Date	Conducted	Number of Participants	Comments

E. Plan Update Cover Sheets

Each time a plan is updated, the new or changed sheets are sent to all plan holders with a coversheet that identifies the pages being replaced. Every plan holder that receives the updates will place the cover sheet in the plan behind this page.

Plan update cover sheets must identify the date of the change, the pages to remove, and the pages to add.

Appendix B

Checklist Testing Sample Documents

There are a few ways that checklist testing can help an organization assure that they are prepared for a disaster recovery scenario. Checklist testing, simulation testing, and test scenarios help ensure that we are prepared for our recovery efforts.

General Checklist Testing

A checklist tests helps to determine whether or not sufficient supplies are stored at the backup site, telephone number listings are current, on-hand quantities of forms are adequate, and a current copy of the recovery plan and necessary operational manuals are available. Figure B.1 gives an example of a checklist that we might use to make sure that we have all of the resources available to us to assist in our recovery. This checklist should be customized for your organization's specific needs.

Another checklist of every step necessary to recovering a given system (or each given system) confirms that the recovery plan can be followed and that all components are available. This checklist test should be followed as if it were an actual recovery situation without actually performing any of the commands necessary to perform a recovery. See Figure B.2.

Figure B.3 shows a completed checklist. This checklist helps you make alterations not only to your disaster recovery plan, but also to the logic *behind* the plan. In this case, the checklist confirms that the correct operating system is available on the recovery hardware and that the recovery steps are properly ordered.

- _______ DR Site
- _______ Printing Supplies
- _______ Toner
- _______ Paper
- _______ Invoice Forms
- _______ Envelopes
- _______ Office Supplies
  - _______ Pens/Pencils
  - _______ Notebooks
  - _______ Envelopes
  - _______ CDs
  - _______ DVDs
- _______ Contact Information
  - _______ Employees
    - Freeman 123-456-8888
    - Leight-Lonny 345-245-4544
  - _______ Vendors
    - June's
    - Vaughn's
    - Stephanie's
  - _______ Clients
    - First Church of God
    - Joy's Diner
    - Crystal's Cards
  - _______ Manuals/Books
    - Microsoft Office
    - Server access documents
  - _______ Backups
    - Most recent date _______
  - _______ Recovery Plan
    - _______ Hard copy
    - _______ Soft copy

FIGURE B.1 Sample checklist.

- _______ Retrieve two most recent backups from safety deposit box at Bank of Your Town
  - _______ Date of these two backups
- _______ Locate recovery hardware
  - _______ Location or access point
- _______ Mount backups in recovery hardware
  - _______ Media compatible
- _______ Identify file structure on recovery media
- _______ Assure media is readable and correct
- _______ Is entire system recovery necessary

CONTINUED ON NEXT PAGE

FIGURE B.2 Blank recovery checklist.

```
_____ Recover necessary system
_____ Copy necessary files
_____ Install necessary software
_____ Install operating systems if necessary
_____ Check software functionality
_____ Check data integrity
_____ Check software/data version compatibility
_____ Bring up system
```

```
_____ x _____ Retrieve two most recent backups from safety deposit box at Bank
of Your Town
        _3/18/2006 and 4/12/2005 not sufficient _____ Date of these two backups
_____ x _____ Locate recovery hardware
        _buy/rent from local vendor _____ Location or access point
_____ x _____ Mount backups in recovery hardware
        _____ y _____ Media compatible
_____ x _____ Identify file structure on recovery media
_____ y _____ Assure media is readable and correct
_____ y _____ is entire system recovery necessary
_____ can't, incorrect operating system _____ Recover necessary system
_____ These steps _____ copy necessary files
_____ logically not in _____ install necessary software
_____ correct order _____ install operating systems if necessary
_____ Check software functionality
_____ Check data integrity
_____ check software/data version compatibility
_____ bring up system
Fail . . .
```

FIGURE B.3 Completed checklist for recovery.

Simulation Testing

All too often, organizations go through the exercise of creating disaster recovery plans, but do not test them regularly or keep them up-to-date. A safe and relatively inexpensive way to ensure that your disaster recovery plan is fairly up-to-date and that it is still viable it to run a simulation test.

As discussed in Chapter 8, simulation testing occurs not only when a *disaster* is simulated (a manager comes in one morning and pulls the plug on any three test servers), but also when the disaster *recovery test* is simulated.

These assumptions can be tested without our ever having a direct impact on the organization as a whole. You can pretend to recover a test or development environment, or you can walk through the process of recovering the entire production system without actually having to touch the servers.

Typically, extensive travel, alternative equipment, or disruption of voice and data communication are not undertaken during a simulation test, just a backup set of hardware (test machines, for example) are impacted and exercised or a scaled-back walkthrough with no actual impact to any of the organization's active processes, even development. This helps limit the financial impact on the organization. Validated recovery checklists will assist in this exercise. However, if no actual recovery is attempted the checklists will only offer minimal assurance that actual recovery will be anticipated.

Simulation testing, regardless of the level of testing that actually is involved, should take into account all lessons learned in any checklist testing as well as any previous simulation testing and even in any higher-level testing that may take place in the organization.

Example Simulation

The following example shows a home-based business's recovery simulation. This business is a Web site design company.

Situation

You awake to find that the storms occurring in your location as well as upstream have resulted in a flash flood, leaving six inches of water in your location. You are not sure if the water is still rising, and it is currently affecting your primary hardware and many of your files.

Process/Procedure

Retrieve emergency laptop, power supply, and backup batteries and cables (phone and Ethernet) from shelf in office closet.

1. Retrieve backups of current in process data from fireproof box in lower attic.

2. Retrieve soft and hard copy of contact information from fireproof box in lower attic.

3. Retrieve financial data from accounting book in closet in office.

4. Retrieve emergency funding information and access from package in freezer marked liver.

5. Retrieve minimal clothes from closet.

6. If car is an option, leave home in car.

   a. If car is not an option, leave with emergency assistance.

7. If car is an option, relocate to recovery location via automobile.

    a. If car is not an option, is air travel an option? If so, relocate to recovery location via air.

        i. If air is not an option, relocate to emergency evacuation location.

8. Upon arrival at backup or emergency location, connect to power and network.

9. Load most current backup of work in process and most recent copy of contact information into laptop.

10. When contact information is loaded, contact most active clients with emergency contact information.

    i. When work in process is loaded, connect to relevant servers and make sure that connectivity is working.

11. Begin work at backup location.

Audit Report

1. Laptop retrieval successful. Although not in the specified location (located it within ten minutes in the loft where Lynn was using it for her homework and to load her iPod). Power supply with laptop, cables, and backup batteries in closet.

2. Successfully retrieved backups of data, contact information (hard and soft copies), financial data, and located liver package still in freezer.

3. Clothing location and retrieval successful. It is Jun,e so opted for both long and short sleeves, casual, and more meeting-like clothes. Probably overkill, as they can always be replaced. Wasted 30 minutes in decision.

4. Car not an option, nor is foot travel. Would have to depend on emergency assistance. Wonder if there would be time. Air should still be an option. Find out how much it would cost for a right-now flight to Oregon. Find out how much hotel rates are this time of year and account for optional cost.

5. Pretend we are at backup site. Laptop connected, and restored backup of work in progress (backup is several weeks old, would have lost significant work but last test they were over a month old, so making progress) and contact information (contact information in soft copy not as current as hard copy, need to be more diligent in backups). Successfully connected via dial-up, wireless, and wired connectivity. Connected successfully in every manner to all relevant client servers, so work would be feasible.

Results

As you can see, the audit report need not be anything formal (depending on the organization) but should take into account all of the steps of the recovery process lined out in the plan. Because you are not necessarily impacting anything directly, you can verify that your current state of readiness is sufficient more often. Where you might only be able to actually perform a disaster recovery test offsite once a year, you could do a simulation test once a quarter or even once a month.

Results of the simulation should be stored with the recovery plan, and ongoing adjustments should be made.

Test Scenarios

When you are having users test the system to assure that it has been successfully recovered, a sample set of recovery scenarios that are always covered in the test should be included. This will assure continuity in the testing as well as make sure that any information identified by the subject matter expert is included in the recovery scenario.

An example of a test scenario follows:

1. Create an invoice. See Figure B.4.
2. Launch Excel.
3. Open company invoice template from c:\invoices\.
4. Create a new invoice.
5. Enter information in customer name, address, city, state, and zip code.
6. Date should fill itself in, but check to make sure date is correct.
7. Enter order number for invoice. Retrieve from orders spreadsheet located at c:\orders\.
8. Enter relevant information into quantity, decryption, and unit price.
9. Save invoice.

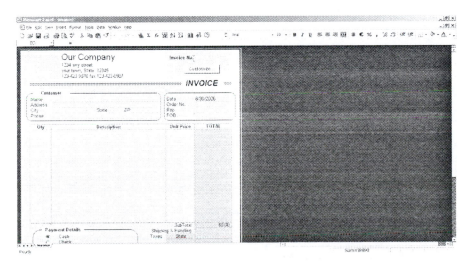

FIGURE B.4 Sample invoice.

Glossary

A

administrative coordinator   A recovery team member who is skilled in the business operations of the organization.

applications coordinator   A recovery team member with a foundational grounding in the current applications of the organization.

application service provider (ASP)   An outsourcing provider of applications to an organization.

asset assessment   An organization's assets (hardware, data, software, and people).

assessment   The act or result of judging the worth or value of something or someone.

B

backups   Copies of data and software of a system.

business continuity   The uninterrupted flow of business or minimally interrupted business.

business continuity plan   A management process to ensure the continuity of businesses, particularly in the event of an emergency or a disaster.

business continuity planning (BCP)   A method that is used to create a plan for how an organization will resume interrupted critical function(s), either partially or completely, within a predetermined time after a disaster or disruption.

business functions   Functions that occur within an organization. Examples include accounts payable and invoice processing.

business impact   The magnitude of the potential loss or the seriousness of the event; by extension, business impact is the magnitude of the potential loss or the seriousness of the event to the organization or the business.

C

commercial off-the-shelf (COTS)   Software that you can buy simply off the shelf with no customizations.

computer operations coordinator   A recovery team member skilled in the day-to-day operations of the systems and the system software, and who has the knowledge and skills necessary to recreate production schedules for application systems and implement new schedules should the need arise.

contingency plans   Plans to put into place in case of a disruption.

critical data   Data that has to be retained and recovered for legal reasons and for the restoration of minimum work levels.

D

denial of service (DoS)   An assault on a network that floods it with so many additional requests that regular traffic is either slowed or completely interrupted.

disaster   A calamity caused by accident, fire, explosion, or technical failure or by the forces of nature that has resulted in serious harm to the health, safety, or welfare of people or widespread damage to property.

disaster declaration threshold   The point at which the organization declares a disaster situation.

disaster recovery   The ability of a company to recover from a catastrophe and to get the company back to business as usual.

disaster recovery plan   An integral part of a business continuity plan, a disaster recovery plan details the steps necessary to simply recover the business sufficiently to get operations restarted.

disaster recovery site The primary location where an organization will recover from the disaster.

disaster recovery planning team The team that plans for the organization's recovery.

disaster recovery team The team that trains to recover the organization.

E

emergency An unexpected situation that demands immediate action.

event An occurrence.

F

facilities coordinator Someone who has hands-on knowledge, but works similarly as a recovery manager.

functional area An area of an organization that functions as a unit (For example, accounting or human resources).

functional area assessment An assessment of an organization's functional areas, their operations, and assets.

H

hazard Anything that can cause harm.

HIPAA Health Insurance Portability and Accountability Act.

hotsite A disaster recovery site.

I

impact A forceful consequence.

Internet Service Provider (ISP) A provider of Internet service to individuals or organizations.

ISO International Standards Organization.

M

malicious disruption A disruption to operations deliberately caused by an individual or individuals. Examples include denial of service attacks, data alteration, or theft.

maximum allowable downtime The absolute maximum time that the system can be unavailable

without ramifications to the organization, either directly or indirectly.

mean time to recover The average time taken to recover.

mean time between failures The average time between failures.

metadata Data about the data in the organization.

N

NAS Network Attached Storage.

network coordinator A recovery team member who has a foundational knowledge in network architecture design and maintenance.

notification directory The document that will help to ensure timely and effective communication.

P

phishing A form of criminal activity characterized by attempts to fraudulently acquire sensitive information (passwords, credit card numbers, bank account numbers, and more) by one entity masquerading as a trustworthy person or business in an apparently official electronic communication.

pharming The practice of one entity setting up a fraudulent Web site that contains copies of pages from a legitimate Web site in order to capture confidential information from users.

R

recovery To return to a normal condition.

restoration To bring back to original condition.

recovery manager The position responsible for overseeing recovery efforts.

Recovery Point Objective (RPO) The point in time to which systems and data must be recovered after an outage as determined by the business unit.

Recovery Time Objective (RTO) The period of time within which your systems, applications, or functions must be recovered (either because of contractual obligations or because of organizational requirements to withstand the loss of productivity) after an outage.

repudiation Assuring the secure legality of transactions occurring electronically.

return on investment (ROI)   A comparison of the money earned (or lost) on an investment with the amount of money invested.

revenue   All of the income produced by a particular source.

risk   The possibility of a person or entity suffering harm or loss because of an event or by a hazard.

risk assessment   A careful systematic examination of the environment and the physical, technological, or human components that could cause harm to organization, staff, or product.

risk management   Prioritizing risks in the order of severity and potential impact on the organization.

S

SAN   Storage Area Network.

SAS   Statement on Auditing Standards.

sensitive data   Data or documentation that is necessary for normal daily operations of the organization but for which there are alternative sources of the same data or data that can be easily reconstructed from other data that is readily available (critical or vital data may be sources for this data).

service level agreements (SLA)   A contract that spells out the terms of service one party can expect from another party.

spoofing   When one person or entity electronically masquerades as another entity.

SWOT   Strengths, Weaknesses, Opportunities, Threats.

T

technical coordinator   Recovery team member with knowledge of interfaces.

threat assessment   The assessment of threats that may present themselves to an organization.

U–V

unavoidable risk   Those risks that an organization cannot avoid or completely eliminate.

vital data   Information that has to be retained and recovered to maintain normal business activities.

vulnerability   The condition of the organization being open to something undesirable or injurious.

vulnerability assessment   An assessment of an organization's vulnerability.

References

Charlotte J. Hiatt, 1999, *A Primer for Disaster Recovery Planning in an IT Environment,* Idea Publishing Group, Hershey PA.

Disaster Definitions from Dictionary.com
http://dictionary.reference.com/search?q=disaster&r=67

Exploring backup alternatives in a SAN environment
www.ameinfo.com/39672.html

Federal Emergency Management Agency (FEMA)
www.fema.gov

FEMA Independent Study Program—Course List
http://training.fema.gov/EMIWeb/IS/crslist.asp

Geoffrey H. Wold, "Disaster Recovery Planning Process," *Disaster Recovery Journal*
www.drj.com/new2dr/w2_002.htm

Government Online Services—Glossary
www.go.tas.gov.au/library/resources/glossary11.htm

HIPAA (Health Insurance Portability and Accountability Act)
www.hhs.gov/ocr/hipaa/

OCTAVE® Information Security Risk Evaluation, Carnegie Mellon Software Engineering Institute
www.cert.org/octave

Overview of the Sarbanes-Oxley Act of 2002
www.ey.com/global/download.nsf/Russia_E/EY_Sarbanes_9_12_02e/$file/EY_Sarbanes_9_12_02e.pdf

Privacy Initiatives
www.ftc.gov/privacy/glbact

Victor Kapella, "Speechless," *Communications News,* November 2004
www.comnews.com/stories/articles/1104/1104coverstory.htm

Index